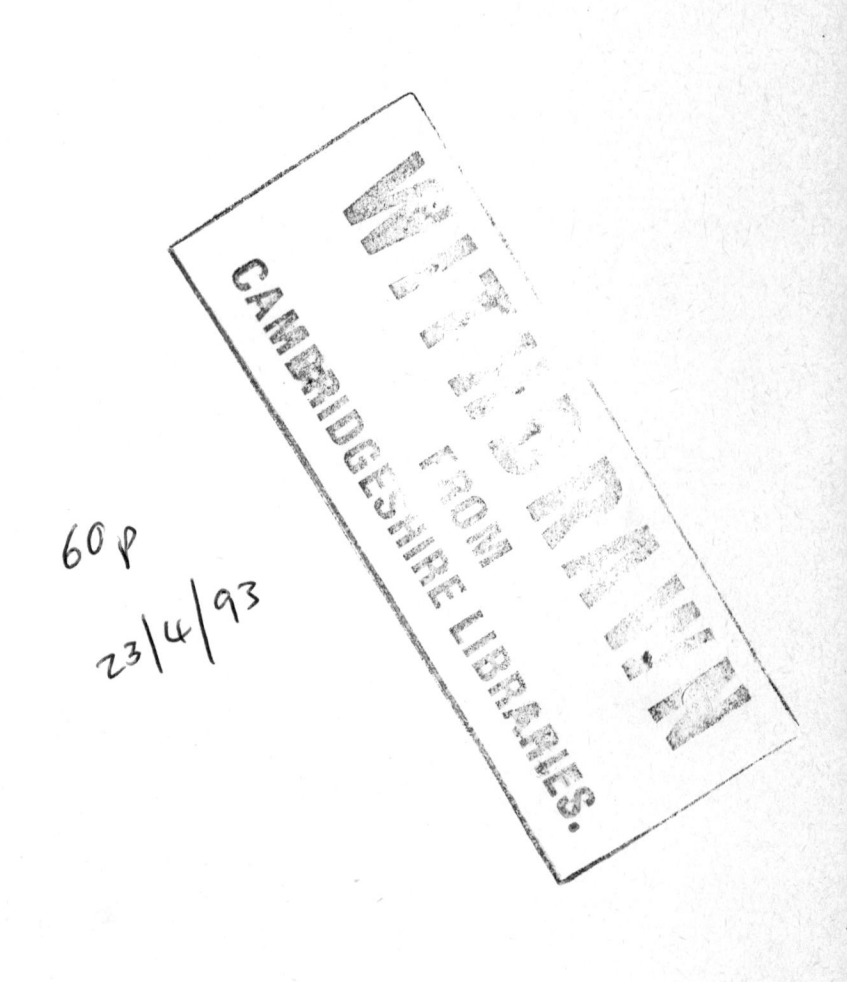
60p
23/4/93

Track
and
Field
Athletics

Track
and
Field
Athletics

WILF PAISH

LEPUS BOOKS
London 1976

About the Author

Wilf Paish is a qualified physical educationist having studied at Borough Road College and Carnegie College of Physical Education. His involvement in the sport has been one of an active competitor, club coach, school coach, county schools' secretary, team manager and county coaching secretary.

Since 1964 he has been a National Coach, employed full-time in the sport by the Amateur Athletics Association and the British Amateur Athletic Board. He has been an official team coach at Olympic, European and Commonwealth Games. As part of his work he has coached international athletes, of the highest calibre, in most of the track and field events.

A keen educationist, he directs the Easter Course at Blackpool, and the Summer Course at Loughborough, for teachers. His interests in the peripheral aspects of the sport are well documented in the many magazines supporting the sport of track and field athletics.

Copyright © 1976
Lepus Books
(An associate company of Henry Kimpton Ltd.)

Standard Book Number 86019 005 6

I.B.M Computer typesetting by
Print Origination Ltd. Hawthorne Road, Bootle,
Merseyside, L20 6NS.
Printed by Photolithography and Bound by
T. & A. Constable Ltd., Edinburgh

Contents

List of Plates

Preface

This manual is aimed at everyone involved in the sport of track and field athletics. It will be of great value to coaches, teachers, students and those involved in specialised studies associated with sport. Not only does it cover all of the track and field events, but includes chapters on the basic philosophy of teaching and coaching, history, diet and strength training.

Each specialised chapter deals with the fundamentals of the event, the mechanical principles involved, ideas for training, teaching and coaching. Certain sections include a very specialised knowledge of work physiology, the adaptation to stress, principles of training, ergogenic aids, aerodynamics, and other peripheral aspects of the sport.

The photographs, taken by some of the most eminent sports photographers, of athletes involved in the highest levels of competition, enhance the text, and the charts, strip sequences, etc., all add up to what I believe to be the most complete text ever produced for this fine sport.

It is only possible to gain the expertise to compile such a text by being completely involved in the sport full-time. For this I would like to thank my employers, the British Amateur Athletic Board, my colleagues for sharing with me a good deal of the expertise they have obtained through their involvements, the international athletes who have made possible such an involvement, and finally my wife who has to live with a person so singularly committed.

WILF PAISH

Section 1

Introduction

Plate 1. Bob Beamon, World record long jump, 8 metres 90 (29' 2½''). The greatest athletic feat to date.

Chapter 1

History of Athletics

Every day, somewhere, someone is practising track and field athletics. This does not mean that it is the most popular sport in the world, with the greatest number of participants; this honour probably belongs to fishing, but it is the competitive sport most common to the majority of nations in the world. From the mighty powers of China, Russia and the U.S.A. to the small islands like Fiji and Bermuda, men and women take part in athletics, and can compete against each other in the most wonderful sporting competition known to the world—the Olympic Games.

The average person in the street only becomes familiar with the sport every four years. This is because the Olympic Games are celebrated quadrennially, and as track and field athletics is the foundation of this "festival of nations", it is given tremendous publicity through the mass media.

The Olympic Games is steeped in tradition and its precise origin is lost in the pre-recorded history of the Ancient Greek civilisations. The Greeks were a nation enamoured by fabulous legends about their gods and heroes, and this, coupled with their love of competitions and festivals of warrior-like activities, encouraged them to weave fantastic tales about their heroes engaged in combat. One such legend says that the first contest staged at "Olympia" was a wrestling match between Zeus and Cronus, the pre-historic king of Olympia. This is only one of the many legends which help shroud the true origin of the Games. However, a fairly common theme suggests that the Games were inaugurated as a form of funeral celebration or to commemorate the death or birthday of a famous person.

Seemingly the first authentic records of the Games date from 776 B.C. At this particular festival Coroebus won the "stade", a race of about two hundred yards, or the length of the stadium. The fact that such an achievement should remain documented for centuries, only goes to show the important place given to successful athletes by the Greeks of this period. About this time Greece was divided into a number of small states who were continually involved in war with one another, or with neighbouring countries. They were a nation of warriors and spectators who obviously enjoyed watching feats of strength and demonstrations of soldiering skills, which were qualities common to all of them and necessary for survival.

Although the Greeks were a nation of warriors, all wars ceased during the celebrations and an "Olympic truce" was observed for the period of the Games. This was usually about a month. It is a great pity that this modern civilisation in which we live cannot keep to such a simple ideal, as two world wars have caused the cancellation of two modern Olympics.

The records attributed to the athletic heroes of this period are typical of such a romantic nation. The title of the greatest athlete who has ever lived must surely go to one Phayllus of Croton who, during the pentathlon leap, landed five feet beyond the "skamma" (landing area) and in so doing broke his leg. This is fairly understandable as the "skamma" was fifty feet in length so making the leap one of fifty-five feet. This even makes the incredible leap of Beamon (U.S.A.), during the Mexico Olympics of 1968, look quite mediocre, and can only suggest that errors were made by the recorders at the time, by the research translators associated with the historic studies, or that the leap consisted of a series of jumps such as the triple jump. The latter is the most probable because, even with the use of hand weights, such a feat would have been impossible.

As far as the Greeks were concerned the most important contest in the Olympics was the pentathlon. It probably held the most appeal because of its all-round test of manliness, a prerequisite for a successful warrior. Women were not allowed to take part, or even observe the early Games, and at one stage contestants and spectators were nude to prevent this from happening. This action was probably taken as a result of a mother who, disguised as a man, tried to gain admission to help her son in a boxing contest. The pentathlon consisted of five events which probably included running the "stade," jumping, throwing the discus and javelin, and wrestling. It is uncertain how the winner was decided, but theories suggest that the victor was the person winning the most individual contests.

Athletics historians have often tried to compare the prowess of the Greek discus thrower with those of the modern era. This would seem to be an impossible task as the dimensions of the ancient discus varied considerably, its weight depending upon the starting size of the bronze or stone from which it was fashioned. The discus event is certainly the only one where any comparisons could be made; times were not recorded in the foot-racing events, the precise action of the jumpers is in considerable doubt, and they used some form of mechanical aid in the javelin event, thus leaving only the discus event even vaguely standardised.

One thing which is fairly certain is that the techniques used in competition, and the methods used in training were fairly sophisticated. For example, some form of starting gate, incorporating a structure similar to the starting blocks used today, was in evidence at the start of the foot racing events. In the javelin throw they used an "amentum", a leather thong which was twisted about the shaft of the javelin in order to produce a rotational, stabilising effect during its flight.

The ancient Games, together with the Greek ideal of sport for sport's sake, continued for several centuries until about the time of the Roman conquest in 146 B.C. Prior to this date the Games went through what is often termed the "Golden Era" when the ancient ideals associated with the Games were fully observed, all wars ceased and standards improved. With the nation's defeat came the decline of the Games, and the ancient ideal began to take on a new meaning. The Romans, more a nation of spectators than participants, encouraged the introduction of the professional athlete, the only person with sufficient time to train to the high standard expected by the spectators. Although this improved the level of the few, it restricted the number of participants and encouraged corrupt practices, so causing the gradual decline of the Games and their ultimate extinction. Thus from the first official records of 776 B.C. until the Games closed in A.D. 369 many celebrated champions are included on the roll of honour, a roll which was to remain closed for 1,503 years.

Although there were several centres where the Greeks staged athletic festivals, the one at Olympia remained the most famous. When the Games ceased, the site was subject to extreme acts of vandalism and many of the buildings were destroyed. The final blows of destruction came with an earthquake early in the sixth century. However, the site was preserved under a layer of silt deposited by the flood waters of the Alpheus, and so it remained hidden from man for about fourteen centuries, until the site was excavated by a group of German archaeologists.

Although the termination of the Games brought about the closing of an important chapter in the history of athletics, it did not bring about its complete death, as athletic competitions still continued in many European countries particularly Germany and the British Isles. This subsequent era is not very well documented, and so most of the records are rather vague. However, there is evidence of an Olympic-type festival staged during the early seventeenth century, in the heart of the Cotswold Hills close to Chipping Campden. These Games, often known as the "Dover's Hill Games" after Robert Dover, a local attorney, were probably "protest games" against the puritanism of the period. They were staged during the Whitsun period, and the programme included casting the bar and hammer, leaping and many other rural sports. These Games continued until 1644 when they were probably stopped by pressure from the Puritans. Several attempts were made to restart them, but none were very successful due to the fact that they often terminated as a drunken orgy that roused the anger of the local inhabitants.

Although the period of the Middle Ages is not well documented as far as athletics is concerned, many people took part in this form of activity in England. Joseph Strutt, in his excellent book "Sports and pastimes of the people of England" written in 1830, makes several references to the practice of athletic events. "In the middle ages, foot racing was considered as an essential part of a young man's education, especially if he was the son of a

man of rank."—"Henry VIII, after his accession to the throne, according to Hall and Holinshead, retained 'Casting of the barre'." There are also other references in this text to the throwing of javelins and heavy objects linking this aspect of the sport with the holiday recreation of Londoners.

The period 1780-1860 forms a fascinating era in the development of the sport, particularly in the British Isles. It is a period that is fairly well documented and includes the development of the sport with the professional pedestrians and leapers, and also its development in the Universities and Public Schools. The study of professional athletics in this country, an aspect of the sport which still remains to this day in Northern England and Scotland, would interest even those people who are only vaguely involved with the sport. The period is not without its heroes, with men like Captain Barclay, a distance runner and walker who performed quite incredible feats for the period, and the legendary "Deerfoot", the American Indian, who frequently enthused crowds in England with his middle distance running. Fascinating as it is, a study of the history of the sport is beyond the scope of this chapter, which is merely to give readers an insight into the background of the sport.

With this extremely brief interlude, which only pays lip service to the development of the sport during the Middle Ages, and later, the professional and University/Public School scene in England, we can return to the ancient idea of the Olympic Games, with the scene set for their revival in 1896.

The idea to start a modern series of Olympic Games was the brain-child of Baron Pierre de Coubertin. Coubertin's childhood was almost certainly influenced by the presence of war and this, together with his love of sport and his philosophy of education, must have aided the germination of the idea. This was strengthened further by tours of the English Public Schools which at the time fully exploited the *Mens Sana in Corpore Sano* theme and included a large amount of athletic activity in their working day. Add to this Coubertin's interest in Greek history and it is fairly easy to see where the inspiration to revive the Games came from.

The revival was not automatic and Coubertin suffered many disappointments during his campaign to re-establish the Games. The final blessing for them came after a meeting of the athletic leaders of the world in 1894 which scheduled the first Olympiad for Athens, Greece in 1896. Once started there followed a struggle for survival, a struggle, which for different reasons, still goes on today.

Although the modern Games has as its foundation the ideals of the ancient Greeks, modern civilisation has found it impossible to live up to them. Two world wars caused the cancellation of the VI, XII and XIII Olympiads and since the 1936 Games, staged in Berlin, they have bowed to political influence. I fear the Olympic movement as it stands at present has only a limited life. With the age of the "professional" athlete fast approaching, the purists must fear that history can repeat itself and cause their

destruction once again. After a break of thirty-six years the Games returned to Germany, to the City of Munich, and the XXIst Olympiad is next scheduled for Montreal, Canada. The aim now seems to be that each successive Games should be larger and more elaborate. The cost to stage the Games, for the host nation, is becoming so prohibitive that few nations in the world will be able to afford the luxury. The Munich Games cost in excess of 600 million dollars and those in Montreal will probably cost more. I expect the movement to limp towards its twenty-first celebration and thereafter I believe it will give way to world-championships in the individual sports. This will be less costly as they can be staged in countries where excellent facilities for the individual sports already exist.

The simple theme, given to us by the founder of the modern Olympics, now seems to have taken on a different meaning in a society where national prestige goes hand in hand with the gold medals. "The important thing in the Olympic Games is not to win but to take part, the important thing in life is not the triumph but the struggle. The essential thing is not to have conquered but to have fought well. To spread these precepts is to build up a stronger and more valiant and above all a more scrupulous and more generous humanity." The idea that all should stand an equal chance of success has long since been forgotten. The rich nations provide their best athletes with bursaries, scholarships or work in government departments so that they can be available to do the extra training essential for those who wish to "live at the top". So athletes from these nations go to the major Games better prepared, having had the added benefits of professional coaching, technologists, pharmacologists and the best that sports medicine can provide to help them.

Because of the cost involved in staging the Games and preparing and sending teams to compete, politicians have become more and more involved. Their involvement has certainly accelerated the presence of "nationalism", now more than ever apparent, and some cynics see the Games as a battle between one political system and another.

The publicity given to the Games through the mass media has made them ideal centres for demonstrations. In 1968 the students from Mexico protested before the Games started, and once underway the negroes from the U.S.A. staged their own mild demonstration. 1972 saw the postponement of the Games for a day because of violent action by Arab terrorists. If all of this is considered in the light of the threatened boycott of the Games by the African nations over the participation of Rhodesia, and the exclusion of certain nations, particularly South Africa, then there is clear evidence that there is now something wrong with the Olympic movement.

For the Games to survive they will have to undergo radical changes. The first move might be to limit them to the individual sports: this would reduce the number of competitors and might decrease the possibility of exploiting the Games for nationalistic and political ends. Ski-ing, equestrian events and

many of the minor sports could all be excluded and encouraged to organise their own world championships. The winter Olympics is only open to those who have the right climatic conditions; the equestrian events are beyond the financial resources of many of the poorer nations; and the minor sports tend to be included at the whim of the organising nation, e.g. judo in the 1964 Tokyo Olympics. For the modern Games to survive, or even return to their simple beginnings, pruning of this kind is essential.

Chapter 2

Athletics in Society

Although this book is concerned with the sport of track and field athletics, much of what is to be said in this chapter will be relevant to all sports. It is based on my own personal philosophy, influenced by my own deep involvement in sport, and I hope that it will be of interest to students and coaches who might like to consider the social implications of sport, and what its future role in society might be.

It is difficult to visualise clearly what place athletics has in our materialistic society. Few people come into direct contact with the sport and the mass media rarely stress the contribution it might make to the mental and physical health of the nation.

Once every four years the track and field scene explodes; society becomes aware of its existence and for a while it has a national importance. With certain nations this awareness is continually stressed, often for political motives. But for most countries in the world it soon becomes history with a very slight revival of interest, in the interim period, through the European and Commonwealth Games.

In an age where the labours of man are being reduced daily, the time is not far off when at least half of his active life will be free for him to indulge in leisure pursuits. Unfortunately, neither man nor society is ready for this leisure age. Man has to be taught how to occupy his leisure time, an educative process which starts at school. Very few people learn new physical skills as adults, mainly because the opportunities to do so do not exist. Of course there are exceptions to this statement e.g. golf and squash. But athletics relies upon teachers to introduce the skills at school, and to provide sufficient incentive to encourage young people to continue to participate in the sport as adults. Because of a diversification of interest in physical education, towards the less competitive sports, such as climbing, canoeing, camping and dance, track and field athletics no longer holds the pride of place it once did. This means that fewer children are being exposed to the sport, in a way likely to encourage future participation. One hopes that the recent awards schemes might change this situation.

Athletics, as a social sport, has many critics. It cannot hope to rival badminton, squash, tennis, golf and fencing, where men and women can compete together. But compared with, for example, rugby football,

association football, cricket and basketball, it has much to offer, in that at international level the sport is "mixed". One hopes that the 1980s will see a change in the administration of the sport which will encourage full family participation, thus enabling it to make an even greater contribution to society.

Violence, in one of its many forms, is every day spotlighted by the mass media. Often it takes the form of wanton damage caused by teenagers who are bored with society; a society which offers them little in the way of recreational and cultural facilities and opportunities. In the case of soccer hooliganism, it is unfortunate that it has become associated with a sport. Soccer is not necessarily at fault; it merely places young spectators in a situation conducive to anti-social behaviour. Psychologists can offer strong evidence to support the theory that those involved in sport are less likely to rebel against society. They support their findings with suggestions that sport offers a good release mechanism for pent up emotions; that it captures their interest, time and money so preventing the conditions which encourage extreme anti-social behaviour. To the layman, the solution seems obvious. If better cultural and recreational facilities could be provided and people, young and old, be encouraged to use them, then the thousands of pounds spent in restoring acts of vandalism could be spent providing better leisure facilities. Is this again an instance of the "chicken and the egg"?

A lot of violence, throughout the world, can be associated with a society which is producing a worker who is bored by the simple repetitive skills of the assembly lines. Sport renders possible the expression and satisfaction of many desires for which the modern world, in its work, can no longer provide an outlet. The situation will get worse as the machine takes over from man, thus giving him more leisure time.

The sport of track and field athletics has much to offer the person who is bored and likely to kick against society. In no other sport does one witness such a wide variety of physiques, temperaments and abilities. Even the obese person, who would have problems with most other sports, is quite "at home" in one of the heavy throwing events. However, apart from cross-country running, athletics is still an "elitist" sport and does not offer competition for the novice and low ability groups. This situation is changing, and must continue to do so at a faster rate, if the sport is to capture the full interest of those who have been enthused by the proficiency award schemes in schools. This will mean that competition, with graded ability groups, must become part of the structure.

In terms of skill and participation levels, track and field athletics can score very highly over its seasonal rivals. Tennis, for example, is a high-skill level game and competition cannot be enjoyed until all concerned are capable of hitting the ball to-and-fro across the net. As soon as a person takes up athletics he can be placed in a realistic competitive situation. Cricket for the batsman is a "single chance" sport. Once he is "out" he cannot contribute

further to the game until the innings is closed. Athletics, on the other hand, is a multi-chance sport where the performer is always given at least three attempts to succeed, and even the shortest running events allow time to make up for any minor mistakes.

Athletics as a sport has much to offer society. It is energetic, calling for a reasonable level of fitness. It appeals to a very wide variety of physiques, abilities and temperaments. It can be enjoyed at low skill levels. Last, but not least, it is a sport that can cater for men, women and children, at the same meeting, thus encouraging family participation.

Chapter 3

Teaching Athletics - A Basic Philosophy

"Mighty oaks from tiny acorns grow", and it is also true that young people can develop into great athletes provided that they are nurtured correctly. But like the oak tree, little happens overnight; it is a gradual process of growth that can be forced, but with disappointing results.

Unfortunately, athletics in schools is nearly always dominated by what happens in the adult version of the sport. In many cases competitions and performance techniques are merely "watered down" versions of what adults do. Whilst this might be acceptable for the gifted few, there is little evidence to suggest that it is suitable for the masses.

For children, athletics must be fun, otherwise they will not want to participate. It should not be a series of stereotyped skills similar to those of the Olympic performer. Instead it should be a series of very simple competitions in which the children have the chance to practise the essential elements of skill only. The inherent dangers of trying to mould on to the immature bodies of children the advanced skills of the world record holder, are obvious to those concerned with education. To illustrate this point further, I must emphasise that certain aspects of skill used by world-class performers, are beyond the capabilities of even the British record holders, who have spent many years trying to develop the necessary strength and coordination. Why should children be expected to mime these people when stronger and more experienced adults find considerable difficulty in attempting to do the same?

Children are not interested in the world of "straddle jumps", "hitch-kicks", etc. They are interested in *How far* and *How fast*. It is this which motivates them and gives them the necessary incentives. Once they have experienced the thrill of performing simple track and field skills, they might be more likely to accept the adult conception of the skill.

Consider for a while the complicated skill of the straddle style high jumper. There are few men in the world who have managed to master this complicated skill, yet it is frequently taught in schools. To most teachers it is a method of clearing a bar, but to the performer it is a beautiful movement which begins the moment the jumper starts his approach run and finishes when he has come to rest on the landing area. The "straddle" position over the bar is not difficult and is well within the compass of most children, but

the preparation stages for take-off, and the take-off itself, are very difficult to master, and mastered they must be if one is to get maximum benefit from the efficient position over the bar. Young children can all jump higher using some form of "scissors" jump, but of course this style has long since been left behind by the Olympic champions because of the inefficient position over the bar. However, the take-off and the preparation stages are simple and efficient and will enable the young performer to get the feeling of jumping high. When asked to justify teaching advanced skills, supporters of this adult approach suggest its long term value. The young performer is not interested in what he might do as an adult; he is concerned with what he does at the present, and the chances are that he might not even be involved in the sport when he has reached physical maturity. If children are intro- duced to the skills in an enjoyable way, they are likely to remain in the sport, so that when the time is ripe the advanced techniques can be introduced. If introduced too soon, children will become frustrated by their inability to master the skills and will rapidly lose interest and desire to participate.

Every year in England, during the summer, one of the largest athletic spectacles in the world takes place. I refer, of course, to the English Schools' championships. This competition involves several hundred competitors, in three age groups, ranging from 11 years to 20 years . . . in both sexes, covering a very comprehensive range of track and field events. All of the counties in England may enter a full team which, because of the total numbers involved, does permit the full entry of two per event, in all events. This means that the athletically strong counties are restricted to the same number of competitors as the weaker counties. Hence some counties are forced to exclude potential champions. Although it is a spectacle that I would not miss, it is little more than a modified Olympic Games complete with its march-past of competitors, presentation ceremonies, the swearing of oaths, etc. At the moment, thank heavens, a flame is not lit and pigeons are not released, but this could well happen in the future as the pattern of each championship being bigger and better has already been set.

Whilst I am an admirer of this championship meeting, which certainly caters for the "elite", I am also one of its harshest critics because of the structure which it imposes on teachers. For climatic reasons, athletics in most schools is restricted to the summer term only. At the commencement of this term, schools interested in taking part in the competition have to start a process. Interest is focused on the "elite" selection whilst the "rabbits" are often forgotten and left to their own devices to practise boring skills that are beyond them. This situation, often found, can be compared with the young and fairly unskilled footballer who is forced to play left wing, and as a result seldom receives the ball to take an active part in the game. Because of the adult version of the game interest is lost and the desire to play gone, probably for ever. The dangers of forcing competition too early can have

quite serious results as far as future competition is concerned. To young children the humiliation of defeat is often more than they can stand,and as a result a rejection of the sport takes place. With the young it might not necessarily be the most skilful or the one most likely to achieve sporting prowess as an adult, who comes out on top. More often it is the precocious child, who happens to be more physically developed than others of the same age. Hence, in terms of competition,the teacher should consider the merits of indirect competition against a series of carefully chosen standards (i.e. Five star award scheme), team jumping, throwing and vaulting competitions decided by aggregate scores. For direct competition, consider handicapping or streaming according to age/height/weight exponents. The reasons for this are that all children must feel a sense of achievement, and all learning should be success orientated and not the reverse. As far as sport is concerned, one does not learn by one's mistakes.

At the present time, age is the only criterion that exists to decide the type of equipment a child should use or the level of competition he should enter. Whilst this might be acceptable as far as competition is concerned, it is not suitable for the teaching situation. In the throwing events, children must feel secure, and the size and the weight of the equipment should be adjusted, as far as possible, to achieve this end. Often it will mean resorting to lighter equipment than the age group specifies,and might even involve improvisation along the lines suggested in the chapters on the throwing events. Hurdling creates similar problems for the teacher who must improvise and adapt the rules to satisfy the needs of the individual in the learning situation.

To conclude this section on teaching, I would like to reproduce a taped interview between myself and a keen teacher of athletics, placed in the situation thousands of other teachers find themselves.

Q. How can I organise a successful programme for athletics in my school?

R. The only way is to plan the whole scheme well in advance of the athletics term. This will involve you in a fair amount of written work to decide exactly how much of your teaching time you are prepared to devote to teaching athletics, how much out-of-school time you will use, the number and types of internal and external competitions you are prepared to hold, (and here I emphasise "types of competition"), incentive schemes, class organisation, lesson planning and the care and improvisation of equipment.

Q. Why did you emphasise "types of competition"?

R. Most teachers only consider using a programme of events identical to that used on a track and field meeting for adults. These are time consuming and are far from ideal in the school situation. I would rather use team jumping, vaulting, throwing or pentathlon competitions.

Q. Can you give me an example of this type of competition?

R. Yes, here is a score card for a long jump competition.

Team long jump competition Class 2A v. Class 2B

	CLASS 2A					CLASS 2B			
Name	1	2	3	Best	Name	1	2	3	Best
Smith	F	16'1"	15'0"	16'1"	Clover	11'6"	12'3"	F	12'3"
Jones	15'0"	15'0"	14'9"	15'0"	Baxter	15'9"	15'6"	15'9"	15'9"
Brown	13'3"	F	F	13'3"	Robson	F	F	13'6"	13'6"
Page	F	12'6"	13'0"	13'0"	Taylor	F	14'3"	F	14'3"
Bell	10'6"	11'0"	11'3"	11'3"	Carter	9'6"	10'0"	F	10'0"
Hobson	9'6"	F	10'0"	10'0"	McNab	9'6"	F	9'9"	9'9"
TOTAL				78'7"					75'6"

In this competition class 2A beat class 2B by 3'1". The individual champion was Smith (2A) with Baxter (2B) second. This type of competition can be organised with any of the events and with any number of children combining to form the team. Often it is wise to combine two events together i.e. long and triple jumps, or shot and discus. Competitions of this nature are ideal for promoting an interest in the less popular events such as the pole vault and hammer throw.

Q. Which events should I teach to my eleven/twelve year olds?

R. The running events do not require teaching, rather they should be encouraged to run by taking part in a series of simple competitions. I would include all events up to 1,500 metres; and of course cross-country running. I would teach all of the field events to these children. This gives you quite a number of events, so you will only be able to afford to teach the children the absolute essentials of technique and place them in simple competitions. I suggest about one lesson per event, a large proportion of which is a form of competition.

Q. How should I organise them for teaching?

R. With the young children, try to keep them together as a complete class. They require the motivation of the class teacher. It will mean that for some of the events like the discus you will have to purchase a lot of equipment or improvise with wooden discus. Teach only the essentials of technique and place them quickly in a competitive situation.

Q. What types of competition are most suitable for this class situation?

R. I suggest that you use a simple three-standard type competition. It is best to use simple marker flags for this. Standard 1 should be low, and all children should achieve this; standard 2 is a good average for the class, and standard 3 should be just beyond the best in the class. Give the children three attempts and suggest that they try to score a total of six points. At the end of such a competition always ask for the results, otherwise the competition is meaningless.

Q. It sounds excellent as there are no failures, but I am worried about placing the best standard beyond the level of the best person.

R. I did not quite mean this. The best will sometimes achieve it on one of

their efforts, but there must always be an incentive to encourage them to try to do better. That is what athletics is all about!

Q. How can I best plan the individual lesson to make full use of the limited time available? In my case the lesson is only thirty minutes long, with the usual delays for changing, etc.

R. The best way is to start the lesson with some form of group running against a time standard. This should never take longer than about ten minutes. The rest of the time should be spent teaching and motivating the other field events.

Q. How can I make sure that the children remain interested in athletics throughout the year?

R. You must develop an athletic awareness in your school. You should make sure that the notice board is informative and interesting. Make sure magazines and books on athletics are available in the library; use some of the feature films, available on hire, to keep the interest going. But the most important thing is to make sure that your programme has built-in incentive schemes.

Q. What do you mean by this?

R. I mean schemes like the Five star system, team jumping competitions, inter-class, -house, -school matches, school decathlon/pentathlon, visits to important fixtures, etc.

Q. I have heard about the group approach for athletics. What does this mean?

R. I suppose it refers to the situation when the class is divided into smaller groups, each group doing a different athletic event. This is suitable for older children, but I do not advocate it for the younger ones, as this age group rely upon the direction and motivation of the teacher. The field events are fairly dangerous if unsupervised and a strict code of procedure must be followed. This procedure is taught and observed in the whole class situation and one then hopes that it will carry over to the group situation. By the very nature of some of the field events, they are fairly dangerous and the welfare of the children must be regarded all of the time. As regards accidents, the high jump area is particularly vulnerable, and special care must be taken to keep this area in a safe condition.

Q. So far most of what you have said is concerned with the class situation. What about the school club?

R. Yes, as far as the teacher is concerned, I am interested that he should be able to do the job effectively which he is paid for. During the lesson time the teacher should be concerned with the whole class. The good performer should be encouraged to come along to an out-of-school session, or to join the local club, so that he can learn more advanced skills and so improve his level of performance. The good teacher should liaise with, and support, the local club.

Q. What have you to say about the traditional school sports day?

R. I regard this as an occasion when most of the school get a chance to compete together on the same day. I do not see it as a day for the "elite". If the athletics programme is organised correctly, the good athletes will get all of the competition they require without having to steal the limelight on sports day.

Chapter 4

Coaching Athletics - A Basic Philosophy

It is not possible to learn the art of coaching from a book. Although reading can give the coach the background knowledge he requires to enable him to coach successfully, the true expertise can only be developed by working with athletes in the practical situation. Coaching is considerably more than advising an athlete on techniques and training. It is a relationship built on respect. The coach will often find that he becomes involved in several aspects of an athlete's life other than steering him towards a better athletic performance. Often the coach becomes a "father figure", and both parties should emerge from a coaching relationship with enriched experience.

Because one has been a successful athlete, it does not follow that one will be a successful coach. Although proven ability as a performer does help, coaching is a little more than just showing "How". The successful coach is a teacher, psychologist, motivator and diplomat all rolled into one. Very few successful athletes continue in the sport and become successful coaches. The psychologist would offer many reasons for this. The successful athlete, who has sacrificed many of the pleasures of life, in order to reach his goal, probably feels that he has given the sport enough when he retires from competition. It could be that coaching does not give him the same satisfaction as competition did, and to be associated with those still able to compete produces a sense of frustration. Some athletes have had to jeopardise their career for the sport, and in retirement devote their time and energies trying to catch up on this aspect of their life. Other psychologists would say that the coach, who was not a successful performer, is better motivated because he can see in others what he never realised himself. In the end it will always come back to the personality of the individual. The coach is probably born and not made; the innate ability to co-operate, motivate, etc. are inborn qualities for which technical knowledge is no substitute.

Coaching is a vocation and not an occupation and in this respect can be viewed in the same light as the medical, teaching and social welfare professions. Whilst there are some professional coaches, the majority do it quite voluntarily. But whether salaried or not, it still remains a vocation. Like the athlete, the coach will have to make many personal sacrifices. He has to give freely of his own leisure time, suffer the hardships and frustrations of

poor facilities, climate, administration, all for the benefit of others. His rewards are the successes of his athletes, and the good coach will not judge these on a win/lose basis. To make an athlete a better person is just as desirable as making a person a better athlete.

To become a coach one must devote a considerable amount of time to study. Not just book learning, but the study of film and athletes performing live. Many ideas in coaching are empirical ones, often arrived at by the coach as a result of trial and error. In producing a successful athlete the coach will have made many mistakes, and probably have restricted the full development of other athletes during his experiments. Unfortunately there is no other way of gaining this knowledge. The study of physiology, kinesiology, psychology and other associated sciences help, but it is the application of this knowledge which determines the success, or otherwise, of a coach. To become a successful coach in the eyes of the public, one must have fortune on one's side. The coach cannot put in what God left out. Good coaching can ensure that true ability is developed to the full, but without talent the coach is very limited. However, as far as the coach is concerned, success is achieved if the athlete improves both as a performer and a person. It is impossible for outsiders to judge these factors and many successful coaches gain true satisfaction away from the "Olympic medals".

To enter coaching, no qualifications are required other than an interest to help others. Once entry has been made, it is up to the coach to decide at what level he wishes to participate. Most governing bodies have a grading system for coaches and it is desirable, though not essential, for coaches to become graded by taking examinations. Unfortunately the system favours the academic approach and often misses the true motivator.

If asked to list the various qualities required of a good coach, the following would rank very high.

1. *Knowledge of the event.* The good coach should have a very thorough knowledge of every aspect of his event; it should include body-mechanics, skill learning, physiology, principles of training.

2. *Photographic powers of observation.* This is an art developed with practice. The good coach can observe a movement, sense its weakness and suggest a remedy soon after seeing the movement. Many coaches can spot the faults in technique, but it takes a good coach to suggest a remedy.

3. *Patience.* Success in athletics can only be achieved after a number of years of hard work. The good coach realises that there are no short-cuts to success and does not waste time trying to seek them.

4. *An ability to motivate.* This quality should head the list as it is the only true essential.

5. *Devotion.* The coach must be prepared to give up considerable amounts of his own free time in the search for athletic excellence in others.

Earlier in this chapter I suggested that the coach needed to be a psychologist. This does not mean that he should have a professional

qualification in psychology, although this might help, but rather through experience he should become aware of the various psychological aspects likely to affect athletes and their performances. Experience is the *key* factor as coaching is a personal relationship between two individuals who are unlikely to react identically when placed in similar circumstances. Hence, no hard and fast rules can be laid down. The coach is bound to make mistakes, they are unavoidable. The good coach learns from his mistakes and avoids making them again. This aspect of coaching can only be gained through personal experience. However, there are a few basic principles which the coach can adopt and modify to suit both his own personality and that of his athlete.

1. *The coach must be a motivator.* He must be capable of stimulating interest and providing the right incentive at the right time. He must be capable of recognising the symptoms of boredom and be able to take the necessary steps to counteract the situation. Training is routine and often boring even for top-class athletes who have numerous incentives. The coach must be on top of the situation all of the time. He must design training schedules and sessions that are varied, interesting and sufficient to stimulate the athlete, so that the maximum benefit can be obtained from the routine. Coaching is 90% encouragement and 10% technical expertise.

2. *The coach must be an organiser.* All coaching sessions should be planned in advance so that valuable time is not wasted. There is nothing worse than arriving at a training venue to find out that certain essential pieces of equipment are not available. Organised sessions will flow easily and the coach will be able to devote all of his attention to the athlete and his training.

3. *The coach must have powers of concentration.* During all coaching sessions the coach must keep in contact with the athlete. At times there are likely to be many distractions, but without this concentration good coaching relationships cannot develop.

4. *The coach must set certain standards.* The coach should cultivate in his athletes favourable attitudes towards training, coaching, competition, officials, etc. This includes punctuality for training and competition, the ability to accept the verdict of judges without outbursts of tantrums. Often the good athlete is selfish, with the present standards he has to be, but undisciplined selfishness can cause undue hardship to others. A degree of co-operation is essential, especially when many athletes have to share common training facilities.

5. *The coach must be a mentor and confidant.* The coach should work with the athlete, letting him know why certain actions are taken; this way he will gain respect. The good coach should not only share the great moments but also the depressing ones. The athlete is capable of shouldering success alone, but failure is best shared. The right encouragement, at the right time, can work wonders with an athlete who has lost confidence.

My final advice relating to this aspect of athletics is to insist that the only way to become competent is through active participation with athletes. This present era is guilty of producing academic coaches thoroughly conversant with all of the associated sciences. Coaching athletics is more of an "art" than a "science" and the art can only be developed by forming a coaching relationship with the best possible athletes.

Section 2

Running and Hurdling events

Chapter 5

Sprinting : 100 metres - 400 metres

Sprinting involves the athlete in an attempt to run at peak speed for the complete duration of the race. By the very nature of the activity the period of the race is essentially short, lasting less than a minute, and even long before this period of time is reached, the killing effect of lack of oxygen, the vital fuel for movement, is starting to paralyse the muscles involved, making them incapable of responding to the demands of such extreme activity.

The chart below illustrates the factors involved in sprinting at top speed.

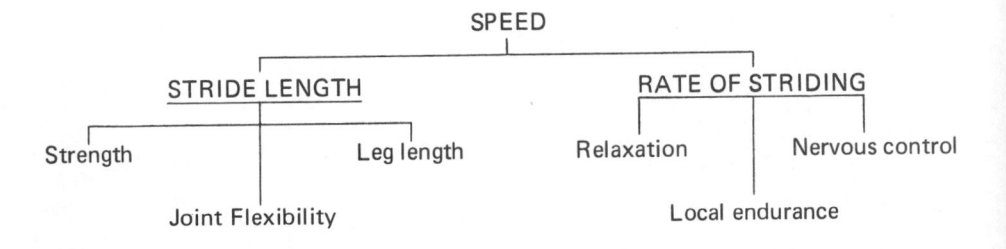

Assuming a standardisation of track surfaces, wind conditions and other outside variable factors, the speed at which it is possible to cover the short distance from A to B is determined by stride length and rate of striding.

Rate of striding

The fact that a sprinter is born is certainly beyond doubt, as the speed at which one can exchange the position of the legs is,, in the first place, dependent upon the speed of the nerve impulse supplying the muscles involved in producing this form of locomotion. That is, man has an ultimate capacity to perform this action, beyond which he is incapable of improving. However, all of those concerned with the sport must assume that man can never draw on his full potential; that he has hidden powers beyond his normal control, that can only be triggered off in the case of an extreme emergency. With this assumption, man can then strive to move as close to his ultimate capacity, as is humanly possible, by adopting a systematic plan for training.

A relaxed co-ordinated style is essential if the athlete wishes to move the legs quickly. This aspect of the training can probably be improved by repeated movements at peak speed, when the body can become adjusted to the stress and will adapt accordingly. The term "relaxation" is a difficult one to interpret as it must be used in a relative sense. One could assume that relaxation means the lack of tension, but if an athlete followed this definition to its logical conclusion he would drop to the floor, as muscular tension is required even to maintain posture. However, it is a concept which the athlete/coach cannot ignore. He should strive continuously towards perfectly co-ordinated movements with the complete economy of effort necessary to preserve the supplies of fuel, essential to complete the full distance of the race. In this introduction to the events, it is not the intention to discuss the ways by which man can improve on his current parameters, as this will be dealt with elsewhere in the text.

Stride length

This factor has obsessed those involved with this group of events for the last decade or so, largely because it is a term that can be subjected to mechanical reasoning, film analysis, etc. and evidence supporting an increased stride length can be easily observed. However, if the stride length is increased to the detriment of leg speed, then the end result might well be a slower performance. An improvement in speed, over a distance, can only result from an improvement in leg speed or stride length without a fall-off in either; or if both are improved simultaneously. From the outset stride length is both strength and flexibility dependent and an improvement in either or both could conceivably increase the stride length. Of course it can be reasoned that stride length is also influenced by an innate factor of leg length over which the athlete has no control.

The sprinting group of events divide naturally into the short sprints, covering races up to and including 200 mtrs. 220 yds., and the long sprints, covering those races between 200 mtrs. and 400 mtrs. 440 yds. The distances mainly contested in the major out-door meetings are:-

100 mtrs. = 109.36 yds. time differential +0.9 secs.
200 mtrs. = 218.72 yds. "   "   −0.1 secs.
400 mtrs. = 437.44 yds. "   "   −0.3 secs.

The differential given in the end·column is the one which is used to convert metric times to those given for a race over yards. For example, if a person does 10.9 seconds for a 100 metres race it is fair to assume that his time for 100 yards would be 10.0 seconds. However, as far as Great Britain is concerned the non-metric distances are history and only the U.S.A. seems to persist with them.

The 400 metres usually involves running one complete circuit of the

Plate 2. A. Neal (G.B.) demonstrates "On your marks".

Plate 3. A. Neal (G.B.) demonstrates "Set" position.

standard track, the 200 metres runner covers half of the circuit with the start usually on the bend, and the 100 metres race is always on the straight track. Hence, the sprinter who races in distances over 100 metres, is usually faced with the added skills involved in negotiating a bend at speed.

The starting official for a sprint race issues the following instructions:- "On your marks"..."Set", followed by the report of the pistol. They are given clearly and precisely, with a time interval allowed between each for the individual athlete to get into an efficient position to overcome the inertia of his own body, when the pistol provides the stimulus. The time interval between each of the commands varies with the individual starter, but all athletes must be steady "On their marks" before the pistol can be fired. The starting movement is the first skill which the sprinter has to interpret, and the variations in styles, employed by athletes in their own interpretation of what is necessary to get them moving efficiently, are fairly considerable.

The sprint start

The only essential of the starting movement is that the centre of gravity of the body must be in front of the feet, which provide the power through their reaction with the ground, when the starting stimulus is given. However, to make the start efficient a number of other factors must be carefully considered. They are:-

  i) The position of the feet relative to the starting line and each other.
  ii) The apportionment of bodyweight relative to the supporting limbs.
  iii) The concentration of the athlete upon the necessary reactions he must make the instant he hears the report of the pistol.

i) The position of the feet

It is impossible to suggest any hard and fast rules, as this factor depends entirely upon the individual. It is considerably influenced by the various lengths of the athlete's body levers, by strength and by flexibility. However, the feet must be positioned so that the athlete is comfortable, thus enabling him to devote his entire concentration to the movements involved in getting away quickly. The positioning of the feet is also influenced by the type of race, as the proximity of the bend for the longer races demands a different positioning. Most other texts, when dealing with this aspect of sprinting, mention three possible positions for the feet:-
(a) The bunch start (bullet start). Here the feet are fairly close together with the toes of the rear foot almost touching the heel of the front foot, the front foot being at a comfortable distance away from the line. (b) The medium start. Here the rear foot is placed about the length of the tibia behind the front foot; again the front foot position, relative to the starting line, is decided by comfort. (c) The elongated start where the rear foot is just over the length of the tibia away from the heel of the front foot. In all starting positions, the position of the front foot must be decided by

experiment. If the front foot is too close to the line, the athlete will be cramped. If it is too far away, extra distance has to be covered. However, most of the work done on starting techniques has been greatly influenced by the research of Franklin Henry, who experimented with four different sets of block spacings, all quite arbitrary, and measured in inches and not lengths of body levers. I am afraid none of the above ideas satisfy my own personal philosophy on the matter and I arrive at all of the starting positions, for my own athletes, by using the medium start position as the basis for experimentation. The vogue at the moment seems to be towards a fairly flat back in the "set" position, without very much weight on the arms; the feet are fairly close together, but some 24 inches between the starting line and the front foot. The final choice is always left to the athlete and it is only taken after numerous observations on stride lengths and stop watch recordings, but the overruling factor is always *comfort*.

ii) The apportionment of weight

To a very large extent this is physique dependent, and the position one adopts will be influenced by length of levers, mobility and strength, but the athlete must always favour the most comfortable position as this will certainly be the most efficient one. A number of authorities on sprinting insist that the weight must be well forward, over the arms that act as the front support. I am personally against this as it will cause tension in the arms. The first really apparent movement from the sprinter comes from the arms. They must move quickly into an efficient sprinting position which they cannot do if they are tense. The sprinting action calls for a flexed arm position and because of this I favour a flexed arm position in the "set", rather than the more commonly adopted straight arm position. There must not be too much pressure on the arms during the "set" position, otherwise they cannot move quickly into the position described.

When the athlete first positions himself for the start, the body must be placed in the most relaxed manner possible, with the legs well bent. From this position the legs could not possibly respond to any fast explosive movement, hence during the "set" position they must shift the bodyweight into a position from which they can react quickly. This will mean that the front leg must extend so that the upper and lower extremities of the front leg form an approximate right angle about the knee joint. This is theoretically an efficient position, although in practice I find that the athlete often needs to adopt an angle in excess of this (see plate 3). Sometimes this will mean that the hips come above the level of the shoulders, sometimes it will mean that the back is fairly flat. It will depend entirely upon the position of the front block from the starting line.

iii) Concentration

A fast "get away" from the start can only follow an efficient relaxed

"set" position, where the athlete has been able to concentrate and channel all of his energy into an instant reaction the moment the report of the pistol triggers off the body mechanisms. Unless the athlete is concentrating on hearing the sound of the pistol, and on what actions to make once the sound has been heard, valuable fractions of a second can be lost. This concentration seems to prime the various systems involved, so that they can act instantly the pressure is applied.

However, the techniques employed at the start are the means by which the body can accelerate quickly from the static position, and although vital fractions of a second can be gained or lost at the start, it must be regarded as a fairly insignificant part of the race. Once the body is moving, full seconds can be won or lost by the actions the sprinter makes to get past the finish. On average, the 100 metres runner makes about forty contacts with the ground during the race. If the body does *not* make full use of each contact with the ground, to propel it forwards, then fractions of a second are lost, and over the course of the race these are considerably amplified as each movement is repeated.

For most people the action of running is a fairly natural one, but running at peak speed is not quite such a natural movement; it has to be nurtured through several years of hard training. The efficiency of the "running machine" is dependent upon the way the body uses its levers to perform this method of locomotion and, if these levers are not used effectively, time is lost. The body is propelled forwards by the reaction of the ground to the combined forces the various body levers exert through the legs. Most of the force is provided by the legs, but the arms contribute particularly during their movement to the rear. Although the legs and the arms are primarily the levers involved, the movement must be regarded as one performed by the body as a whole. If the trunk and head, which on the surface appear not to contribute, are not kept in correct alignment then wasteful movements, retarding speed, can ensue. At this stage it is worthwhile to analyse the precise movements made by the major segments of the body:-

The legs. Here we are concerned with the actions they make and not the speed at which they operate, as this must always be kept to a maximum. Hence, one must accept that in this respect the means by which the body levers exert their force will largely influence stride length.

When one observes cine film of great and novice sprinters together, a most significant difference in running style is immediately apparent. The great sprinter uses his driving leg to the full, getting complete extension, whereas the novice has started to recover the leg well short of the optimum drive position. As both are in contact with the ground for approximately the same time, it follows that the good sprinter has this unique ability to do more work during this brief moment when the foot strikes against the track surface. Most sprinters can manage to get full extension of the knee joint, but only those of exceptional class can get full ankle extension. The athlete

Plate 4. The powerful driving action of the Olympic 100/200 metres champion for 1972, V. Borzov (U.S.S.R.)

must be made aware of this final small, fast, extension that can contribute so much to the quality of performance. Therefore, the most important part of the running phase is the way in which the leg, in contact with the ground, performs the driving action. A number of authorities on the subject suggest that there are two types of sprinters, "drivers" and "strokers": the former giving the overall impression of driving the ground away behind the body with strong, powerful, leg movements, and the latter that of stroking the ground away. It would appear that this is a misinterpreted analysis, with the observers confusing tension and fluidity and that both are really performing the same movement. It must always be accepted that the talented performer executes the skill with complete relaxation so making it look easier, and this can confuse the observer into misinterpreting the skill.

The important thing is that, while the foot is in contact with the ground, every scrap of useable energy must be obtained from it. This will mean that the leg must extend rapidly about the hip, knee and ankle joints. Most athletes experience little difficulty in extending the leg about the first two mentioned joints, but the final ultra-fast action about the ankle region is obtained only by the elite. Often the athlete is unaware of this phase of the movement, because it must happen so quickly, if it is to happen at all. However, by systematic conditioning, outlined later, it can be achieved.

The running movement is so organised that while one leg is driving the body forwards, the other leg is recovering, ready to be forced to the ground to take over propulsion. Frequently, attention is focused on the mechanics of this event, particularly this action of recovery, making it seem as important as the driving phase. The only essential is that the leg must be recovered at speed and this will mean that it has to be brought through to a position, in

front of the body, so that it is bent ready to exert a downward force. If the driving action is correct, the heel of this leg will naturally pick up behind the thigh. The powerful muscles acting about the hip joint will then have to pull this bent lever through to the position ready for driving. This position will be determined by joint flexibility and strength. It is often thought that the higher it is picked up the more forcibly it can be pushed down. Theoretically this is the case, but often there is not time to recover it to such a position before it is required to take over from the driving leg. During conditioning work it is possible to get a fast powerful knee lift, but this is of secondary importance to the action of the leg while the foot is in contact with the ground. However, it is a phase that must not be ignored as the athlete must perfect all movements if he is to achieve technical excellence and with it, we hope, improved performances.

The trunk. During the leg cycle the trunk is locked in a position about the hip joint so that it can help absorb some of the movements of the legs and arms. If this were not the case the efficiency of the movement would be reduced, as the muscles which work the legs could also be used to perform unwanted movements of the trunk. There must not be a forced lean of the trunk as this will only restrict the action of the muscles acting about the hip joint. Many inexperienced teachers and coaches see the running actions of athletes soon after the start and think that the lean of the trunk, during this phase, is one that is kept for the duration of the race. Once the athlete has picked up speed, the trunk gradually becomes fairly erect and remains so unless a dip finish is used.

In running the arms are used to balance the movements of the legs. Their movement is, at all times, co-ordinated with the legs and it is virtually impossible for them to get out of phase, other than for a brief moment at the start. Theoretically it can be reasoned that the arms can contribute to the drive via a reaction through the legs; it is best to think of them solely as a balancing mechanism that plays a most important part in relaxed sprinting. At all times the arm movement should be fast and to achieve this they should be kept bent about the elbow joint, with most of the movement taking place in the shoulder girdle. The upper and lower arm should form an approximate right angle about the elbow joint, this angle slightly increasing on the backwards movement and slightly decreasing on the forward movement. My only concern is that the arms should be free of tension, particularly in the shoulder region. Tension in this area is often reflected in the neck and it seems to have a disturbing effect on the whole fluidity of the running movement.

Once the athlete has got over the embarrassment of having to move at speed from a static position, there is little he can do except rely upon muscular memory. The chances are that if the athlete strives for speed he will become tense and the movement might well become less efficient. It is best to rely upon the investment made during training, to keep relaxed and

to allow competitive situations to draw on extra reserves, which are not really possible to tap during self-imposed training.

The period of a race, directly following the start, is often termed the "pick-up" phase, during which time the athlete is accelerating to peak speed. With some athletes this can take as little as fifteen yards and others require as much as forty yards to reach peak speed. Each accelerating stride is longer than the previous one and they continue to increase in length until peak speed is reached, when the stride length will remain constant until fatigue starts to take over. It is impossible to lay down any hard and fast rules as to how long each stride should be, as the precise distance is influenced by a multitude of factors which include physique, strength, mobility, etc. However, the good coach must learn to recognise the pick up pattern for his athletes, analyse it to see if it is consistent and if it can be improved upon. I feel that it is a phase of a race that should be recognised but without considering it as a priority, unless it is clearly a restricting factor. I am convinced that the best sprinters are those who can maintain their maximum speed for the greatest part of the race. From observations it would appear impossible for an athlete to remain at peak speed for the entire duration of a race. That is, there is bound to be some fall off in speed approaching the finish. The great sprinter is the one who slows least. Some coaches suggest that this phase of a race, when an athlete starts to tire, requires great concentration, others suggest that the athlete should strive for leg speed. I am of the opinion that the athlete is alone with just the memory of what he has done in repeated training and racing situations. The only way for a sprinter to develop to maximum potential is when the running is performed under the stress of competitive pressure. By frequently experiencing this pressure, the athlete is likely to adapt the body to perform the most unnatural task of running at peak speed. This does not mean that *all* running is performed flat out. This might cause a break-down and not an adaptation. Unfortunately few sprinters are made; conditioning, etc. can improve one's performances but it is impossible to put in what God left out.

As mentioned earlier in the text, the sprinting group of events concern the 100 metres, 200 metres, and 400 metres. Although they are considered as a group, the 400 metres event must remain an individual event since it involves the athlete in an attempt to run for a period beyond which the normal process for providing energy breaks down. Certain groups of people also argue that the two shorter sprints are quite different and they suggest that in the future the short sprint double is less likely to happen. This is a theoretical possibility, but at the moment both men and women are still achieving this.

100 metres. This is a short dash that only permits the athlete to run at peak speed for about 60 metres. It involves the athlete in the normal, straight sprint start, a very rapid pick-up sustaining the peak speed until the tape is breasted. The 100 metres, which takes only a little longer to run than

Plate 5. A close finish for the 1972 100 metres for women.

it does to say it, is often won by fractions of an inch, or hundredths of a second if a time interval is used. Because of this the athlete cannot miss any opportunity that is likely to save these vital fractions. The only specialised technique other than that of running, is at the start and the finish. The race itself is over so quickly that the athlete seldom gets a chance to appreciate fully what is happening. It is a subconscious movement, almost reflex, which is elaborated by frequent practice. In most top-class races it is rare to see a sprint race without one or more of the athletes attempting a dip finish. A dip finish is made in the heat of a competition, in an attempt to gain a verdict. It is often made necessary when an athlete's final stride, before the line, lands marginally short. To take a further stride, when probably a distance of about a foot is all that is involved, would force the athlete into a time wasting leg cycle when a dipping of the body would save all of this. There is no doubt that the dip finish, timed correctly, is a race winner and so it must always remain part of the top-class sprinter's "armoury".

200 metres. This event demands considerably more technique and judgement on the part of the athlete than does the shorter sprint, as it involves the added skill of being able to negotiate a bend at speed. The athlete still attempts to run the race flat-out, but wasted energy caused by undue tension, becomes more evident the longer the race lasts.

The start. For the conventional race the start is always on the bend, hence the normal straight facing position for the blocks cannot be used. The reason for this is that the athlete, forced to run on a curve directly he has started, has to try to get as many of the early strides, as possible, in a straight line. To achieve this the blocks are positioned at an angle across the lane, in such a way that it is possible for the athlete to strike the inner curve at a tangent. Other than this offsetting of the blocks, the only other way the conventional sprint start is modified is in the positioning of the hands relative to the scratch line. Because the blocks are at an angle to this line the hands have to be offset to keep the shoulders square to the direction of the run. (See figures 1-2.) Apart from the very slight change in the pattern of the arm movement, caused by speed running on a curve, the pick-up and running action is similar to that for the straight sprint. Although the action is slightly modified, the start must still be as fast as possible.

The bend. It is often true to say that the long sprint is won or lost by the way the athlete runs the curve. As sprint race verdicts are gained by fractions of an inch, the athlete cannot afford to waste them by running wide on the bend. The closer the curve is hugged, the more likely is the athlete to run the scheduled distance. If the curve is run wide, a greater distance is run, and unless all athletes make the same mistake the athlete concerned is at a disadvantage. The good sprinter has the ability to hug the bend all of the time until the final straight is reached. Lesser mortals run the whole curve wide, or run wide off the curve, wasting vital inches. The important thing about bend running is that it should be relaxed speed. If there is any sign of tension, the athlete is unlikely to have the necessary energy left to pick up

4   3   2   Figs. 1

8   7   6   5

even more speed on the straight. The whole secret of bend running rests with the ability to run at speed in a relaxed manner. In some texts it is stated that the athlete must "coast" the bend ready for the final "gather". This dated philosophy would gain little support in our present world of high standards. Never, at any stage during a full-effort sprint, can the athlete afford to coast. Some might argue that it is a play on words because to them coasting means running without tension. To me the term "coast" means running at sub-maximum effort, that is slower, and this cannot be accepted. During a sprint race there must always be maximum effort but with minimum tension.

The straight. The athlete will meet the straight at almost top speed which has only been restricted by the curve. However, peak speed is reached very early on in the straight which still leaves a considerable distance of sustained speed running. The athlete who can sustain this speed the longest is assured success. As in the 100 metres there is very little the athlete can do except rely upon the muscular memory of hours spent training and conditioning for this situation. The well conditioned athlete, with experience, will find that the straight appears to become shorter, the fitter and more confident he becomes. I refrain from saying "easier" because sustained running at speed can never become easy and will always remain a physical effort, the side effects of which become less with good conditioning.

To summarise, 200 metres running is for the superbly fit sprinter who has mastered the ability to run a bend with relaxed efficiency. It is very simple to say, but it is the truth which few short sprinters will accept.

400 metres. This event is often termed the "killer" and indeed it is in terms of physical effort. The race is a sustained sprint, demanding vast supplies of energy giving materials which are not readily available. Because of this, the athlete will experience some discomfort towards the end of the race and for a period during recovery. In many respects it is wrong to call it a sprint because, although theoretically possible, full speed for the entire race is not achieved. It would appear that an athlete can run at full speed for something short of the full 400 metres. If an athlete attempted to go flat out from the start he would certainly be in a state of collapse before the finish and would certainly be overhauled by athletes who succeed in proportioning their effort. So the 400 metres runner is faced with considerable pace judgement which in turn is influenced by the natural demands of the race, i.e. the early burst of speed from the blocks and the "Cast all to the wind" attitude towards the finish.

Most texts offer quite confused and conflicting opinions on how a 400 metres race should be run. Firstly there are those who suggest a flat out first 200 metres and then rely upon competition, etc. to help withstand the crippling effects of sustained speed running. Then there is the group who favour an even paced race, where the time difference between the first half and the second half of the race is small. Theoretically, this is a sound plan which seldom works out in practice. The ideal is obviously to produce a

Plate 6. The relaxed stride of D. Jenkins (G.B.) 400 metres.

fit, strong, aware athlete capable of winning the race whether it is run slower or faster than his existing capabilities. An aware athlete is capable of interpreting correctly the feedback from the race itself, and from his body, to help him judge the pace correctly and make use of his fitness to react to the situation, and later rely upon strength to help him pull through when other faculties are being paralysed by fatigue products.

However, a glimpse at the way recent Olympic winners have run the race might throw some light on how the race might be run. The 1972 winner ran the first 200 metres in 21.3 and the final 200 metres in 23.3 seconds, that is a differential of two seconds. The 1968 winner ran the first 200 metres in 21.2 seconds and the final 200 metres in 22.6 seconds, a differential of 1.4 seconds. The average differential for all of the men who competed in Mexico (1968) was 1.5 seconds, with a range of 0.2 for the best differential to 3.2 seconds for the poorest. The most interesting point to note from the study of the 1968 finalists is that the winner of the men's 400 metres ran to within 0.6 seconds of his personal best 200 metres for the first 200 metres of the race. This supports my own ideas that the first two hundred metres of the race should be the fastest and that it should be about one second slower than the athlete's personal best for the 200 metres. If the race is judged correctly, the final 200 metres should be the slowest section due to fatigue. Women, who have not quite the same capacity as men for this type of endurance, obviously run the final 200 metres quite a lot slower. For example the average differential between the first 200 metres segment and the second 200 metres segment, for all of the women who competed in the 400 metres in 1968 Olympics, was 3.0 seconds, exactly twice the average differential for men.

To summarise, the 400 metres runner who is fully conditioned, and this must be emphasised, should run the first 200 metres at slightly sub-maximum speed in order that the final sections of the race can be completed with reasonable form. The whole situation demands a very specific type of fitness that can be developed through systematic training, outlined later.

Sprinting for the novice. The essential thing for the novice is that the activity is enjoyable. The novice is mainly interested in immediate success and is motivated by this. This philosophy must influence the way sprinting is introduced to the young. Most young people react favourably to competition and, if this is of the right kind, it can do much to motivate them. I rely on this natural instinct when introducing sprinting to young people. All children, unless physically handicapped, are capable of running between fifty and one hundred metres, so races of this order should be organised. For children to beat an opponent, or an imposed standard, they will try to run at peak speed. Since competition is so important, children should be placed in ability groups and made aware of the type of competition. Initially, I favour indirect competition where the child is competing against an imposed standard and not against a person.

A very suitable type of competition, designed to motivate and not select, is a race, preferably over a straight distance, for a period of ten seconds using three marker flags to indicate levels of achievement. For example,14 year-old boys might be asked to run over a straight course with marker flags at 60 metres, 70 metres and 80 metres from the start. From a standing start, an audible signal (a blast on a whistle) is given after a running period of ten seconds, and ideally this should take all children to a position within the zone bounded by the standard flags. The competitors should have been previously warned to take notice of which marker flag they are passing the instant the signal is given. If points are awarded for each flag position, i.e. one point for the near flag, two points for the central flag and three points for the flag remote from the start, a simple points grading can be given to each person. Ideally the run should be repeated several times, with a recovery period between each. A suitable number of repetitions is three, and if a target total of six points is suggested to the group further motivation can be applied. If competitions of this nature are used, the teacher/coach must take note of the results and praise all concerned. If the standard markers are carefully selected there will not be any failures as all should achieve at least three points, and again they should be such that none can get nine points. This way there is motivation for all of the competitors. Once children have been motivated, and enjoy running, other less important aspects of sprinting, such as a method for starting, can be introduced. However, speed will always remain the dominant factor and this timed run is but one of the methods available to the teacher/coach to serve as motivation. There are many other methods, which include handicap running, all of which the good teacher/ coach should experiment with to sustain interest.

TRAINING FOR THE ADVANCED SPRINTER

It is not the intention of this book to put forward schedules alleged, or known to be used by top class sprinters, but rather suggest the various avenues open to the discerning coach/athlete,who can then plan a schedule to include all or some of the ideas put forward depending upon the needs of the athlete, the environment, facilities, etc. To make the presentation logical and uniform, I will follow the basic theory pattern of the event outlined in the opening paragraph of this chapter, and examine the ideas on training which might affect the factors that ultimately determine speed.

Stride length

Provided the rate of striding is not decreased, any increase in the length of the stride, for all or part of the race, will improve the standard of performance. The basic length of an athlete's stride is determined by the length of the lower limbs, strength and mobility. As the former is something over which the athlete/coach has little if any control, for the purpose of this treatise on training it can be ignored. The only other factor to affect stride

length, assuming a standardisation in all outside influences such as track surface, wind, etc. is one of fitness, which could possibly help the athlete sustain maximum stride length for longer or for the duration of the event.

Strength

In all athletic events I am convinced that there are two main areas of strength. A pure strength, which I often term "animal" strength, refers to the ability to exert a peak force for a single contraction. Then there is the "specific" strength which is probably the way a degree of "pure" strength is utilised in the event situation. For example,running is not a single maximum contraction but rather a multi-impact situation demanding a number of sub-maximal efforts. However, I feel that it is difficult to develop the true "specific" strength until a reservoir of "pure" strength has been developed.

(a) Development of "pure" strength. I am convinced that the only way to develop this kind of strength is through a form of progressive resistance exercises, using weights or some other form of resistance. At the moment most track and field athletes use barbells, etc., with discs as the most common method for applying a resistance; but looking to the future, I believe that the use of a "multi-gym" incorporating cables, pulleys and keyed weights will supersede this form of training because of its greater reliability and safety factor. (See Plate 34.) In this area the athlete should use conventional exercises, utilising accepted lifting techniques and systems. Ideally the weight should be kept high and the number of repetitions low, but this will be dealt with further in the section on strength training. When working for "pure" strength I suggest that the body be considered as three major parts: arms, trunk and legs, and a balanced schedule should be drawn up to bring about complete and harmonious development of the whole body.

(b) Development of "specific" strength. It is in the area of "specific" strength where I feel that the greatest advances can be made. In this area exercises are performed against a resistance in such a way that they might have a carry-over to the event itself. It is impossible to say that there will be a direct transfer of training from one form of activity to another related form of activity. However, it is generally accepted that a transfer of training is more likely when two activities are very similar to each other in their method of performance.

i. Specific weight training exercises

(a) Timed method. The average good class sprinter probably runs fast for a period of 11.0 seconds, 22.0 seconds or 50 seconds, depending upon the event being performed. Better class athletes perform for a shorter period and those with less ability perform for a longer period of time. With this method of training the athlete performs an exercise with weights for a period relative to the time he is likely to spend racing. For example a good class sprinter

might do a stepping-up exercise, onto a standard bench, for a period of ten seconds before taking a recovery. Ideally the rhythm should be as fast as the safety factors will allow. Similarly the 400 metres runner would perform an exercise like the straddle dead-lift for a period of 48 seconds before taking a rest. In this case the athlete will suffer considerable stress almost identical to that which he is likely to experience during a very fast race. The weight lifted should be sufficient to produce the "overloading" effect. Similar exercises incorporating the arm movement, close to that used in sprinting, can be performed using dumb-bells, for identical periods of time. This type of strength training also helps to develop the specific endurance necessary to keep the stride length up for the duration of the race.

(b) Contact frequency method. This method is very similar in its application to the timed method. Instead of using a time as its controlling factor, it uses a number of repetitions relative to the number of contacts or complete cycles the limbs are likely to make during a race. For example, an athlete might take about forty strides during the course of a 100 metres race. In this case the athlete should perform the resistance exercise for a number of forty repetitions before a period of recovery is taken. Again the resistance must be carefully chosen to produce the required level of stress.

In the case of the above systems the athlete/coach must be on guard not to do an excess amount of this work otherwise an adaptation to the stress might not take place and instead a breakdown could occur due to fatigue.

ii. Exercises using other forms of resistance

(a) Harness running. This is excellent work for sprinting but again too much of it should not be recommended. It should only be done during the strength-build-up period. I suggest this because the nature of the activity causes the athlete to run at a considerably reduced speed and sprinting is only concerned with fast movements. Basically the athlete performs the movement with a belt secured about the waist. The belt is attached to ropes which are held by a partner who provides a resistance proportionate to there being effective movements coming from the performer. Harness runs can be performed for a period of time or for a distance. It is most helpful if the coach can apply the resistance as he can place certain emphasis on movements by calling to the performer from behind. e.g. greater ankle extension, higher knee lift, etc. The resistance does not have to be applied by a partner. It can be applied by weighted sleighs which have the advantage that the degree of resistance can be measured and standardised, but I favour the greater flexibility of the partner method.

(b) Uphill running. With this type of training the athlete attempts to sprint up a slope. The duration of the run will depend upon the gradient, but as always, I feel that it should be associated with the performance time. The important thing is that it should not be too long otherwise it becomes an

endurance exercise. I prefer a slope of about sixty degrees as this forces a high knee pick-up and an extensive drive.

(c) Sandhill running. This type of activity is similar to the above only it is more strenuous due to the power lost in displacing the sand during the driving phase.

(d) Running against an elastic resistance. This method of training might be termed gimmicky but it is the author's opinion that it has a very definite place in the systematic training for sprinters. It requires a good deal of improvisation and can really only be performed in a gymnasium with standard wall bars. The contraption is constructed from an elasticated waist belt secured by ropes to two elasticated feet harnesses. (See Plate 36b.) A skill factor is involved in running in the harness effectively but it is soon learned. It has an advantage in that a double transfer effect is likely. When the knee is picked up in the running action, against the resistance of the elastics, a strength factor is involved. Once under stretch the elastic takes over and forces the foot to the ground very quickly, much faster than the athlete would normally be capable of. I cannot make any rash claims for the apparatus other than the fact that most athletes like it as a part of their winter indoor conditioning.

Mobility

This is an area of athletic endeavour which is sadly neglected, probably because its effect upon performance is more difficult to recognise, but it is nevertheless a factor that can contribute to the complete development of a sprinter. Most athletes will claim that they do mobility work as part of their warming up routine prior to training and racing. This usually takes the form of a most boring routine of free-standing exercises and is more a mental preparation than a physical one. The truth is that because of the way most athletes perform these exercises, they can have little if any effect upon promoting greater flexibility. Once the mobility of youth has been lost, often through systematised strength work, the only way to obtain greater mobility is to stretch the joint artificially. I believe there are three ways by which the athlete might improve mobility. The first is to perform stretching exercises with a weight or a medicine ball and rely upon the momentum to produce a stretching effect in the joint. The weight should only be just sufficient to promote the degree of stretch below pain level but above the normal range of movement. There are, of course, inherent dangers with this type of work and great care must be taken not to stretch the joint beyond the elastic limits of the ligaments and supporting tissues. The second method involves using a partner to provide the stretching force and this type of work is extremely valuable once a pair have worked out an understanding with each other. The third system involves a series of carefully selected exercises, which isolate unwanted movements and concentrate the force on to a specific area or joint. In some cases the weight of a

limb, or muscles acting about an isolated joint, places the joint under pressure. If this type of work is performed to music or a beat rhythm, it can be made more interesting and can bring about improved results. This system is probably the safest in that the effort is always under full control. But of course this is also its weakness in that the athlete can release pressure at a time when the exercise might be producing the greatest effect.

Rate of striding

For a number of years I supported the established theory that this factor cannot be improved upon, and theoretically this is the case once the athlete has reached his physiological maximum. However, during training sessions I now place a good deal of emphasis on it and only facilities restrict the avenues I would like to explore. I believe that the rate of striding is influenced by the ability to relax and so overcome the natural resistance offered by muscles and joints, and of course by the innate factor of nerve impulse. By their very nature they are areas that are not very tangible, but they must not be ignored. The word "relaxation" is probably the most abused word in the coach's vocabulary. It is impossible to relax fully, and at the same time exert muscular effort. The aim should be to cut out unnecessary tension that uses up vital foodstuffs and often produces unwanted movements. It is an extremely difficult area to train for because so many factors are involved. An increase in strength and mobility could bring about a better sprinting style and this, together with other factors, could improve confidence and help the ability to relax. Outside this almost automatic improvement in the ability to relax, I feel that by repeating movements, at speed, with the coach often calling for a freer arm shoulder action, etc., will focus attention on the problem, make the athlete aware of it and, one hopes, able to do something about it. However, it is an area so much related to the psychological problems which the athlete encounters that it is not easy to give a simple straightforward answer.

It might be possible to help an athlete increase his stride rate if he is placed in a situation which will help him to run faster. I have in mind where an athlete could be towed by a specially prepared yoke secured to a bicycle or a motorised vehicle, or by placing the athlete in a slipstream created by a motorised vehicle. I can see both of these methods as being feasible and would like the situation where I could experiment. Other than this I have experimented with fast sprinting down a gradual incline and believe that it can help in the preparation for a sprinter.

To date all of the training ideas put forward have been what one might term "supplementary exercises" and do not directly involve the athlete in the true sprinting movement. Although the athlete must be conditioned correctly at least fifty per cent of the time which he spends training should be devoted to the sprinting movement. This will vary slightly depending upon the time of the year. During the winter more time might be spent on the

conditioning aspect and less on the actual speed running. Then as the season approaches, considerably more of the work will be directed towards running at speed. In an athlete's training schedule, time must be allowed for sprinting training and all of this work must be done flat out. If, during training, the athlete is involved in anything other than flat out running, then that training cannot be termed sprint training. I am not suggesting that all sessions involving running should be done at peak speed. There is a place for over-distance work being done slightly slower to help improve stamina as part of the general conditioning work. A sprinter must perform some flat out speed work the whole of the year round. Often athletes have made the mistake of merely including strength promoting work during the winter, only to find that they emerge in the spring slower than the previous year. It is essential that speed, strength, stamina and suppleness are developed together otherwise it is possible to arrive at the situation whereby a new skill has to be educated in order to match the improved strength levels.

Sprinting training

(a) Short sprints. The 60 metres dash, repeated a number of times, probably forms an important part of all sprinters' training programmes. It can be done from blocks or from a rolling start. Since the emphasis is on speed of movement, a fairly long recovery must be given in order that the quality of the running can be kept as high as possible. The athlete's desire to repeat the movement is often the best guide to the time taken for the period of rest. However, it should not be so long that the athlete would need to warm-up again before performing the activity. The quantity of this type of running, in a single session, will vary from athlete to athlete, but I have never asked for more than eight in a single training session.

(b) Up and down the clock short sprints. This is a mixture of distances between 60 metres and 100 metres. Ideally the distances chosen should be in ten-metre steps, then a guide to performance can be kept. For example, I often include the following in a sprinter's schedule:- 60 metres slow walk back recovery taking about three minutes, followed by a 70 metres sprint with a similar recovery; then followed by an 80 metres sprint, 90 metres sprint and a 100 metres sprint. If a challenge of 1.1 seconds is offered for the ten-metre differential, then it can act as an incentive and a guide to the performance. This type of session should always be timed preferably with a watch capable of recording one hundredth of a second. If the above scheme formed a training session it would be termed "up the clock". A 400 metres runner might go up to 100 metres in ten-metre intervals and come back down to 60 metres. Using the same step intervals it would be termed "Up and down the clock". A training programme of 60.80.100.80.60 metres, with a sufficient recovery between each, is an interesting session for the short sprinter. An attempt to make the respective times equal can provide an incentive and a guide to fitness.

(c) Repetition 150 metres. For me this is an essential training distance for all sprinters. I frequently give sprinters a training programme of six repetitions of 150 metres calling them emphasis runs. Although the aim is to run very fast on each, the athlete is given just one other aspect to think of. For example, this could be a longer ankle movement, a longer more relaxed arm movement, an attempt to run faster off the bend, etc. For this type of work the distance does not have to be exactly 150 metres. It is often best run from a point on the crown of the bend to the end of the straight. If the same starting position is used for each subsequent session, then any stop watch timings are meaningful.

(d) Up and down the clock medium distance sprints. This is identical to those described earlier only the distance of the run is greater, varying from 120 metres to 200 metres. This type of work is excellent for the 400 metres runner, and carefully selected distances between these can be ideal for the short sprinter, provided the recovery is sufficient and the number of fast runs kept to a few.

(e) Overdistance work for the short sprinter. I do not think that the short sprinter should be asked to perform many training distances in excess of 300 metres. However, I firmly believe that a few repetitions, usually three, performed weekly during the conditioning period are of value to the short sprinter.

(f) Overdistance work for the long sprinter. For the 400 metres runner the variety of this type of work that can be performed is endless. I would personally include distances of up to 600 metres as part of the all-year-round training scheme for a 400 metres runner. In this area differential 500 metres is an excellent training system. Here the athlete is given set targets to complete various sections of the race. For example, it might be suggested that the first 300 metres be completed in a time of 45 seconds followed by a final 200 metres taking 22 seconds approximately. The variation of differential running is almost endless; it adds variety and can be used to bring about specific effects.

(g) Short recovery work. This work is essentially for the 400 metres runner who has to condition the body to function, without an adequate supply of oxygen, for a fairly sustained period. Fast sprint turn-arounds are ideal in this situation. They involve running distances between 60 metres and 100 metres with a recovery period sufficiently long only to slow down, turn round, and start sprinting back to where the first sprint started from. This system can be fitted into an "up and down the clock" scheme very effectively. Repetition 200 metres, with a recovery period of about twenty seconds, often done in groups of three, is another way to condition the body to this type of stress.

There is a tremendous amount of variety in the work which a sprinter can do. The only problem is how to blend it into a training scheme so that it can be of maximum benefit. This problem can only be solved between the coach

and the athlete who must work together to produce athletic excellence. The only word of advice I will offer, on such an individual matter, is to suggest that more athletes should be made to work harder on their weaknesses. It is very common, and easy, for a sprinter to work only on his strong points because this is often the area which he enjoys most. But in good class sprinting, where fractions of a second are involved, the athlete cannot afford to have a single weakness.

(h) Coaching the sprinter. The sprint's coach is not unduly concerned with the technical aspects like his field events counterpart. This is because, apart from the starting situation, sprinting is a fairly natural function. This does not mean to say that the sprint's coach is inferior in any way to his counterpart who specialises in the field events. The sprint's coach is more a trainer and a motivator. In his striving for speed he has to be able to encourage the sprinter to produce peak effort frequently during training. In sprinting, the coach's first aim is to produce a fit, strong athlete. This is something that cannot be achieved in a period of weeks, or even months. It is a gradual build up which can often take years. With many sprint's coaches the work pattern changes very little with the season of the year, and many only pay lip service to the essential conditioning programme. Often it is easier to take a group to the local track and attempt to sprint, even though weather and track surfaces might be against this, rather than prepare a true conditioning programme, including a number of the ideas mentioned earlier. If the coach can be present for the majority of the conditioning sessions then it is helpful, as he can provide the necessary motivation to pull the athlete through this often dull and boring routine. It is possible to add variety, but if one wishes to succeed it is not possible to shirk hard work. So the coach is faced with drawing up a work routine, which has only just sufficient variety to prevent boredom and not to distract in any way from the prime aim of producing a fit, strong frame that can handle the demands of the sprinting activity.

Apart from the systematic planning of the training schedule, the sprint's coach must be frequently present at the track during the sprint training. Although his most important role in this situation is that of a motivator, the trained eye of the experienced coach should be able to spot instantly any weaknesses in running style or wrongful interpretation of the running schedule.

During starting practices, or fast running from blocks, the sprint's coach will nearly always find himself in the situation of being the starter. Although such a situation is far from being ideal, the coach can vary the timings of his commands, his voice inflexion and even give the commands in a foreign tongue, all of which can help the athlete prepare for the pressure of competition. Unfortunately, when filling this dual role, the coach cannot give both jobs his full attention, hence it is certain to be a compromise. The good coach will enlist the aid of a local, qualified starter, so that he can

concentrate upon the movements the athletes make from the blocks and during the vital pick-up strides. Here the tape measure, stop watch and cine camera are very valuable aids but the most valuable aid of all is the coach's appreciation of fluency, and this can only be developed over a period of years by being practically involved.

However, the coach should not think that his only duty is during the technical aspect of the starting movements. This is just a very small part of the training with which he must become involved. During longer runs, timed sections of a sprint, words of encouragement, providing an external stimulus such as a blast on a whistle to bring about a certain response or to shift emphasis, all have their place and the good coach, through experience, will know just what to do at the right time. This is an aspect of the coach's work which cannot be written about, or learnt from a book. It is a feeling, a relationship which the coach builds up with the athletes.

Chapter 6

Relay Racing

Relay racing is where one team of runners attempts to beat another team of runners over an identical distance. The race can be of any duration, with any number of people making up the team. More often than not a baton is carried and passed from runner to runner, but this is not essential and a simple touch of the hands will suffice. Apart from the very popular road relays, the most common race is one where a team of four runners completes a single lap of the track, or four laps of the track. The former is the sprint relay and each runner covers about 100 metres with the baton. The second is the 4 x 400 metres where each runner completes approximately one full lap with the baton. The important thing is that the baton must complete the full distance in the hands of the runners. Hence it cannot be thrown, and if dropped it can be retrieved but valuable time will be lost.

I am not an enthusiast of relay racing. To me it seems like an attempt to make something that is essentially a sport for the individual into a team event. However, relay races are often used to terminate a major meeting and as such can be enjoyable. Runners often compete in them after their own individual event is finished; they can take part in a relay free from the pressures associated with direct, individual, competition. Also the inter-club road relays, often designed to give the harrier runner a little extra variety, have much to commend them.

The historians might suggest that the relay race is of ancient Greek origin where one could conceivably argue an association between the torch races that formed part of a religious rite and the baton carrying races of today. Relay races are of modern design and while they appeared in the late 1800s in the United States of America, they did not find their way into the Olympic programme until 1912 in Stockholm where both the 4 x 100 metres and the 4 x 400 metres were held.

As far as the sprint relay is concerned it is true to say that slick baton changing can win a race, but it is equally true to say that four "hacks" cannot blend into a winning team by merely perfecting the baton exchange. There are several methods for passing and receiving the baton; some of the popular ones have equal merit and the selection is a matter of personal preference. However, there are certain fundamentals that must be observed in order to keep the baton moving at speed. They are:-

i) The speed of the outgoing and incoming runners must be matched so that both are travelling at speed when the baton is exchanged. For this to happen, the running styles of both athletes should be as near to a sprinting action as relay racing will allow.

ii) The exchange must take place within the stipulated zone otherwise disqualification will result. To prevent disqualification, there must be a margin of safety with the exchange method used.

A. Blending of speed and style

The first essential is that the exchange should be non-visual. That is, the outgoing runner does not run with a twisted trunk to look for the baton. Hence the placing of the baton in the hand is entirely the responsibility of the incoming runner. The early strides of the outgoing runner must be those of a sprinter, complete with the vigorous arm movement, and the receiving hand should not go to the receiving position until the cue mark has been reached. If the cue position has been chosen correctly, the instant the outgoing runner's hand reaches the receive position the baton should be placed in it. This will very seldom happen.

Plate 7. The relay "Up-sweep" with G.B. team members.

Plate 8. The relay "Down Sweep" with G.B. team members.

The method for exchanging the baton used by most international teams, at the moment, is known as the "up-sweep" (see plate 7). It is safe and permits a good sprinting action for most of the race. Here the outgoing runner's hand, for receiving the baton, is taken to the rear by an arm bent at about 90 degrees, and the hand is cocked slightly forward so as to make sure that the baton receives a full palm. The outgoing runner pushes the baton up into the hand, in the gap between the thumb and fingers, and ideally the respective hands should touch to make sure that there is sufficient baton length left for subsequent changes. However, a certain amount of juggling with the baton, to produce this free baton length, is nearly always necessary.

While the up-sweep into the down turned palm is considered safe and ideal should runners "overshoot" each other, it is not the only method used in international competitions. The down-sweep into the upturned palm (see plate 8) is probably more efficient in that it permits a greater free distance, as the change is effected at a full arm's distance and in theory a full running stride can be saved. But the position of the hands is so critical that to get just one good change in a race is an achievement. Because of this critical factor, which can only be perfected by frequent practice, something difficult for most teams, it has been dropped in favour of the "up-sweep" pass.

B. The place of exchange

In a very good relay baton exchange, the outgoing runner's hand should go

back, the stride before the centre of the box, and the stride after should see the completion of the exchange. For this to be possible, check or cue marks must be used; their precise position being arrived at by trial and error. However, the basic starting position for the mark is one of 25 foot lengths before the start of the accelerating zone (see diagram p. 61). The outgoing runner should stand just inside the accelerating zone and watch the incoming runner until the 25 foot pace mark is reached. Without looking back again, the outgoing runner should sprint away from the incoming runner, placing the hand back at the centre of the zone, when the change should be effected. If an exchange does not take place then, the position of the check mark must be adjusted until it does. Most of the current British team use a check mark of between 28/30 foot lengths.

C. Safety measures

The best safety measure is to adjust the cue mark so that the exchange is effected on the centre line, allowing the second half of the box to adjust for errors. A system of calling is often drilled with good squads; the simple call for "hand" when the incoming runner is ready to deliver the baton, and "wait" meaning the reverse, can often save a race. There is the danger of the baton being dropped, particularly if the runner changes the hand grip on the baton while running fast. This can be avoided by getting the first and third runners to carry the baton in the right hand, and the second and fourth runners to carry it in the left hand. This staggering will also mean that the first and third runners use the inside of their lanes, during the exchange, and the other runners the outside of the lane. It is also essential to remain in lane until all runners, competing in other teams, have passed by.

The individual skills involved in the event are:-
   i) The starting procedure.
   ii) The placing of the baton.
   iii) The receiving of the baton.
This of course assumes that the skill of top speed running, as described in the section on sprinting, is taken for granted.

i) The starting procedure

The normal sprint start is used for the first leg with only the modification made necessary to carry the baton in the right hand. The starting position for the remaining runners should be a modified sprint start, using only one hand for support, the incoming runner being viewed under the free arm which should be raised slightly. As there are no commands after the initial start, the other runners must rely upon visual cues to take their place. It is important that the athlete does not remain in the unsteady "set" position for any length of time. Hence the outgoing runner should rise to the set position as the incoming runner approaches the check mark and then sprint away once the mark has been reached.

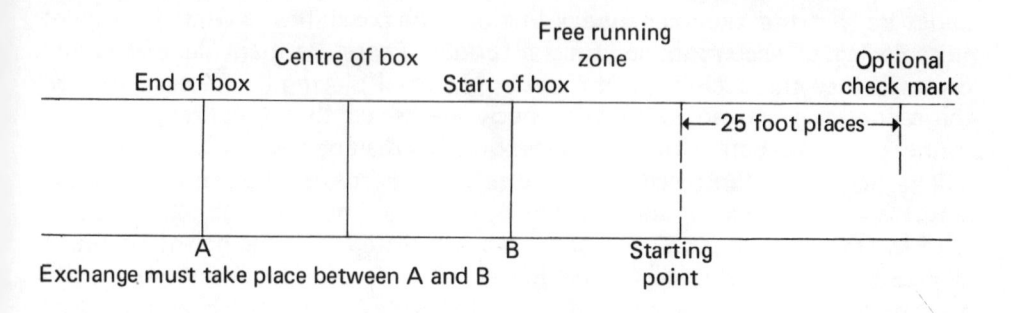

Exchange must take place between A and B

ii) The placement of the baton

The passing of the baton is the responsibility of the incoming runner. It must be a precise positive action, always permitting sufficient free baton length.

iii) Receiving the baton

Once the outgoing runner has sprinted away from the start, the only concern is to give the incoming runner a stable hand. This is difficult as the arm is required to help balance the sprinting movements.

Teaching relay racing

It must be emphasised that the sprint relay, covering one lap of a conventional track, is not the only type. The basic philosophy with young children must be to ignore take over zones. The only essential is that the baton must be carried all of the way.

In the large class situation a continuous relay lasting five or ten minutes can be good fun. The difficulty of selecting teams of sufficiently equal ability to provide competition for the entire duration of the race can be overcome with coloured batons. All that is required is a duplicate set of the same coloured batons, the competitors representing only a colour. The teacher/coach keeps the spare set of batons close to the finishing line. Should one team gain a considerable lead their baton can be exchanged, as it passes the finishing line during one of the laps, for the colour baton of a trailing team. The trailing team being given the baton of the leading team.

The important thing with children is that relays must be free from the possible risk of disqualification. The adult rules, methods, etc. can be taught to the school team should this be required.

Coaching the advanced team

The first thing the coach has to decide is the running order of the team. In dealing with the sprint relay the coach might decide to put the best starter first, a capable 200 metres runner on the second and third legs (in theory

these cover the greatest distance) and the "fighter" on the "Glory" leg. It could be that the team has a weak link and the coach has to decide the most suitable leg to accommodate such a runner. There are many factors which can influence the decision, but I am in favour of placing the "weak link" on the second leg and adjusting the check marks, so that the first and third runners have the baton for the longest possible distance.

The main function of the coach is to make sure that the time and energy is not wasted during training sessions. Hence they must be well planned. It is wise to start each session with some work directed at changing the baton. It is possible to get four very slick passes, at speed, in the length of a 100 metres straight. Once the method of passing and receiving has been rehearsed the often tedious task of calculating check marks should take place. If the coach has an assistant, the team can be split up with one coach carefully observing the actions of the first to the second runner, and the other coach doing the same with the third and fourth runners. Once the possibility of an efficient exchange seems likely, then the remaining exchange, runners two and three, can be drilled. The check mark runs can be done with the incoming runner approaching at speed from about 50 metres. The session should always end with a complete full effort run, as only in this situation can the true blending of the combination be evaluated. All exchanges should be rehearsed at the track position where they will take place during a race.

The coach must observe where, in the box, the take-over is effected. He must notice whether the outgoing runner actually commenced running as the check mark was hit and if the running action was at speed. All of these things have an effect upon the efficiency of the take-over. Therefore, the job of the relay coach is a very demanding one.

With the 4 x 400 metres the coach has an identical decision to make concerning the running order. It might not always be favourable to keep the strongest runner until last. A race is often decided well before the runner takes the baton for the final leg. As the race is run partly in lanes he must make sure that the runners know where to receive the baton and when to break for the inside.

As the exchange involves a fairly tired runner and a fresh runner, I favour a completely visual exchange for the 4 x 400 metres race. The outgoing runner should receive the baton in the left hand and immediately change it over to the right hand for carrying. The baton is best received with a downward facing palm and the outgoing runner reaching to take the baton from the slowing incoming runner. As the event is not carried out at such speed the margin for errors is greater.

Chapter 7

Middle Distance Running:
800 metres - 10,000 metres

The middle distance races, particularly the shorter ones, are the most popular throughout the whole world, both from the numbers of competitors taking part and the spectator response. The reasons for this popularity are simple and obvious. The skills involved in sustained running are very simple, and the competitor is not faced with the frustrations of trying to master a complex skill. Because of this it appeals to the less physically gifted, those lacking the co-ordination, or the patience to master the co-ordination, necessary for technical sports requiring intricate skills, and such people form the majority of the population. This statement is not made in any derogatory sense, and there will always be exceptions, but the general observation appears to be empirically true. Neither does it mean that the middle distance runner is a second grade athlete, far from it. He must spend many hours training very hard, to condition the body to withstand the stress placed on it during fast sustained races. It would be fair to say that about eighty per cent of the athletes in the United Kingdom are associated with middle distance or harrier running, and as such from the most dominating part of the sport. In countries not noted for the provision of facilities for athletics, it is obvious that a sport only requiring natural facilities is bound to attract a large interest. True harrier running, which is the foundation for all middle distance running, only depends on the natural environment of roads and fields, and even with the most adverse weather conditions it is nearly always possible to train at peak quality. So the two factors of maximum enjoyment at low skill levels, and facility requirement, are certain to ensure that this aspect of the sport will always have a large and healthy following.

Its spectator appeal is equally obvious. The running events are the only ones that present the spectator with the chance to view direct competition with all of the rivals taking part at one and the same time. The sprint races are over so quickly that they cannot possibly sustain interest, and a blink of the eye could make one miss the key feature of the race. On the other hand the longer distance races, lasting more than about five minutes, can become a monotonous procession of runners unless a number of them remain in contact to compete for the final placings. The middle distance events such as the 800 metres, 1,500 metres, and the mile, capture the imagination as they last long enough to observe tactics without becoming boring.

The process of running is a simple one, but to run faster and further calls for complex changes in the body, the precise nature of which is unknown. To run fast for a sustained period calls for a high degree of endurance on the part of the athlete. The term "endurance" is vague and requires some elaboration; its nature can be understood from the simple chart given below.

Total endurance

Cardio vascular	Local	Oxygen debt
Efficient heart	Strength of performing muscle	Toleration of waste products
Efficient circulation system	Efficiency of blood supply in that muscle	Removal and resynthesis of waste products
Efficient breathing mechanism		
Efficient exchange of gases		Acid/alkaline balance
Efficient transportation of gases		

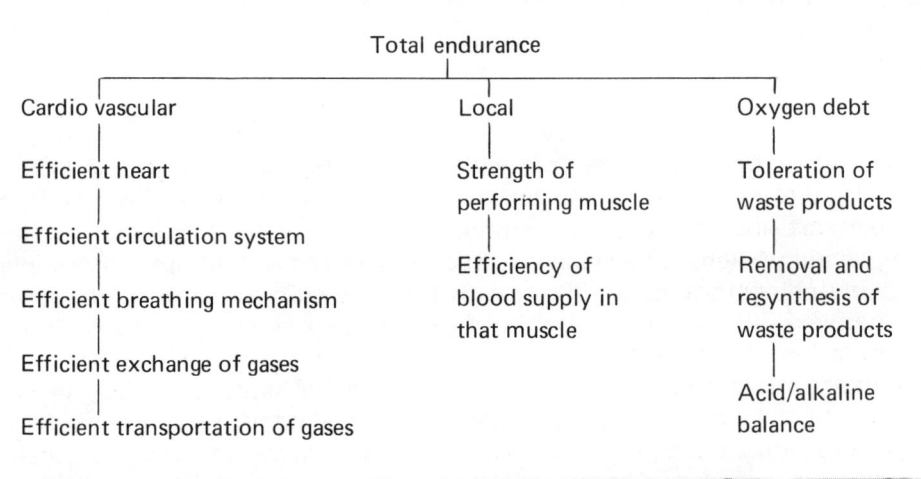

Plate 9. D. Wottle (U.S.A.) wins the 1972 Olympic 800 metres.

When the body takes exercise increasing amounts of oxygen, proportional to the severity of the exercise, are required by the active tissues. This is followed by a similar change in the type and amount of waste products found in the tissues. Basically the body adapts in two ways:-

1. There is an immediate increase in both the rate and depth of breathing which has the effect of making more oxygen available in the alveoli, the final unloading and loading compartments for the transportation system.

2. There is an increase in the output of the heart achieved by a greater stroke output and a faster beating rate which has the effect of pumping more blood to the active tissues. This action, together with a closing down of unwanted areas of circulation, speeds up the transportation of the gases from the lungs to the active tissues and vice versa.

The combined system for the gaseous exchange and for transporting the gases around the body for disposal, or use, is frequently termed "the cardio-respiratory system". It is towards development of an efficient cardio-respiratory system that most of the endurance training is directed. I say "most" because total endurance, as the athlete understands it, is not just a cardio-respiratory response.

The human body is a marvellous machine capable of performing work when it is partly deprived of essential energy-providing substances. The vital fuel for muscular work is oxygen and under certain circumstances the body can perform work without an adequate supply of it for a limited period. When the body is forced to perform work in this way it is inefficient and the term frequently used to describe this situation is "oxygen debt" or anaerobic work. The term "oxygen debt" is slightly inaccurate as it implies a debt which can be repaid later and this is only partly true. However, the simplified term does help to convey to the layman an understanding of this phase of muscle action. All athletic events call for the muscles to work anaerobically, but the degree is dependent upon the severity of the exercise. Very severe work can only be performed for a short while before fatigue, and later exhaustion, sets in. In the middle distance events, the duration of the run basically determines the degree of "oxygen debt". For example, in a fast 800 metres run the athlete will incur a larger "oxygen debt" than, say, in a fast 10,000 metres. The graph on page 66 illustrates the energy requirements for the various middle distance events and from this the approximate proportion of "oxygen debt" work can be calculated. The precise nature of what happens when the body is forced to work anaerobically is not fully understood. However, it is possible to present a layman's impression of what happens in order that the coach/athlete may understand the principles of training for the middle distance events.

When the body is forced to perform work beyond its normal aerobic (work performed with an adequate supply of oxygen) limits, the exchange of gases becomes inefficient, the chemical balance of the body is upset, and as a result paralysing acids start to accumulate. During aerobic work the quantity

of acid formation is low and the body can cope with its dispersal and removal. However, with very high levels of work the system is stretched to its physiological limit. During training the athlete must place the body under a similar stress to that which he is likely to experience during a race, so that the adaptive mechanisms can be triggered off and a degree of tolerance developed. The tolerance of the fatigue products is probably the most important single factor the athlete has to train. The much bandied phrase "fatigue is purely in the mind" is only partially correct but to the athlete it is a very significant one. There is always a stage during a fast race when the athlete starts to feel distressed. This phase is often termed the "pain barrier", and for an athlete to be successful he must break this psychological barrier fairly frequently. The athlete has to develop a callousness towards fatigue. He

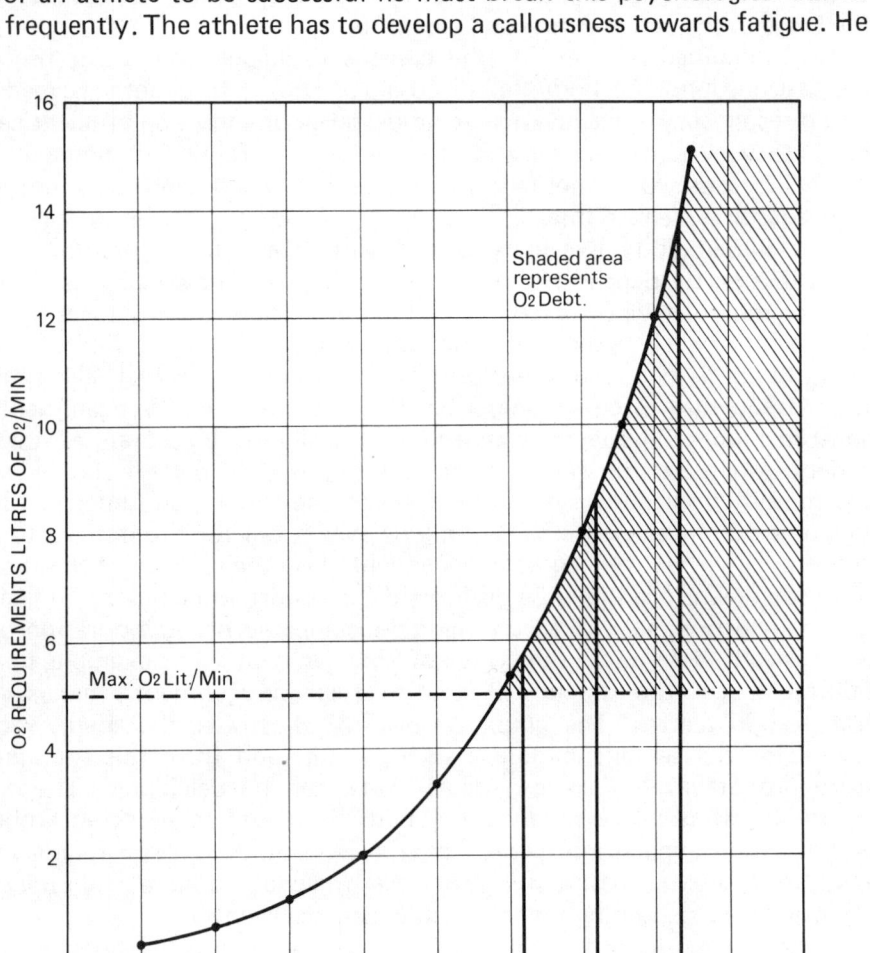

must be the complete master of his body and will it to go on when all other mechanisms are trying to encourage it to give in. The extreme limits of fatigue can only partially be approached during training. It requires the added incentives of competition to force the body almost to a state of exhaustion. Hence the ultimate can only be experienced in the competitive situation.

However, during training the athlete can approach the limits of endurance and so condition the adaptive mechanisms other than the tolerance already discussed. The basic problem with high levels of work is the accumulation of acid products. The body has its own method for dealing with the situation although the precise nature of it is not fully understood. To deal with this aspect of the chemical changes within the body is beyond the understanding of most coaches actively involved in coaching, but a layman's understanding is all that is required.

When acid products start to accumulate the chemical composition of the blood changes. The various receptor mechanisms in the body are very sensitive to the changes so they start to trigger off adaptive mechanisms. The first adaptive mechanism is that the rate of beating, and stroke output, of the heart is increased and unnecessary subsidiary circulations, such as that supplying the gut, are temporarily closed down. The total effect of this is to increase the amount of blood going to the active tissues, taking more oxygen to the tissues and transporting more waste products away from them. Associated with the increase in blood supply there is an increase in both the rate and depth of breathing which is triggered off by the deposits of carbon dioxide found in the blood as a result of increased activity. The increased rate of respiration both in the lungs and at tissue level, more fully charges the blood with the gases necessary for work or as a result of work. However, the system rapidly reaches its maximum. There is a limit to the speed at which the heart can force out blood to the active tissues; there is a limit which restricts the rate at which the blood can return to the heart and again be charged with oxygen and give off its waste gases. If the rate of blood flow is excessive the gas carrying pigment never becomes fully charged with oxygen, neither does it ever become fully charged with carbon dioxide during its circulation through the active tissues. This means that the muscle ultimately becomes starved of oxygen and saturated with deposits of carbon dioxide and waste products. Hence this is a severely limiting factor.

If the acid bi-products are allowed to accumulate, the muscles ultimately become paralysed and are no longer capable of functioning. The bulk of the acid products are excreted through the various systems the body has for disposing of its waste material. Some of it is released in the form of carbon dioxide and is released during breathing, some is released through the kidneys and a proportion is resynthesised into useable material again. So there is a system which hopefully can be stimulated during training to dispose of any unwanted materials likely to limit performance.

Another possible mechanism which can be brought into play is one involving neutralising agents known as blood buffers. At all times the body must establish a balance between the acids and alkalis in the blood. To do this the body calls upon what is known as an alkaline reserve in the form of blood buffers and these have the effect of neutralising an acid situation. With training, one hopes that the total reserve of blood buffers can be improved.

So during training the middle distance runner is attempting to stimulate the various adaptive mechanisms outlined above. It is fairly certain that the majority of the adaptive mechanisms only respond to the extreme levels of fatigue, hence, during training, the athlete must occasionally subject himself to an identical stress to that which he is likely to experience in a race. Only in this way can he be sure that an adaptation can take place. However, such forms of work are extremely fatiguing; they cannot be performed frequently otherwise a breakdown rather than an adaptation will take place.

Very little is known about the effects which various methods of training have upon the organs of the body. However, the physiologists can certainly suggest with some confidence what the likely effects are to be. It is worthwhile to review the various training regimens and suggest the possible adaptive response.

1. Long slow sustained runs

These are often termed L.S.D. and they usually refer to distances in excess of ten miles. As the athlete is essentially running quite slowly he never embarks upon the "oxygen debt" phase of muscular activity, hence the effect is most likely to be upon the heart and associated aspects of circulation. This does not mean that the athlete does not incur an "oxygen debt", he does, but it is built up gradually. Because the activity is sustained the heart is kept pumping at an increased rate for an extended period of time, placing a natural overload on the heart muscle, which has a strengthening effect. The effect is likely to be an enlargement of the heart which will permit more blood to be pumped from it per contraction. At tissue level there is a sustained demand for energy providing materials, particularly oxygen. Here the training effect is likely to be one of improved capilliarisation; existing and functioning capillaries enlarged and dormant ones revitalised. Almost any form of exercise brings about a fast and full response from the muscles controlling respiration. With this form of running the demand is sustained, hence the greater is the strengthening effect upon these muscles.

2. Intermittent running

This form of running is where periods of effort are spaced with intervals for recovery. The recovery periods can be active in the form of a walk or a jog, or they can be taken as a complete rest. The former has the advantage in

that for the walking activity muscles are used, and these can help to squeeze the blood back to the heart through the veins. There are several forms of intermittent running which are directed at stimulating various aspects of the running machinery and adaptive mechanism.

(a) Interval running. This is almost essentially a heart conditioner. In this form of running the athlete runs for a period of about 30 seconds, sufficient to raise the heart rate to a level of about 180 beats per minute. This period of activity is followed by a rest interval during which the heart rate drops to a level of about 120 beats per minute before a subsequent effort period is undertaken. This is a scientific form of training which does allow the coach to monitor the effect fairly carefully. However, it is a form of training which has been misunderstood by most coaches throughout the world who use the term to mean any form of intermittent running. The theory associated with interval training is that the training stimulus occurs during the recovery period and *not* during the period of activity. Once the period of activity is terminated, the heart continues to beat at an elevated level for some time during the recovery period. This has a two-fold effect. The first is to put a natural overload on the heart muscle, and the second is to enable the muscles to be cleared of waste products quickly, due to the elevated rate of blood flow when there is little demand for activity from the tissues. With this type of training it is important that the period of activity should not be so intense as to produce heart rates above the 180 beats per minute threshold. Intense activity would cause an excessive build up of waste products that could not be fully removed during the period of recovery.

(b) Speed endurance running/tempo. The difference between this type of training and the interval method is that the training stimulus is thought to be present during the period of effort. This means that this type of training is almost certainly directed at the various aspects controlling anaerobic efficiency. Here the distance of the run is either extended to last for a period in excess of 30 seconds, or the speed of the run is considerably increased to produce the high activity fatigue products, or the actual period of recovery is shortened. Whichever method is used the athlete is forced to become involved in anaerobic work and the distressing side effects of anoxia.

i) Increased distance

Because the distance of the run is increased fewer repetitions of the fast effort can be undertaken. The distance of the fast sector can vary from 300 metres to 800 metres or even more. Most coaches regard distances of 300 metres and 600 metres as the most suitable and these are the distances that I favour myself. They are certainly ideal for the 800 metres and 1,500 metres runners as both can be performed at faster than racing tempo. I am personally against doing repetitions of distances in excess of 800 metres during tempo training sessions, as I feel that an identical effect could be gained by doing a fartlek (see page 70) run away from the regimented

situation of the track. For training runs of this nature the recovery period should be about four times the duration of the fast effort period. This type of running is essentially fast and is intended to make the athlete feel distressed.

ii) Increased speed

With this type of training the speed of the run is considerably increased, hence the distance of the fast sector and the number of repetitions have to be decreased. Here the distance of the fast effort usually covers the range from 60 metres to 200 metres. Most coaches, including myself, favour a distance of 150 metres. The period of rest is just sufficiently long to allow recovery so that a subsequent fast run can be attempted.

iii) Decreased recovery period

This is probably the most fatiguing of all of the training regimens. The distance of the fast sector is between 60 metres and 200 metres but the duration of the recovery period is 30 seconds or less. The speed of the run is also kept fast in order to produce the desired effect.

So it can be seen that in speed endurance or tempo training there are five variables which the athlete or coach can experiment with in the hope of bringing about a specific adaptation to this form of stress. They are:-

(a) The number of fast periods of effort (repetitions).
(b) The distance of each fast sector.
(c) The speed of each fast sector.
(d) The duration of recovery.
(e) The type of recovery, i.e. Jog, walk, complete rest.

3. Fartlek running

This could almost come under the heading of intermittent running. It is a type of running training developed in Sweden by Gosta Holmer, a national coach in the 1930s. The word "fartlek" means speed-play, suggesting that it is a method for enjoying speed training and indeed that is what it is. Fartlek running is always done away from the track in the most inspiring and enjoyable surroundings that can be found. The total distance can vary from about three to eight miles, the run being divided into fast and slow sections depending upon the feeling of the individual. Fartlek training is an excellent relaxing form of running, ideal for the really committed athlete who is able to inflict self-punishment.

I feel that the three classifications of running mentioned cover all of the necessary training a middle distance runner should be required to do. Of course there are many variations on the theme that might not fit very conveniently into the classifications I have used, for example, cross-country running, hill running, sand-hill running and short sustained runs lasting about

fifteen minutes. All of these have a place in any middle distance runner's training programme, but I feel that the bulk of the schedule should be planned around long sustained runs, the various types of intermittent running and fartlek running.

PLANNING THE SCHEDULE

The most important work of the middle distance coach, other than provide motivation when inevitably morale gets low, is to plan the programme for daily training. The good coach will spend many hours with the athlete, referring back to training diaries, in order to blend together the various aspects of training into the "schedule" designed to bring the runner to peak racing condition at the right time. The good coach/athlete will firstly devise a plan for the complete year. This will include recognition of all of the important races which the athlete has to run, together with the way the training emphasis should shift from month to month. With the basic plan to act as the guidelines, the weekly training programme is designed and modified from week to week to allow for any specific interruptions, such as illness, injury, work pressure, etc.

When planning the programme for the year, the coach will have to keep in mind all, or most, of the following factors:-

1. The specific event, i.e. 800 metres, 10,000 metres, etc.
2. The specific weaknesses of the individual athlete.
3. The training environment—proximity of track, etc.
4. The various external demands such as place and type of employment, and domestic responsibilities.
5. The diet of the athlete and training times relative to meals.
6. The total amount of time available for purposeful training.

When all of these have been considered the various programmes drawn up might look like any one of the following schemes. They are based on ideas for athletes in the Northern hemisphere who normally compete for the period May-September.

800 metres

SEPT./OCT.

Period of rest spaced with enjoyable slow runs, fartleks, etc. to get over the stresses and strains of the competitive season.

NOV./FEB.

Period of general conditioning. This should include long sustained runs, fartlek runs, circuit training for local endurance, specific weight training activities and one weekly track session to keep in contact with speed. The total mileage run should increase gradually throughout the period to reach

a peak of between 30 miles and 60 miles per week depending upon the individual.

MARCH/MAY
Period of specific conditioning. The long runs will give way to demanding track sessions directed at the various phases of anaerobic efficiency and leg speed. The change over should not be too abrupt otherwise the legs will suffer from soreness such as shin-splints. It will probably mean three track sessions per week spaced with enjoyable sustained runs.

JUNE/SEPT.
The racing period, when it is essential to maintain the beneficial effects of the specific conditioning period. What is done during this period will depend considerably upon the frequency of racing.

I believe that the good 800 metres runner should train twice a day for at least four days in the week's cycle. During the racing period at least two days of resting is required prior to an important race, and of these two days one should be a complete rest void of any real physical activity.

1,500 metres

SEPT./OCT.
As for 800 metres runner.

NOV./FEB.
Basically the same as the 800 metres runner only with a greater emphasis on the total mileage recorded. Depending upon the athlete this should vary between 50-100 miles a week.

MARCH/MAY
As for the 800 metres runner although the distances covered in training will tend to be greater and the emphasis on "oxygen debt" work less apparent.

JUNE/SEPT.
As for the 800 metres runner.

The general comments made concerning frequency of training and rest periods, for 800 metres, apply equally to 1,500 metres.

5,000 metres

SEPT./OCT.
As for the 800 and 1,500 metres.

NOV./FEB.

An extensive period of stamina training and conditioning work. The emphasis must be on sustained runs with a weekly speed session, away from the track, over a distance of 2-4 miles. This speed session is ideally done as part of a longer sustained run, only with the desired section done very fast. The good performer will clock about a four-minute mile speed for a section of this effort period. The total weekly mileage should be in the region of 80-120 miles per week. Cross country running can form a part of this conditioning period of work, but the tendency to race every week should be avoided.

MARCH/MAY

Period of speed conditioning. The athlete should start to include one or more track sessions per week during this period. Ideally one of the track sessions should be fast, over a short distance of about 200 metres, and another should be one calling for fast sustained running over a distance in excess of 600 metres. In each case the speed of the fast sector, number of repetitions and recovery period will vary according to the quality of the individual. As the emphasis is on speed the period of recovery must be sufficiently long to allow repeated quality. The popular road relays can play an important part in this vital speed conditioning period. The emphasis on the weekly mileage total will not be so apparent although the good runner will always approach 100 miles per week in training. Towards the end of the period the sustained runs should be shorter with extended bursts of speed over distances ranging from 2-4 miles. There should be at least one long run over a distance in excess of 10 miles, kept in the programme.

JUNE/SEPT.

The racing period for the 5,000 metres runner is a very critical one. The body cannot take many races over this distance in a short space of time. Hence races over 5,000 metres have to be selected wisely. The athlete should be encouraged to race over 800 metres and 1,500 metres to provide added competition. Such races also serve as the track speed training sessions, so permitting the athlete to do most of his training away from the track. Ideally the training should be enjoyable fartlek and short sustained runs, over good grass, with at least one sustained run in the week lasting over one hour duration.

The top class 5,000 metres runner will require to train three times during the day for at least three days during the week. A period of three days' rest is required before a major competition with one of the days as a complete rest and the other two days fairly short, easy, sustained runs.

10,000 metres

SEPT./OCT.
As for the 5,000 metres runner.

NOV./FEB.
As for the 5,000 metres runner except that there will be a greater emphasis on distance. The good runner over this distance really requires to run something in excess of 100 miles during a single week. The training should include a fast, sustained, weekly run of about five miles which can form part of a longer training run.

MARCH/MAY
During the period there should be a slight shifting of emphasis towards speed which can be done with a single weekly track session. For this single outing on the track repetition 200 metres is a good standard session. Again road relays and cross country over fast courses can be beneficial.

JUNE/SEPT.
If the race planning for the 5,000 metres runner is critical then that for the 10,000 metres runner is more so. It is difficult for the body to stand more than about four races over the full distance, during the competitive season, without there being some fall off in the standard of performance. The races must be carefully selected and spaced with the odd race over 5,000 metres or 1,500 metres. The peak mileage achieved during the build-up period will obviously drop but it should be kept reasonably high and should not drop by more than one third.

    The top class 10,000 metres runner will almost certainly require to train three times during a single day, for several days during the week. This type of training is very difficult to fit in relative to meals and the normal working duties of most male athletes. Ideally the first session of the day is a very easy sustained run taken early in the morning, and serves more to prepare the body for the stresses likely to follow during the day. The quality session is usually performed in the evening which is not the most ideal time of the day to do it. Hence the current world-class performer, over these distances, often finds it very difficult to train at the intensity required and still keep down a job of work.

With the basic format of the year's programme the coach/athlete can then plan the various day-to-day training sessions so that they offer variety, incentives and as much enjoyment as is possible.

INTERMITTENT RUNNING
As mentioned earlier this is a means of performing a greater work load by

spacing each period of effort by a suitable rest or recovery period. It was also mentioned that with this type of training there are five variable factors which could provide a different training stimulus. In the world of middle distance running there exists some interesting yet conflicting opinions on the interpretation of the training variables. Most of the confusion here exists because of the apparent misinterpretation of the term "interval training" which has been fully described in an earlier section. Another reason is that at the moment coaching is an almost empirical field, with various coaches forming their opinions by trial and error, working with small groups of good quality athletes. Because all athletes are individuals, often working in completely different environments from one another, it is quite obvious that no one can suggest hard and fast rules. In view of this I consider it worthwhile to review some of the existing opinions.

1. Distance of fast sector

The main body of opinion suggests that the distance of the fast sector should be one quarter of the racing distance. That is 200 metres for the 800 metres runner and about 400 metres for the 1,500 metres runner. On the other hand Gerschler, the originator of interval running, suggests that it should always be done over a distance of 200 metres or less. In terms of pure interval work, where the training stimulus is during the recovery, I would completely favour the idea supported by Gerschler. Away from true interval work the distance of the fast sector should be varied to include fast work over distances up to 1,500 metres. However, although the training schedule must contain a lot of varying types of work, it is essential to do at least one regular standard session in each week. For this single session I tend to favour a speed sector of approximately one quarter of the racing distance. So an integral part of an 800 metres schedule would be eight repetitions of 200 metres.

2. The speed of the fast sector

Most coaches, and these include Valste, Igloi and Gerschler, insist that the fast sector should be done at faster than racing speed; that is, faster than the calculated speed for the shorter training segment. For example, an 800 metres runner whose racing speed is two minutes would do a 200 metres training segment in less than 30 seconds, i.e. 2 minutes ÷ 4 = 30 seconds.

Hollmann stresses that it should be run at a speed that is 80% of a person's best time for the training distance. For example, the best 200 metres time for a middle distance runner might be 24.0 seconds.

$$\frac{80}{100} \times 24 = 19.2$$

$$24.0 - 19.2 = 4.8$$

Training time = 24 + 4.8 = 28.8 seconds.

This is a very reliable training guide for the person who has not developed the experience to understand the training times that can be done by individual athletes.

3. The number of fast repetitions

This is the most empirical aspect of all of the training variables. Of course the number of repetitions is limited by the speed at which they are performed. In true interval work the number of repetitions is determined by the ability of the heart to return from its elevated level immediately after the period of effort, to approximately 120 beats per minute during a reasonably short period of recovery.

For work which is outside the definition of interval training the main body of coaches favour a number which will approximately double the racing distance. For example, an 800 metres runner would perform eight repetitions of 200 metres in a training session or a 1,500 metres runner would perform five repetitions of a 600 metres.

The training programmes which I devise certainly fit in fairly closely with both of the ideas mentioned in this section. Unfortunately there is a common tendency all of the time to do more than is really necessary. It does not always follow that because something is good, more of the same thing has to be better. There always comes a time where there is a breakdown rather than an adaptation to the stress and this has to be avoided.

4. Recovery period

There are three main opinions in this area.

Holmer and Karpovitch suggest that the recovery period should be three times the duration of the effort period. This would mean that an athlete running repetitions of 200 metres in 30 seconds would take a 90 seconds recovery period. This can only work if the effort is fairly low as it is in true interval running or during the sustained effort periods.

Nocker suggests that the recovery period should be long enough to allow the heart to return to one third of the difference between rest and activity. For example, an athlete who has a resting pulse rate of 55 b.p.m. and during the effort period it elevates to 170 b.p.m.

$$170 - 55 = 115$$

$$115 \times \tfrac{1}{3} = 38.3$$

$$170 - 38.3 = 131 \text{ approx.}$$

Therefore, the heart beat should be allowed to return to 131 b.p.m. before another period of effort is attempted.

Gerschler whose approach was more scientific actually performed tests on

a fairly large sample of athletes. Gerschler suggests that the period of effort should elevate the heart rate to 180 b.p.m. and the recovery period should allow it to return to 120 b.p.m.

All of the above ideas will provide the coach with a base for experimentation. Athletes are all individuals and do not respond to the same training stimuli in identical ways. Hence the only suitable compromise is to rely upon experience and this the good coach will build up over a period of years, by being actively involved with good athletes and learning to recognise the true symptoms of stress.

With this added information on training variables, together with the various forms of training and plans mentioned earlier, it is time to suggest ideas on the actual schedule itself. To help with this I will list the exact training schedules which I know have been completed by three international athletes, one from each of the categories—800 metres, 1,500 metres and 5,000 metres. Obviously a training schedule must vary from week to week throughout the year and as it would be impossible to give fifty-two schedules for each athlete, I have chosen a typical week during October and April, suggesting an out-of-season scheme and a pre-season scheme. I realise the many dangers inherent in listing the schedule of an individual athlete, but at least it will give the discerning coach/athlete an idea of the work undertaken by good international athletes.

800 metres. Athlete's best time = 1 min. 48.0 sec.

OCTOBER

Day 1   (i) 3 miles easy sustained run.
            (ii) 10 x 150 metres fast sprints walk back recovery.
Day 2   (i) 3 miles easy sustained run.
            (ii) 5 miles fartlek.
Day 3   (i) 3 miles sustained run.
            (ii) Weight training. 6 x 60 yards harness running.
Day 4   (i) 3 miles sustained run.
            (ii) 5 miles fartlek.
Day 5   (i) 3 miles sustained run.
            (ii) 30 minutes steep hill work.
Day 6   (i) 8-10 miles sustained run.
Day 7   (i) 3 miles sustained run.
            (ii) 2 x 80 metres fast with one minute recovery.
                 2 x 100 metres fast with two minutes recovery.
                 2 x 200 metres fast with three minutes recovery.

The Day 7 (ii) was performed on an all-weather track and used as a standard session during the complete winter.

Day 8   As Day 1.
Day 9   (i) 3 miles sustained run.
      (ii) 8 miles fartlek.
Day 10   As Day 3.
Day 11   (i) 3 miles sustained run.
      (ii) 3 x 600 metres @ 95 seconds lap jog recovery.
        3 x 300 metres @ 45 seconds 100 m. walk recovery.
Day 12   As Day 5.
Day 13   Rest
Day 14   (i) 3 miles sustained run.
      (ii) As many fast 200s with 200 jog recovery as possible in 30 minutes. (Graphical record kept.)

APRIL

Day 1   (i) 3 miles easy run.
      (ii) 5 x 300 metres @ 38 seconds. 3-5 minutes recovery.
Day 2   (i) 3 miles easy run.
      (ii) 2 x 80 metres fast with one minute recovery.
        2 x 100 metres fast with two minutes recovery.
        2 x 200 metres fast with three minutes recovery.
Day 3   (i) 3 miles easy run.
        3 miles quality fartlek.
Day 4   (i) 3 miles easy run.
      (ii) Up clock 120 .. 140 .. 160 .. 180 .. 200 walk back recovery.
Day 5   (i) 3 miles easy fartlek.
      (ii) 5 miles sustained run.
Day 6   (i) 3 miles sustained run.
      (ii) 4 x 600 @ 85/87. 5 minutes recovery.
Day 7   (i) 10 miles easy sustained run.
Day 8   (i) 3 miles easy sustained run.
      (ii) 2 x 3 of 200 metres 26 seconds, 30 seconds recovery. 5 minutes between sets.
Day 9   (i) 3 miles sustained run.
      (ii) 5 miles quality fartlek.
Day 10   (i) 3 miles easy run.
      (ii) 10 x 150 sprints walk back recovery.
Day 11   (i) 3 miles.
      (ii) 1 x 200 .. 1 x 300 .. 1 x 400 .. 1 x 300 .. 1 x 200. Fast with 3 minutes recovery make "up" times equal "down" times.
Day 12   (i) 3 miles sustained run.

(ii) Weight training . . 6 x 60 yards harness running.

(iii) 5 miles fartlek.

Day 13   REST

Day 14   8-10 miles sustained run.

The schedule is only listed to indicate the variety of work and the way the schedule is based on a fourteen day cycle. It is essentially for an individual athlete who does not thrive on excessive distance work and who really enjoys the very hard speed sessions. Any schedule should never be followed blindly and to the rule. Many things such as injuries, the chance to train in a completely new environment, etc. all make last minute changes absolutely necessary. The athlete concerned often fitted in a number of short weight training sessions, designed to strengthen the ankle joint, as extra periods of work.

1,500 metres-1 mile. Athlete's best time 3 min. 41.0 sec. and 3 min. 58.0 sec.

OCTOBER

Day 1   (i) 5 miles sustained run.

    (ii) 8 miles fartlek.

Day 2   (i) 5 miles sustained run.

    (ii) 4 miles sustained run.

    (iii) 8 miles sustained run.

Day 3   (i) 5 miles sustained run.

    (ii) 1 hour forest and hill running.

Day 4   (i) 5 miles sustained run.

    (ii) 10 x 200 metres fast 200 metres jog recovery.

Day 5   (i) 5 miles sustained run.

    (ii) 5 miles quality fartlek.

    (iii) 5 miles sustained run.

Day 6   (i) 8 miles fartlek.

Day 7   (i) 10-15 miles sustained run.

Day 8   As Day 1.

Day 9   As Day 2.

Day 10   As Day 3.

Day 11   (i) 5 miles sustained run.

    (ii) 3 x 600 @ 90 seconds. 3 minutes recovery jog.

        3 x 300 @ 45 seconds. 100 walk on recovery.

Day 12   As Day 5.

Day 13   As Day 6.

Day 14   As Day 7.

APRIL

Day 1	(i)	3 miles sustained run.
	(ii)	15 x 150 metres walk back recovery.
Day 2	(i)	3 miles sustained run.
	(ii)	5-8 miles fartlek.
Day 3	(i)	3 miles sustained run.
	(ii)	4 x 600 metres 85 seconds approx. 3-5 minutes recovery.
Day 4	(i)	3 miles sustained run.
	(ii)	5 miles fartlek.
Day 5	(i)	3 miles sustained run.
		1 x 200 @ 28 . . 200 jog. 1 x 300 @ 38 . . 110 walk.
		1 x 200 @ 28 . . repeat to a total of 3 x 300 m.
Day 6	(i)	3 miles sustained run.
	(ii)	Road relay leg.
Day 7		10-15 miles sustained run. 6 minute mile pace.
Day 8	(i)	3 miles sustained run.
	(ii)	3 x 600—90 seconds. 3 minutes recovery.
		3 x 300—40 seconds. 110 slow walk recovery.
Day 9	(i)	3 miles sustained run.
	(ii)	8 miles quality fartlek.
Day 10	(i)	3 miles sustained run.
	(ii)	3 x 3 of 200 @ 26 seconds. 30 seconds recovery 5 minute sets.
Day 11	(i)	3 miles sustained run.
	(ii)	3 miles fast sustained run over grass.
Day 12	(i)	3 miles sustained run.
	(ii)	200 . . 300 . . 400 . . 600 . . 400 . . 300 . . 200
		Make "down" times equal "up" times.
Day 13	(i)	Rest or 3 miles sustained run.
Day 14	(i)	10-15 miles sustained run.

5,000-10,000 metres. Athlete's best time 13 min. 32.0 sec. and 28 min. 33.0 sec.

OCTOBER

Day 1	(i)	3 miles sustained run.
	(ii)	10 miles sustained run—6 minute mile pace.
Day 2	(i)	3 miles sustained run.
	(ii)	3-5 miles with a VERY fast one mile segment.
	(iii)	8 miles sustained run.
Day 3	(i)	3 miles sustained run.
	(ii)	20 x 200 metres 28 seconds 200 jog recovery.
	(iii)	8 miles fartlek.

Day 4	(i)	3 miles sustained run.
	(ii)	8 miles quality fartlek.
Day 5	(i)	3 miles sustained run.
	(ii)	5 miles sustained run.
	(iii)	10 miles sustained run.
Day 6	(i)	3 miles sustained run or rest.
	(ii)	Cross Country race or 10 miles sustained run.
Day 7	(i)	15-20 miles sustained run.
Day 8		As Day 1.
Day 9		As Day 2.
Day 10	(i)	3 miles sustained run.
	(ii)	8 x 600 @ 98 seconds lap jog recovery.
	(iii)	5 miles sustained run.
Day 11	(i)	3 miles sustained run.
	(ii)	5 miles sustained run.
	(iii)	8 miles fartlek.
Day 12		As Day 5.
Day 13		As Day 6.
Day 14		As Day 7.

APRIL

Day 1	(i)	3 miles sustained run.
	(ii)	5 miles quality fartlek.
	(iii)	10 miles sustained run.
Day 2	(i)	3 miles sustained run.
	(ii)	4 x 300 metres 40 seconds or less. 3 minute recovery between each. 5 minute rest. 4 x 200 @ 26 seconds. 1 minute recovery.
	(iii)	5-8 miles sustained run.
Day 3	(i)	3 miles sustained run.
	(ii)	8 miles fartlek on golf course.
Day 4	(i)	3 miles sustained run.
	(ii)	200 . . 400 . . 600 . . 800 . . 600 . . 400 . . 200 Make "up" times equal "down" times.
	(iii)	5 miles sustained run.
Day 5	(i)	3 miles sustained run.
	(ii)	3-5 miles with a VERY fast 2 mile sector in it.
	(iii)	5 miles sustained run.
Day 6	(i)	Road Relay/or 10 miles sustained run.
Day 7	(i)	15-20 miles sustained run.
Day 8		As Day 1.
Day 9	(i)	3 miles sustained run.
	(ii)	4 x 800 in 2 min. 8 sec. with lap walk recovery.

2 x 1,000 metres 2 min. 40 sec. lap walk recovery.

4 x 150 flat out walk back recovery.

Day 10		As Day 3.
Day 11	(i)	3 miles sustained run.
	(ii)	4 x 1 mile on track 4 min. 40 sec. 5 minutes recovery.
Day 12	(i)	3 miles easy run.
Day 13	(i)	Road relay race followed by 8 miles sustained run.
Day 14	(i)	15-20 miles sustained run.

TACTICS

There is probably more irrelevant information given about racing tactics, for the distance runner, than for all of the other branches of athletics put together. It is impossible for the athlete/coach to decide in advance any hard and fast rules as they will almost certainly change from race to race. For example, it is unlikely that the tactics employed in winning an Olympic final will be identical to those used in winning a club race, where there is less pressure. Racing tactics have to be viewed with this philosophy, as pre-arranged racing plans do not take into consideration what the opposition is likely to do. Many well intentioned plans have had to be scrapped very early in a race because the racing situation has made it necessary. This does not mean that there cannot be any such thing as racing tactics, as all athletes must go into a race with an idea of what they are going to do if the opposition will permit it. So I would rather regard racing tactics as a number of cardinal rules which should be observed if the racing situation and desire to win make it possible.

If the race is to be a tactical one, and the most important races develop into this, the best place for the athlete to remain, during most of the race, is at the shoulder of the leading runner. This means that the pressure is on the leader as he can only rely upon his hearing to decide how close the rivals are. The runner "sitting" in this position can at least see what the leader is doing and can respond quickly to any changes in running rhythm. The positional runner should *never* run directly behind a person in front, in the "pole" position, as it will almost certainly lead to being "boxed in" when other positional runners start to overtake. The "boxed in" situation is a very difficult one to get out from and it will involve changing the running rhythm, to allow the outside runners to overtake, and then an increase in speed in an attempt to catch them again. So the golden rule here is—avoid being "boxed in", although it is certain all athletes will make this fatal mistake more than once.

With the present high standards in these events a yard or less can separate the medallists from the "also-rans". Hence it is important to save vital inches by running as close to the full racing distance as the rules will permit. This will mean running close to the inner kerb, particularly round the bends, for the entire duration of the race. However, one has to decide between the

dangers of being "boxed in" and running slightly wide to avoid it. The circumstances of the race might demand that the runner has to go wide, particularly on the final bend. But the rule is one which should be observed as far as possible.

The feed-back mechanisms which operate from within the body during a race demand great concentration from the athlete, and the degree might be at its maximum level when the body is tired and not ideally suited for concentration. A slight lapse in this crucial area could mean that a rival has made a break and it could be several yards before it is realised. So the runner must always be aware of the situation at any stage during a race, and must always remain with the leading group of runners. The gamble that a leading runner will break down as fatigue takes hold is not really worth considering. Remember the ultimate in distance running is to set such a fast pace, from the front, that no other runner could stay with it. However, this is a "pipe dream" and unlikely ever to happen, although Vladmir Kuts successfully employed this in the 1956 Olympic 5,000 and 10,000 metres.

During a race, an athlete must always keep in mind his particular weakness. For example, the runner lacking basic speed will never be successful in a fast finish, hence he must build up a lead during the race to compensate for those who might overtake because of a faster finishing speed. Or he must set a fast enough pace throughout to remove the "sting" from any fast finishers. It is unlikely that, in the future, any Olympic medals will be won by athletes who lack a reserve of finishing speed. This does not mean that athletes who fit into the other category will not be successful; indeed it is likely that world records will continue to fall to those who lack finishing speed. However, in an Olympic final, where there is so much at stake, there will always be a fast finisher, capable of hanging on, with sufficient left in reserve to sprint past all rivals at the opportune moment. So the golden rule here is to train for speed as well as stamina.

Many races are won or lost by athletes who are not decisive enough. If a runner decides he is going to try to make a break from the rest of the field by increasing his running speed, then such a break must be decisive and sustained for long enough to achieve the object of the exercise. It is very energy-consuming to have to keep changing running rhythms because a short attempt to break the field failed in its objective.

The final point in racing tactics might be better termed strategy, as the term implies a knowledge of the racing habits of the opposition. All good athletes study their opposition, they are aware of their best times relative to their own, and also of the common racing tactics which such runners employ. For example, the racing tactics of Keino, Olympic 1500 metres champion in 1968 and Steeplechase champion in 1972, always appeared to be consistent and this could have led to his defeat in the 1,500 metres final in Munich 1972. If the athlete is aware of this, his own predetermined racing plan is more likely to be successful.

To conclude this section I must emphasise that any racing plan must be flexible to allow for the specific situation. The aim of the athlete should be to win. If he cannot win, then the aim should be to run faster than he has ever run before as both are a true measure of success.

In this early discussion on tactics I have only thought about general situations likely to occur during a race. One section of a race that is always fairly constant, and must demand some consideration from the athlete, is the start. This is particularly significant for the 800 metres runner as this race is becoming more of a sprint as the years progress. Also the change in rules insisting that athletes run in lanes for two complete bends in international 800 metres races, puts a very special emphasis on starting techniques and should favour the 400/800 metres runner rather than the 800/1500 metres type. The 800 metres race will probably soon demand a crouch start and this should be left to personal preference. All other middle distance races should involve the runner in a relaxed "dab" start. For this type of start the athlete places whichever foot he likes close to the starting line, lowers the trunk and puts the opposite arm forwards so that an instant running rhythm can be obtained.

Most people involved in the physiology of exercise, particularly middle distance running, are adamant that the most economical way to run a race is by using a constant speed approach. That is where each specific lap time is similar if not identical. To help in this consideration I will list a number of important races over recent years to illustrate that this is only partly true.

800 metres

			Lap 1	Lap 2	Diff.	Time
P. Snell	World record 1962	MEN	51.0	54.1	(3.1)	1.45.1
R. Doubell	1968 Olympic Final	MEN	51.0	53.3	(2.3)	1.44.3
D. Wottle	1972 Olympic Final	MEN	52.3	53.5	(1.2)	1.45.8
A. Packer	1964 Olympic Final	WOMEN	58.6	62.5	(4.1)	2.01.1
M. Manning	1968 Olympic Final	WOMEN	59.1	61.8	(2.7)	2.00.9
H. Falk	1972 Olympic Final	WOMEN	58.3	60.2	(1.9)	1.58.5

1 mile

			Lap 1	Lap 2	Lap 3	Lap 4	Time
R. Bannister	First sub 4 min. mile	MEN	57.5	60.7	62.3	58.9	3.59.4
D. Ibbotson	1957 World record	MEN	56.0	60.4	63.9	56.9	3.57.2
P. Snell	1962 World record	MEN	61.0	59.5	55.3	54.9	3.54.4
J. Ryun	1966 World record	MEN	57.7	57.7	59.4	56.5	3.51.3

Plate 10. L. Viren winner of the 1972 Olympic 5,000/10,000 metres. A product of the new Finnish school of running.

1,500 metres

			400	800	1,200	Finish
P. Snell	1964 Olympic Final	MEN	58.8	2.00.7	2.59.7	3.38.1
K. Keino	1968 Olympic Final	MEN	56.0	1.55.3	2.53.4	3.34.9
P. Vasala	1972 Olympic Final	MEN	61.4	2.01.4	2.56.5	3.36.3

In the 1972 Olympic 5,000 metres, won in a time of 13 min. 26.4 sec. the fastest lap was the last one completed in a time of 57.2 sec. and the slowest lap was the sixth in a time of 68.6 sec. The last 800 metres was completed in 1 min. 56.2 sec. and the first 800 metres in 2 min. 14.2 sec. In the 10,000 metres at the same Games the race was again won by Lasse Viren (Finland) in 27 min. 38.4 sec. The fastest lap was the last, run in a time of 56.6 sec. and the slowest was the sixteenth lap in a time of 71.2 sec. The average lap time for each race was 64.6 sec. and 66.5 sec. respectively.

It would appear that there is a fairly uniform approach to top class races. In the 800 metres event the first lap is usually faster than the second lap by approximately two seconds for both men and women. The mile and 1,500 metres is closer to even paced running with the first and last 400 metres segments fairly equal. In the longer events the tactics are considerably different and it would appear that in the major races the pace speeds up considerably towards the end.

Some general points about training and training schedules

The aim of a training schedule is to build the body up so that it can adapt to the stresses likely to be placed on it during a very fast race. At times this will mean pushing the body very close to its physiological limits. However, there is a definite danger of placing too much stress on the body during training, hence instead of adapting to the stress it starts to break down. The dividing line between adaptation and breakdown is a very fine one and both athlete and coach must be very aware of the breakdown symptoms. If the schedule is well planned, a careful eye kept upon the state of health and diet, then only adaptation should take place.

It will be noticed that on most days the training schedules listed start with a sustained run over about three miles. It is essential that this is the first training session of the day. The body does not take very kindly to sudden sustained periods of effort like that done in middle distance training. Hence the morning run of about three miles should be regarded as a means of preparing the body for the greater stress which is likely to be placed on it later in the day. All of the runs must be carefully planned around the meal times and diet, but more of that later.

An athlete should not be kept on a very hard schedule for fifty-two weeks of the year. I personally favour a schedule which is planned for a two-week period. Once the two week period of very intense work has been completed

it is followed by a single week of less intense work before a subsequent two-week period of intense work, to a different schedule, is tackled. This period of two-weeks intense followed by a week of fairly easy work would seem to be a prophylactic against the possibility of a breakdown.

It is frequently said by dieticians that the standard diet of the British people is more than adequate for those who perform even the heaviest of work loads. I am afraid I am not one of the people who share this opinion. The middle distance runner is a very active person, with a very high energy requirement, who is continually breaking down the various forms of tissues, etc. all of which require special elements of food during the repair process. I am a firm believer in health foods, particularly pollen and honey. Pollen is a very rich source of protein and honey is a good provider of fairly quick energy.

Recommended daily intakes of energy and nutrients for the 18 years—35 years age group

Person	Energy Requirements K. Cals.	Protein Gms.	Thiamin Mgs.	Ribo-flavin Mgs.	Nicotinic Acid Mgs.	Ascorbic Acid Mgs.	Vit.A. Ms.	Vit.D. Ms.	Calcium Ms.	Iron Ms.
Sedentary	2,700	68	1.1	1.7	18	30	750	2.5	500	10
Moderately Active	3,000	75	1.2	1.7	18	30	750	2.5	500	10
Very Active	3,600	90	1.5	1.7	18	30	750	2.5	500	10

This table was compiled for residents in the United Kingdom. The Canadian authorities, on the other hand, suggest that the daily intake of Thiamin, Riboflavin and Nicotinic acid can rise to 1.5, 2.5 and 15 mgs. respectively for the very active. Apart from illustrating that the world's authorities differ, it also becomes apparent that the very active do require considerably more of certain nutrients than sedentary people. The Canadian authorities list a very active person as one requiring close on 5,000 k. Cals/day while those in Poland suggest that a distance runner can use up to 6,400 k. Cals/day. It would certainly seem that the U.K. assessment for the very active is on the conservative side and that our top-class middle distance runners are more likely to approach the Polish estimation of 6,400 k. Cals/day. It is interesting to note that Vitamin C is omitted from the above table and it is fairly certain that the distance runner, left to his own devices, might well become very short of this vitamin. For this reason athletes should visit their doctor fairly frequently, and if in doubt take extra vitamin A, D and C or multivitamin tablets, all of which are available over the chemist counter.

Whenever a group of physiologists and athletics' coaches get together an

interesting discussion can always be centred around iron therapy. Iron affects the oxygen-carrying pigment of the blood and should an athlete's iron reserve become depleted, then he has less oxygen-carrying potential than the non-anaemic person. This is surely a critical factor in middle distance running. The athlete should try to submit himself to a physiological testing centre, or a doctor interested in sports medicine, fairly frequently in order to have a blood count. Again, the problem arises, that what is normal for the average person in the street might well be below what is required for sustained endurance events. On the other hand there is a small group of people who suggest that a lower haemoglobin level might be part of an athlete's adaptive mechanism and extra dietary iron can only increase the viscosity of the blood and so slow down the circulation rate. Of one thing I am certain: athletes should only take iron preparations under medical supervision.

The whole problem of dietary considerations and the athlete is a fascinating one and quite beyond the scope of this text. However, one aspect with which the coach/athlete must concern himself is not only *what* should be eaten but *when* it should be eaten relative to training. The truth is that the athlete is unlikely to train efficiently on a full stomach or even an empty one. The preparatory 3 mile run taken in the morning should be done after a very light meal containing a fair amount of simple sugars and starches. The act of training disturbs the digestive system and it could well be that eating cannot be resumed until several hours after the training run. Ideally, I suppose, one should eat, rest, train, rest, eat, etc. in that order and this ultimately brings us to the stage of the full-time athlete. When training is to follow a meal, the diet should be fairly weighted towards carbohydrates; when training is not to follow directly, the diet should be weighted towards protein, making use of protein extracts. The use of powdered fructose or glucose drinks has a place in the dietary considerations of the middle distance runner. It is fairly true to say that the dietician and the pharmacologist will play an increasingly important role in the future performances of track and field stars.

The athlete, who is continually placing the body under quite abnormal stresses, is prone to injury. Injuries can be extremely time consuming and more often than not they can determine success or failure. The athlete must never ignore an injury, or take it to one of the many unqualified people who are in practice. At the first signs of an injury he should try to get an X-ray to determine that it is not structural. Once this has been established the correct physiotherapy can then follow, or if necessary other forms of rehabilitation treatment.

However, there is a lot the athlete can do to insure against injury by using the correct footwear for the surface in use and to treat all unfamiliar situations with extreme care. The desire to join in a "free-for-all" football match can often reduce a gold-medal potential to an "also-ran".

Any coach with an interest in middle distance running will always be asked if weight training can be of benefit to a middle distance runner. The most important thing for the middle distance runner to do is to run, and this is his first concern. If, during the day, the runner can fit into his programme a certain amount of strength training, which will not in any way restrict his running programme, then it is to his advantage that he should do it. In this area I favour the combination system or timed system. The distance runner does not require the pure strength of the thrower; it is more a local endurance strength, hence I prefer a high number of repetitions with a relatively light weight. Correctly performed circuit training exercises can be of value. Some of the exercises described for the sprinter will also be of value to the distance runner and those not naturally endowed with strength. Those who feel that their performance is limited by a lack of strength should consult an authority on strength training, although a good deal of advice will be given in the relevant chapter in this book.

Teaching middle distance running

There is very little need to teach a person to run as it is a most natural body function. However, to run fast for a sustained period requires a high level of fitness. I believe that middle distance running for young people must be based on a foundation of cross-country-type running. This activity will appeal to certain types of children and, generally speaking, these are the ones most likely to take up the distance events.

However, when the period of competition arrives, the good teacher/coach has to seek out all of the various incentive schemes necessary to motivate children to take part in what many find is a boring activity. It is best to stimulate interest through some form of competition, using handicap systems, relays, "devil takes the hindmost", "Indian files" and 30 seconds runs. Most are self-explanatory, although the latter might need some explanation:-

Devil takes the hindmost. This should be done around a circuit with two marker flags at opposite points on the circuit. As the runners pass the markers the last person is eliminated, the race being won by the last remaining runner.

Indian files This can be done in almost any situation. The runners must start in single file and it is wise if the best runners are in the middle. The object is for the last runner in the file to keep taking over the lead. Once the rear runner fails to be able to do this he is eliminated.

30 seconds runs A marker is placed on the track 190 metres away from the 200 metres and this, together with the finish, makes up the zone. The object is to start at the 200 metres start and get within the zone when the 30 seconds signal is sounded (whistle blast). Failure to reach it, or get beyond the zone, results in the penalty of having to miss a run. All runners who reach the zone at the signal must walk back across the track ready to take

part in another run. The winner is the person who has recorded the most runs in a stipulated period of time i.e. 20 minutes.

Coaching the top-class middle distance runner

A better name for a middle distance coach would really be "trainer" since there is very little technique work involved in the event, and the role of the coach is mainly one of preparing a balanced training schedule. However, it does require a very thorough understanding of the event as well as the situations of stress, physiology of exercise and applied psychology. I am not suggesting that coaches of other events do not require this knowledge, but it is of paramount importance to the middle distance coach, who is primarily concerned with making an athlete adapt to the stress of running fast for a sustained period. It is very time-consuming as the coach should be present at most of the timed sessions to observe how the adaptation is taking place. Hence, it is not just a task of writing out a training schedule. The coach must carefully plan a programme of training, in consultation with the athlete, and observe many of the sessions to ensure that the training is producing the desired results; and if it is not, he must modify it until it does so.

Chapter 8

Hurdling : 100 metres - 400 metres

Hurdling is often aptly termed "rhythm sprinting" in that the event is essentially a sprinting one, with ten hurdles carefully placed in each lane, so demanding a very precise rhythm to clear all of them successfully.

Like steeplechasing, it would appear that the sport has inherited this event from the horseback equivalent. Many of the early races were held over the conventional wooden hurdle used for retaining sheep, but the progress of time has presented the athlete with a less formidable barrier, made to topple over if an undue force is applied to the top rail. As the sheep hurdle was securely hammered into the ground the runner had to make sure that he did not strike it, thus leading to a jumping style. The fluent style, as we know it today, came with the safer hurdles so that now the events vary little from their flat, sprinting, equivalents. The first record of hurdling events being held comes from Eton College, and the sport was later popularised at the major universities in England.

Today's event can be divided into two groups; the high hurdles over a distance of 110 metres (120 yards) using ten barriers, each 1.06 metres (3 feet 6 inches) high; and the 400 metres (440 yards) hurdles, again over ten hurdles, each 91.4 centimetres (3 feet) high. Due mainly to the influence of the British universities the low hurdles, over a distance of 220 yards using ten hurdles, each 2 feet 6 inches high, became very popular for a period between the wars.

The women's version of the sport has not enjoyed the same consistency as that for the men, whose rules have remained almost unchanged since the event was first introduced. The women have experimented with a number of variations but it would appear that the 100 metres version is now standardised. They have also experimented with longer versions including a 200 metres and a 400 metres equivalent. It seems obvious that the event will follow the same evolutionary pattern as for the men and that the 400 metres hurdles, for women, will be fully accepted at international level.

Younger age groups run over shorter distances, lower hurdles, and in some cases fewer hurdles. The precise position for each hurdle is carefully calculated so that once a hurdling pattern is established, it can remain with the athlete as the transition is made from one age group to the next. Full details of the specifications can be found in the section on teaching.

To clear a high hurdle, at speed, demands great skill and confidence. It also calls for a fairly tall physique, or better still an athlete with sufficiently long legs to straddle the hurdle fairly comfortably, and to produce a stride pattern to fit in with the specifications for the event. It is possible for a hurdler to be too big, making it essential for him to "chop" the stride length in order to fit in with the imposed rhythm. An analysis of the 1968 hurdles event reveals that the average height of the finalists in the men's event was in excess of six feet compared with a figure of five feet ten inches for the finalists of the 100 metres event.

Perfection of clearance style is of secondary importance to basic speed. While an efficient clearance style might make a good sprinter a top-class hurdler, it cannot even make a mediocre sprinter into a good hurdler. Speed is of paramount importance and without this basic quality all else is lost.

The rules of the event are few and simple to apply. Adult men and women all run over ten hurdles spaced as follows:-

Distance	Height	Approach to 1st	Interval between	Run in
110 mtrs.	1.06 mtrs.	13.72 mtrs.	9.14 mtrs.	14.02 mtrs.
400 mtrs.	91.4 cms.	45 mtrs.	35 mtrs.	40 mtrs.
100 mtrs.	83.7 cms.	13 mtrs.	8.5 mtrs.	10.5 mtrs.

Imperial distances have not been given as these are now almost a thing of the past. Most organisers use the international-type hurdle which is made to exact specifications, and counterbalance weights are used to ensure some form of standardisation in the "knock-down" force, partly to safeguard athletes. With this type of hurdle there is no restriction on the number of hurdles that can be toppled, provided the athlete does make an attempt to clear them. The starting procedures are identical to the sprint event. During the race the whole of the body must pass over the hurdle, thus preventing the "lazy" trailing leg which could be possible in the 400 metres event. The athlete must remain in his own lane for the entire duration of the race.

The technique of high hurdling

For ease of description the technique of hurdling can be broken down into four parts. They are: (a) Approach to the first hurdle, (b) Movement across the hurdles, (c) Running between the hurdles and (d) The run-in. However, it must be emphasised that hurdling is a continuous movement and not a series of parts.

(a) The approach to the first hurdle. The distance from the start line to the first hurdle is such that most hurdlers can get eight fast accelerating strides before the hurdle is straddled on the ninth. This is usually the case irrespective of age and sex. It is possible for the long-legged character to get seven strides before negotiating the barrier. At the top level of the sport

anything in excess of eight strides must not be permitted as this would call for "chopping" the stride length.

With the normal eight strides, this will mean that the leading leg is the one to the rear in the standard sprint start position. Sometimes this is contrary to an athlete's normal starting habit, but for fluency's sake it must be adhered to. Everything written about the starting procedure for the sprinting events is applicable to the hurdler. Comfort in the starting position is of prime concern, once the bodyweight is in front of the driving leg.

It would be wrong to say that the first strides of the hurdler are identical to those of the sprinter, although they are similar enough for comparison. Soon after the start the hurdler must be in a position to view the hurdle, thus meaning that the trunk will become erect sooner. Many athletes find that the early strides have to be stretched in order to develop any hurdling rhythm. One seldom finds that the athlete requires to shorten the early strides. It is generally recognised that the eighth stride is slightly shorter than the seventh stride, and while this produces a feature that helps in hurdling, it is merely part of a preparation forced on the athlete by the presence of the hurdle.

(b) Movement across the hurdle. After eight strides the hurdler should be poised to drive across the hurdle. It must be emphasised that time spent in the air is time wasted, as the athlete can only exert a force when in contact with the ground. The lead-leg must be picked up fast, high, and bent at the knee and then driven across the hurdle so that it becomes athletically straight. The whole movement is a forward driving one, hence there is an associated trunk lean and a compensatory movement of the opposite arm. The arm movement (see plate 11, and fig. 10) keeps the trunk square, permitting a straight, line running movement.

The instant the athlete breaks contact with the ground he will be about seven feet away from the hurdle. This will vary slightly from hurdler to hurdler, and will get less as the race progresses due to fatigue, and is likely to become more during the early flights as the speed builds up.

The power to cross the hurdle is derived from the vigorous knee pick-up of the leading leg which is similar to an exaggerated sprinting action, coupled with the driving force of the contact leg. There must not be a conscious effort to delay the action of the driving leg in order to produce a more efficient clearance. Rather, the lead-leg should move faster to produce the same effect. If it is all done correctly it will produce the beautiful position characteristic of the good hurdler (see plate 12).

The high point of the clearance will be slightly in front of the hurdle. As the crotch approaches the hurdle, the trailing leg must start its forward swinging movement. It is in the action of the trailing leg where the greatest deviation from sprinting is noticed. As the crotch is barely above the height of the hurdle, the trail leg could not be recovered in the normal position directly under the body. Instead it is recovered, with the sprinting flexion,

Plate 11. D. Hemery (G.B.) demonstrates a balanced position over the high hurdle.

Figs. 9   10   11

12   13

only at 90 degrees to the normal plane in sprinting. The emphasis of the trailing leg must be one of speed, as it is this action which provides a good deal of the speed away from the hurdle. However, it will place the leg in an unnatural position, and it must be taken to the normal position for sprinting directly after it has cleared the hurdle. The trailing leg action

produces three essential features of good hurdling. It aids the pivoting movement over the hurdle, essential to get the lead-leg down to the ground quickly. It gives the body added momentum, and finally it assures a good stride away from the hurdle landing.

The landing position of the body should be approximately four feet away from the hurdle, thus producing a flight stride of about eleven feet. There should only be a slight variation in the length of this stride otherwise the rhythm will be affected.

So far the emphasis of the movement has centred around the leg action. As in normal sprinting the arms make complementary movements which aid the balance of the body during the driving, flight and landing positions. The action of picking up a single leg, at speed, could cause the hips to rotate away from the normal "square-on" position, making straight-line running very difficult. To compensate for this action, the arm makes a similarly exaggerated movement as the elbow of the opposite arm reaches towards the leading knee. This will set up a counter rotation, keeping the chest and trunk square to the front. During flight the free arm remains fairly passive, while the active arm performs a very vigorous sweeping back action to coincide with the movement of the trailing leg. The elbows must stay close to the hips otherwise stability is affected, and will cause the hurdler to meander.

(c) Movements between the hurdles. The high hurdler has a distance of 9.14 metres (10 yards) between each flight. Of this distance some 3.30 metres (11 feet) can be accounted for during the hurdle clearance, thus leaving approximately 5.84 metres (19 feet) to be covered by three running strides. The stride off the hurdle can seldom be in excess of 1.55 metres (5 feet) so making each of the following strides 2.15 metres (7 feet) in length. The long-legged hurdler can manage this stride length without undue stretching, but the shorter hurdler will have considerable problems should the length of the follow-up stride drop much below the recommended 1.55 metres. As the strides between the hurdles are fairly lengthy ones, the efficiency of the driving levers must be exploited. Such an action will force the hurdler up on to the toes calling for a long fast movement about the hip joint, knee joint and particularly the ankle joint.

(d) The run-in. Many races are won or lost during the final obstacle free section of the race. Speed off the final hurdle is essential and the action of the trailing leg cannot be over-emphasised. The act of clearing ten hurdles spaced over 82.26 metres is a very tiring one, hence fatigue is bound to set in even with the very best hurdlers. When the hurdler reaches the final barrier, he will have less speed than normal, making it an extra effort to strive for speed over this final section of the race. Observations indicate that most hurdlers take six strides for the final section of the race, and that frequently this stride lands them slightly short of the finishing line, thus making the dip finish an essential part of the hurdler's skill. This is preferred to the time loss involved in executing another stride.

The 400 metres hurdles

This event has been revolutionised in the last decade by superbly fit men, with a fast flat time, taking up the event. Not only have they reduced the world record by a significant margin, but they have introduced stride patterns which hitherto would have been considered impossible. As in the high hurdles, a fast basic flat time is essential and races are nearly always won by the speed of running between the hurdles. The time spent hurdling, compared with that spent running, is quite insignificant, so while a good technique is important it cannot be regarded as paramount. It must also be realised that as the tempo of the race is slower any slight error during clearance can be rectified during the free running distances.

The clearance style is a slower replica of the one used by the high hurdler and as the tempo is slower, the movements involved call for less muscular effort.

The 400 hurdler must complete one lap of the track, and as the hurdles are evenly spaced, some must come on the bend, so producing the added skill of bend-hurdling. In this case it is better if the athlete leads with the left leg; then the trail leg action helps to compensate for the effect of centrifuge, keeping the athlete closer to the inside of the lane. The skill is also aided by quite a natural compensatory movement coming from the arms.

While the stride pattern to the first hurdle is not too important, it would seem that most athletes can take 21 or 22 strides before straddling the hurdle. However, the stride pattern between the hurdles is of prime importance. A decade or so ago most athletes took a standard fifteen-stride pattern between each hurdle. This probably meant that when fresh, soon after the start, strides were chopped a little, and when tired the pattern called for extra effort. A very sound exception to this rule came when Potgieter (South Africa) lowered the world record using an unconventional fourteen-stride pattern, and again in 1960 he lowered the record further, using a combination of thirteens and fourteens. Such an approach demanded the ability to lead over the hurdle with either leg, something quite difficult to do in practice.

The following stride patterns emerge from the survey compiled by the British National Coaches in Mexico:-

1. Hemery 13 strides to hurdle 6, 15 strides for the rest.
2. Hennige 13 strides to hurdle 6, 15 strides for the rest.
3. Sherwood 13 strides to hurdle 6, 14 strides to eight, 15 strides remainder.
4. Vanderstock 15 strides all of the way.

I feel that we are fast approaching an era when we might see a hurdler doing a thirteen-stride pattern for the entire duration of the event, or even a twelve/thirteen pattern.

Initially the hurdler/coach might adopt a fifteen/seventeen rhythm, but as strength, ability, etc. improves it will be necessary to move towards one of the more demanding, yet faster, patterns.

Hurdling for women

Good women athletes frequently make fine hurdlers. This is probably due to the greater flexibility afforded by a different angular tilt of the pelvis. In all athletic events their performance techniques are identical to men, and although they lack the same degree of strength, the events are made less demanding to match this.

The fairly low hurdle does not really challenge the good hurdler, hence there is likely to be a greater clearance margin. However, all other movements are almost identical to those described for men.

The 400 metres version is still in its experimental stages. At the moment the description given to the men's version, about ten years ago, would be descriptive of the event. In those days it was termed the "man killer". This is because it attracted two types of athletes. In the first case it attracted the slow high hurdler and similarly it attracted the slower 400 metres flat man. With this situation prevailing it is obvious that it would cause such athletes some distress. The fit woman athlete, experimenting with this event, might adopt a seventeen/nineteen pattern, but with the progress of time I think we will see at least a constant fifteen rhythm.

Teaching the hurdles events

The conventional hurdle, even in its lowest position, is quite a formidable obstacle. A hard knock, on a tender part of the body, could soon ruin confidence and with it an aptitude for hurdling. Therefore, this event should be learnt over very light, low hurdles or even canes. Improvised hurdles can be made from three bamboo canes and two spring-clip pegs. The pegs form a ledge on the vertical for the horizontal rail.

The event is best introduced in the competitive situation using the grid illustrated below. It will be noticed that 24 hurdles are used in eight lanes, three to each lane, with the distance between the hurdles varying slightly from lane to lane.

With the young age group I find the 75 metres spacing quite a good point to start from. The event is a competition to clear first the third hurdle, of lane one, in five seconds. A whistle provides the time signal. If this can be

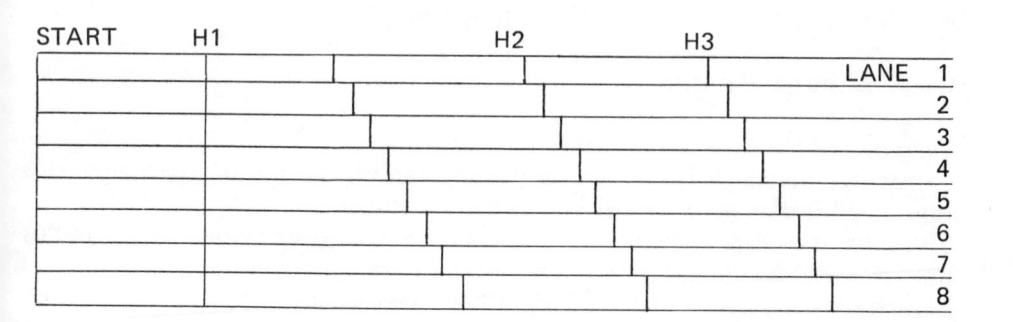

achieved, the pupil should attempt the same time standard in lane two and subsequently in lane three, four, etc. The competition is to see which lane can be reached before it becomes impossible to keep to the five seconds' time standard. Hurdling technique must be ignored for this practice, although the competition imposes the greatest quality of a hurdler, that of speed.

Using the most suitable spacing, observed from the first practice, the eight plus three rhythm must be taught, that is, eight strides to the first hurdle, with a three-stride pattern between the hurdles. The important thing is to arrive at the first hurdle balanced, hence a starting technique must be adopted. All of the time the five second theme, for three hurdles, keeps the essential speed quality.

The basic philosophy that must prevail during the early stages of learning is:-

    (a) Use light improvised hurdles.
    (b) Use a hurdle lower than racing height.
    (c) Use less than the racing distance between each hurdle.
    (d) As confidence and technique improve, the height and interval can be increased, until they reach the racing specifications for the age group concerned. These are:-

Age Group	Distance	Height	No. Flts.	Approach	Interval	Finish
Boys under 15 yrs.	80 mtrs.	84 cms.	8	12 mtrs.	8 mtrs.	12 mtrs.
Boys under 17 yrs.	100 mtrs.	91.5 cms.	10	13 mtrs.	8.5 mtrs.	10.5 mtrs.
Boys under 20 yrs.	110 mtrs.	99.0 cms.	10	13.72 mtrs.	9.14 mtrs.	14.02 mtrs.
Boys under 20 yrs.	400 mtrs.	91.5 cms.	10	45 mtrs.	35 mtrs.	40 mtrs.
Girls under 15 yrs.	75 mtrs.	75 cms.	8	11.5 mtrs.	7.5 mtrs.	11.0 mtrs.
Girls under 17 yrs.	80 mtrs.	76 cms.	8	12.0 mtrs.	8.0 mtrs.	12.0 mtrs.
Girls under 20 yrs.	100 mtrs.	84 cms.	10	13.0 mtrs.	8.5 mtrs.	10.50 mtrs.

Those who show the necessary aptitude should be encouraged to do the event over the conventional hurdle, increasing the number of flights to five, then to seven and finally the full flight. The motivation provided by a target time should be present all of the time, otherwise a "slow motion" technique could develop. Once this situation has been reached, the event will no longer be a class activity, and it should be catered for as a "club" event.

Coaching the good hurdler

The high hurdles
Initially the coach finds that he has to take on the job of a groundsman and carry hurdles to the most suitable lane, adjust the heights and at times carry out temporary repairs to the weathered hurdles. However, it is no chore as it can be done during the athlete's preliminary warm-up.

Once a reasonable basic technique has been established, the role of the

coach becomes that of a trainer, motivator and director of training sessions.

The best work the hurdle's coach can do is associated with stride-lengths and split-times, as these two factors combine together to indicate the quality, or otherwise, of the technique. A stop-watch, capable of recording in one hundredth of a second intervals, is a valuable aid.

It is most convenient to do the bulk of the work over three or five hurdles, but it should be emphasised that training must also be included over more flights than this, otherwise the athlete is stepping into the unknown once the fifth flight has been cleared.

The ideal training distance is 60 metres. This permits the correct start, five hurdles and a run-in of 9.72 metres, when the conventional high hurdles' spacing is used. It is wise to establish target times. The following are within the ability range of the good hurdler. As the various attributes improve, so too must the target times. Times are given at foot contact the far side of each hurdle.

		Differential
Start to hurdle 1	2.5 seconds	—
Start to hurdle 2	3.7 seconds	1.2 seconds
Start to hurdle 3	4.9 seconds	1.2 seconds
Start to hurdle 4	6.0 seconds	1.1 seconds
Start to hurdle 5	7.1 seconds	1.1 seconds
60 metres	8.2 seconds	

With this basic information the coach can set on a course to improve the various sections of the race. At first he might focus attention on the start, where a little work can improve the time to 2.3 seconds or less. However, this will not indicate an improvement in hurdling. The difference between a 14.8 seconds hurdler and the 13.3 seconds one is seldom recognised in starting times. For example in the 1968 Games a 15.0 seconds hurdler recorded 2.5 seconds to the first hurdle, during a heat, while a 13.8 seconds man had a 2.4 seconds-split. Nevertheless 0.2 of a second saved here will ultimately produce a faster time. To get an improvement in this area the coach will need to study the starting technique and check every stride length to the first hurdle. The following stride pattern might serve as a guide to the coach in this matter:-

Strides 1 and 2	3' 6'' approximately
Strides 3 and 4	4' 6'' approximately
Strides 5 and 6	5' 6'' approximately
Strides 7 and 8	6' 6'' approximately

The measurements are based on the common eight stride approach. As mentioned earlier the eighth stride will be shorter than the seventh, and generally speaking all other even strides will be slightly longer than the odd

strides. The pattern will vary from athlete to athlete, day-to-day, track to track, etc. The take-off stride will be between 6' 6"-7' 0".

When examining the interval splits the following pattern might help the coach decide on a line of action:-

Landing stride	4' 0" approximately
Follow up stride	5' 0" approximately
Stride 2	7' 0" approximately
Stride 3	6' 9" approximately
Take off	7' 0" approximately

These are approximate, and like the approach strides, will not add up to the precise distance.

A tremendous amount can be obtained from these figures. If the follow-up stride is less than four feet the distance has to be made up somewhere and this will usually be reflected in an increase in the length, hence style, of strides two and three. This could indicate a weakness of the trailing leg action. If the take-off mark is more than seven feet it could indicate the inability to stride out on strides two and three.

By experimenting with the variable stride patterns and keeping a constant reference to the split-times, an improvement should follow.

With this complete there only remains the endurance factor of the race and this is the most difficult aspect to cater for. It can be done in two ways:-

1. Over a full flight of ten hurdles, keeping a check on split-times, especially for the hurdles 6-10. It is often this phase of the race which makes great hurdlers what they are. They have the ability to keep their form with fatigue in the body. The very good hurdler will often record split-times of 1.0 second up to the eighth, with a slight drop-off to 1.1 seconds for the final hurdles. Lesser mortals will probably record 1.1 seconds and 1.2 seconds respectively.

2. To use just five hurdles to 60 metres, a quick jog back to repeat the same five hurdles. Again split times must be kept and the aim should be to keep the differential between the first run as close as possible to those of the second run. This method offers variety and incentive, and as such it is probably more suitable as a training distance.

However, training over hurdles alone will never assure success. The athlete must improve speed, strength, stamina, mobility, etc. by adopting a carefully planned training scheme.

Identical work can be done with the 400 metres hurdler. While there is little point in measuring each stride, the overall pattern must be examined carefully. By experimenting with the various stride plans, within one's capability, and associating them with split times, the most efficient formulae can be deduced.

To help the coach understand split times for this event I will list those of

David Hemery, in winning the 1968 Olympic final, in a new world record. All are touch-down times:-

Hurdle	Time	Differential
1	6.0 (6.2)	
2	9.8 (9.9)	3.8
3	13.6 (13.8)	3.8
4	17.5 (17.7)	4.0
5	21.5 (21.8)	3.9
6	25.4 (26.1)	4.2
7	29.6 (30.3)	4.3
8	33.9 (34.8)	4.4
9	38.3 (39.4)	4.5
10	42.8 (44.2)	
Run in	5.3 (5.4)	
Time	48.1 seconds (49.6 seconds)	

Those in brackets belong to Steve Tziortsis (Greece) and are taken from the 1972 Olympic Games final in Munich where he was placed seventh. I had the pleasure of working with Steve for a year while he was a student in England (see plate 12).

The good coach must keep an accurate record of touch-down times in order to provide an indication of progress and to be used for motivation.

Women's hurdles

The coaching formulae is identical with work centred around stride lengths, split-times, etc. The only times I have in this area are those of Christine Bell (plate 13), in a year when her best time was 13.4 seconds. These are the best times recorded during training:-

Hurdle	Time	Differential
1	2.2 seconds	
2	3.3 seconds	1.1
3	4.3 seconds	1.0
4	5.3 seconds	1.0
5	6.4 seconds	1.1

Her approach strides were fairly consistent at the following marks, so too was the interval stride pattern, also shown.

Stride No.	Length
1	2' 9''
2	3' 3''

Plate 12. S. Tziortsis (Greece) a relaxed 400 hurdler.

Plate 13. C. Bell (G.B.) demonstrates a good trailing leg action.

Stride No.	length
3	3' 10"
4	4' 8"
5	5' 6"
6	5' 6"
7	6' 0"
8	5' 9"
Take off	5' 6"
Landing	3' 7"
1st stride	5' 5"
2nd stride	6' 8"
3rd stride	6' 8"
Take off	6' 2"

Training for sprint hurdlers

In very simple terms, training for this event is identical to training for the sprints, only the added factors of hurdling skill and extra mobility must be catered for. The hurdler must have dynamic flexibility developed through callisthenics, partner assisted exercises and ballistic movements using medicine balls or weights. The hurdler, therefore, has to allow sufficient time in his training programme for all of the five "S" factors—Speed, Strength, Stamina, Skill and Suppleness. The precise amount of each will vary with the individual and will be influenced by the total amount of training time available, facilities, specific weaknesses, etc. The only way to give the reader an understanding of this is to list some fairly typical schedules for two different times of the year. However, it must be emphasised that training schedules are very personal things; they will vary from week to week. For my own squad I have a printed sheet which lists the proposed schedule and allows space for the actual schedule which has been completed. The form is divided into 28 squares, the top line of fourteen squares containing the proposed training load, the bottom 14 squares being for the athlete to record the actual training load. Such a variable situation is essential, as the athlete might find it impossible to follow a schedule to the letter because of varying external circumstances.

Typical Schedule for October/March

Day 1   (i) Fartlek run 2 miles.
          (ii) Gymnasium work:
                 a)   Dynamic mobility.
                 b)   Weight training.
                 c)   Harness running.
Day 2   (i) Fartlek run 2 miles.
          (ii) Track work:
                 a)   Warm-up, mobility work
                 b)   8 x 60 metres from blocks . . 2 x 150 metres.

Day 3   As Day 1.

Day 4   (i)   Fartlek run 2 miles.
             (ii) Track work 5 x 5 hurdles spaced with 4 x flat sprints over
                   same distance. Note differential: 3 minutes recovery.

Day 5   (i)   Fartlek run.
             (ii) Weight training . . fast timed method . . mobility work.

Day 6   Rest, indoor race or game.

Day 7   Track work:
             a)   Warm up mobility work.
             b)   1 x 3 hurdles, 1 x 5 hurdles 1 x 7 hurdles repeat in same
                   order; 3 minutes recovery period.
             c)   6 x 30 metres from blocks.

The schedule indicated assumes that the athlete can train twice a day. The
first session should consist of a fartlek run done before mid-day, with the
second session taking place during the late afternoon or evening.

Typical schedule for May

Day 1   (i)   Fartlek run.
             (ii) Indoor work: Fast weights timed method, harness running.

Day 2   (i)   Fartlek run.
             (ii) Track work: 10 x 5 hurdles as follows. Sprint five hurdles, jog
                   back to start, repeat immediately. Rest 5 minutes. Repeat.

Day 3   (i)   Fartlek run.
             (ii) Track work: 6 x 150 metres sprints 5 minutes recovery.

Day 4   (i)   Fartlek run.
             (ii) Track work: 8 x 3 hurdles concentrating on technique, split
                   times etc.

Day 5   Rest or easy run.

Day 6   Competition.

Day 7   Track work: 1 x 1 hurdle; 1 x 2 hurdles; 1 x 3 hurdles; 1 x 4
                   hurdles; 1 x 5 hurdles . . repeat in reverse order. Recovery
                   period 1 minute per hurdle.

Typical winter schedule for 400 metres hurdler

Day 1   (i)   Fartlek run.
             (ii) Indoor work: weights timed 50 seconds. Harness running.

Day 2   (i)   Fartlek run.
             (ii) Track work: Up clock—120, 140, 160, 180, 200 metres, walk
                   back recovery.

Day 3   (i)   Fartlek run.
             (ii) 3 miles sustained run or 30 minutes hill work.

Day 4   (i)   Fartlek run.
            (ii)   Indoor work: circuit training, mobility training, shuttle runn-
                 ing over hurdles.

Day 5   (i)   Fartlek run.
            (ii)   Track work: 4 x 600 metres, 3 minutes recovery period.

Day 6   (i)   3 miles sustained run.

Day 7   (i)   Track work: 6 x 5 hurdles 400 spacings; 3 minutes recovery
                 each. 10 minutes rest; 6 x 60 metres from blocks walk back
                 recovery.

Typical schedule for 400 metres hurdles for May

Day 1   (i)   2 miles fartlek.
            (ii)   Track work: 2 sets of 3 x 200 metres fast, 30 seconds recovery
                 10 minutes rest, hurdle technique work.

Day 2   (i)   2 miles fartlek.
            (ii)   Track work: 6 x 400 metres with hurdles 6-10 in place. 5
                 minutes recovery.

Day 3   (i)   2 miles fartlek.
            (ii)   Track work: 10 x 150 metres fast, walk back recovery.

Day 4   (i)   Fartlek run.
            (ii)   Track work: 3 x 600 metres, 5 minutes recovery; 15 minutes
                 rest. 4 x 3 hurdles from blocks.

Day 5   Rest or easy run.

Day 6   Competition, over flat distances.

Day 7   Track work: 6 x 5 hurdles 400 spacing from blocks. 5
                 minutes recovery.

The schedules are devised with the idea that the athlete would like to reach peak form for the international season in the northern hemisphere during August/September. It must be accepted that the schedule is only listed to illustrate a general theme. If taken over the period of a full year the emphasis will shift according to the proximity of the competitive period. The variety can be introduced by changing the nature of the sessions in order to produce a superbly fit athlete at the correct time of the year.

Chapter 9

Steeplechasing

The exact origin of steeplechasing as an athletic event is very difficult to trace, although its history makes humorous reading. An affair at Exeter College, Oxford, in 1850 is well documented when one Halifax Wyatt, referring to a horse race over obstacles, remarked "I would prefer to go over that two mile course on foot rather than mount that camel again." The challenge was taken up.

However, it is fairly certain that the event was established in the English public schools before 1850 as the Eton College records list the event being won by C. Foster in 1846. The nature of the courses used were not documented, so they could have been little more than a Cross Country course with the odd gate, hedge or ditch for variety.

It would be very easy to dismiss the history of the event as the poor man's attempt to copy the rich, who probably made the horseback version popular. The "steeple" part of the word might be significant in that village life of the early nineteenth century was often centred around the Church, the steeple of which was probably a local landmark visible for several miles.

As a track event it was introduced around 1860, there being a record at the Sandhurst Military Academy for the year 1862. It became very popular as an event in the 1870's, but this was more as a spectacle than as a test of athletic ability and was probably staged as amusement for the spectators. The water jump was often made a formidable barrier, almost impossible to clear when fresh, let alone after a period of fast running. Hence the competitors always emerged from the water jump muddy and soaked.

As an Olympic event, it was first introduced to the programme for the Paris Games of 1900. But right from the start it was bedevilled with inconsistent and muddled thinking. Even this Games saw two steeplechase events, one over a course of 2,500 metres and one over 4,000 metres. In the next successive three Olympics it suffered a very mixed fate. In 1904 the distance was 2,500 metres, at the London Games of 1908 it was made as close to the British standard distance of 2 miles, over a course of 3,200 metres, and the event was not included in the programme for 1912. However, in 1924 there was an attempt to standardise the distance at 3,000 metres, but fate played its part because in 1932 an error, on the part of the lap scoring official, caused the distance to be 3,400 metres. In

all subsequent Olympics it has been a standard distance of 3,000 metres.

With a history like this, it is fairly natural that the event did not appeal to the "cream" of middle distance runners, although names like Paavo Nurmi and Ville Ritolo do appear on the lists of medal winners. Until fairly recently the event has been regarded as a soft option for 5,000 metres runners who could not quite make the grade. This is not meant as a sad reflection on very talented athletes like Volmari Iso-Hollo of Finland, Gaston Roelants (Belgium) and our own Christopher Brasher. But the Olympic Games of 1972 saw the best ever runner over 1,500 metres, Kipchoge Keino (Kenya), win the event on running speed alone, as his barrier clearance was far from efficient. I am certain that the win of Keino will revolutionise the event and in the future it will appeal to very good 1,500 metres runners.

The history of the event is full of the odd incidents of the great names of middle distance running making a single attempt at the distance without being persuaded to specialise in it. Some have admitted that the event is too hard, requiring a specific type of running fitness and a fair degree of technique beyond that which they were prepared to achieve. It presents the talented middle distance runner with the risk of losing dominance in his proven event and possible failure in a new one—a risk few runners would accept.

The steeplechase must be set on a sound foundation of middle distance running that might be termed a good cross between 1,500 metres and 5,000 metres training. One thing is certain, the steeplechaser of the future will have to be a very competent performer over both of these flat distances. All of the material presented in the section on middle distance running is applicable to the steeplechaser. Hence the rest of this section will be devoted to the techniques of barrier clearance and the specific training necessary for this aspect of the event.

The single three foot, solid, barrier presents quite a formidable obstacle to the athlete. While it can be classed as a hurdle, and the clearance technique of the best could be compared with that of the high hurdler, the race situation is entirely different. The steeplechase hurdle is solid and if struck is unlikely to topple over, hence collision can only affect the runner. As it is a single barrier, cleared by all competitors, who are jostling at one and the same time for the best advantage point, extra pressure is placed on the athlete. A clear approach to the barrier might be suddenly blocked by another athlete, calling for a complete change in stride pattern, direction of approach, etc. In the early stages of the race the hurdle is little more than a challenge but with fatigue it becomes a test of skill and courage. The water jump presents an extra hazard and unless the clearance technique is efficient vital seconds can be lost, and the fate of many important races has been decided at this barrier.

The senior steeplechaser is called to negotiate twenty eight hurdles and seven water jumps in the course of the 3,000 metres race. It is impossible to

lay down any hard and fast rules concerning the location of the hurdles, because it depends upon the position of the water jump which, by the very nature of its construction, has to be on the inside, or the outside, of the normal running circuit. The international rules insist that the water jump is the fourth in each lap and they recommend that there should be sufficient free running before the first hurdle, and after the last hurdle, to prevent unfortunate circumstances that might arise from groups of athletes, or very fatigued athletes, approaching these important barriers. The distance from the starting point to the commencement of the first lap has to be free of all obstacles, hence they have to be removed from the track and replaced once the first lap proper has been started.

As mentioned earlier, the hurdle clearance technique has to be a very economical version of that used by the high hurdler. Although the hurdle is lower, it is more solid, hence the very close clearance used by the high hurdler is modified to suit this event. The approach to the hurdle is all-important, and athletes have to sight the hurdle several strides out and try to negotiate for a free run-in. Several years ago athletes used check marks to

Plate 14. M. Herriot (G.B.) demonstrates a good hurdling action in the "Chase"

help them adjust their strides before driving across the barrier. These are seldom, if ever, used by current steeplechasers who, through constant practice, can judge their stride pattern relying on the visual senses only. This is made easier if athletes can negotiate the barrier equally well from either leg, as this will make any last minute alterations to stride patterns less obvious. Should circumstances prevent the athlete from judging the stride pattern correctly, then the athlete, as a last resort, can place a foot on the solid barrier. Indeed this method for negotiating the hurdle was a feature of steeplechasers of just over a decade ago; and some less efficient hurdlers, but good runners, have resorted to this method of clearance. The important thing is to judge the stride pattern correctly and drive in faster to attack the barrier. The lead knee should be picked up high and the trail leg recovered in the running position round the side of the body in order to produce a fluid movement from the hurdle (see plate 14).

The water jump is impossible to clear completely on each and every lap. While it might be possible for a strong, fast athlete to clear completely the three foot high fence, followed by a twelve foot trough of water, once, it is unlikely that any athlete could completely clear it seven times, often with extreme fatigue in the body, particularly towards the end of the race. Hence all good athletes have developed a technique where one foot is placed on the barrier and the other foot placed towards the water's edge as part of an exaggerated running stride.

Again a very important part of the technique is to judge carefully the final strides leading up to the barrier. The cadency of these strides must be increased to provide sufficient momentum to clear the barrier and water. Most athletes judge the approach so that they can place the foot, of their strong leg, on top of the hurdle. In approaching the hurdle, the knee of this leg must be picked up high and fast to help provide lift, so that the foot can be placed on top of the hurdle. The bodyweight must be kept low as it pivots over the supporting foot. Once the bodyweight is in advance of the foot it should push the body out and across the water. During the flight from the barrier the thighs of the legs must be kept split so that on landing the trailing limb can be pulled through to provide the slowing body with extra momentum. The first stride can then be taken on dry land and the running action quickly resumed. This means that the steeplechaser gets one foot wet, while ideally the other foot remains dry (see figs. 25-26).

Teaching the steeplechase

With the limited amount of time for teaching athletics, and because this event requires very specialist equipment, it can legitimately be excluded from the formal teaching programme in schools. Potential steeplechasers should be encouraged to join a club with the specialist facilities. However, timed runs of 800 metres, or other suitable distances, can encourage the event, provided five adjustable hurdles are placed in each lap. The motiva-

Plate 15. "One foot wet". The field during the 1970 Commonwealth Games.

Figs. 14   15   16   17   18   19

20   21   22   23   24

25   26

tional training schemes described in the section on middle distance running can be used, placing the light adjustable hurdles as obstacles to be cleared.

Coaching the top-class performer

As this is primarily a running event, the role of the coach is more that of a supervisor of training, only concentrating on the technical aspects when the barrier sessions are being done. All that is written under the section on coaching middle distance running is applicable to this aspect of the steeple-chaser's schedule.

The first thing the coach must do on the technical side is to help establish a confident approach to the hurdling work. Apart from a weekly speed endurance session, using barriers, I find this work best done after a sustained run, fartlek, or interval track session. To help give confidence, hurdle sessions can be done using the conventional track hurdle at a height of 3 feet. If these are placed on the normal hurdling straight, at double the spacing used for the high hurdles, five hurdles can be completed in the course of one hundred metres. The spacing of 20 metres is just sufficient to enable the athlete slightly to increase cadence in order to attack the hurdle. It also permits an easy ten stride interval, thus permitting an alternate leg clearance should this be decided advantageous.

The technical work for the water jump is best done by placing a portable barrier on a long jump approach board, using the approach runway to gain speed and placing a marker in the sand to indicate the position the water's edge would be in. The imprints made in the sand serve as an instant check on the landing and follow up strides. These "dry runs" save the filling of the water jump, considered as a chore by most groundsmen, and those left perman-ently full are likely to be unsafe.

A lot of very useful barrier work can be done in a conventional school gymnasium using the beams in place of the barriers, and rubber landing mats' should one wish to simulate the water jump.

Training for the steeplechaser

This section will be limited entirely to the extra specific work the steeplechaser will be required to do over and above the middle distance training.

As the steeplechaser is required to place himself in positions similar to those performed by a high hurdler, a degree of dynamic flexibility work is demanded. Other than those performed as part of a warm-up routine, additional exercises are best done as part of a stamina circuit, using most of the conventional circuit training exercises, including sit-ups, "Burpees", and sit-ups with an alternate knee flexion. Such a circuit should be performed at least once a week during the winter conditioning period.

Once the period of stamina build-up has been completed, and for most northern hemisphere countries this will be soon after the beginning of a new

calendar year, training runs incorporating barrier work should be introduced. Initially I find it convenient to standardise on just a single session and performance times can be used as a guide to this area of fitness. The session I find most suitable is intermittent 800 metres, with the first lap free of barriers and the second lap containing five hurdles. The hurdles should be placed in lane two, leaving the inside lane for the first lap. The first lap must be done reasonably fast, in order to produce a degree of fatigue, so that the barriers have to be cleared in a stressed condition. The good steeplechaser should aim to complete the free lap in 60 seconds or less. The sequence should be repeated four or five times allowing some five to ten minutes for recovery. The same lay out of the track can be used for doing 600 metres or 1,000 metres. When doing 600 metres it is best to do the first 200 metres using the inside lane. With the 1,000 metres it is often a good idea to do the first and final 200 metres using the inner lane. However, with the longer distance it can be adjusted to produce a desired effect or to add variety.

Other than these specific sessions the steeplechaser is well advised to concentrate on building up a fast flat time. In the early part of the competitive season the steeplechaser should seek out competitions over 800 metres, 1,500 metres and 5,000 metres. A fast time recorded over one of these flat distances will add to the confidence. The situation in the flat race is that the steeplechaser is likely to be challenging a specialist, probably not of international status, but often more than good enough to extend the non-specialist: in this case the proficient steeplechaser.

Section 3

Jumping events

Chapter 10

Horizontal Jumps

The term "horizontal jumps" is the one given to the group comprising the long jump and triple jump. The term is given to differentiate them from the vertical jumps, where the aim is to project the body vertically rather than horizontally. The term "horizontal jumps" also indicates the direction in which the speed is applied, and the emphasis is on speed. The long jump, in essence, appears to be a very simple event but it is not the automatic choice for reject sprinters. Most good long jumpers are also good sprinters but very few good sprinters ever make the grade in the long jump.

To a certain extent the horizontal jumper has to make a compromise, which probably explains why the sprinter does not readily adapt to these events. In theory all that the long jumper has to do is to jump high at the end of a fast approach run. Indeed, if we could combine the qualities of the world record high jumper, and the world record sprinter, the record for the long jump would be in the region of *36 feet,* some twenty per cent more than the existing record. If the horizontal jumper approached the take-off board with the speed of the sprinter, the body would pass so quickly over the fulcrum, that lift would be minimal. If in turn he wished to develop the vertical lift of the high jumper, then approach speed would have to be considerably reduced, with a drastic effect upon the distance jumped. So it can be seen that the events are a compromise with the balance weighing heavily in favour of horizontal speed.

The long jump

The long jump competition is one for distance, and the jumper who can record the longest jump during a series, the maximum number of which cannot exceed six and must not be less than three, wins the competition. There are, of course, a number of other restrictions to help standardise the event throughout the world. The athlete, in theory, can take an unlimited length of approach run. This can never work out in practice as the stadium itself, and its associated event areas, etc. must impinge on the long jump area. However, the true limiting factor is that all athletes reach peak speed within fifty yards, so any additional length would be superfluous. The jumper must take-off from behind a scratch line which is the part of a board nearest to the landing area. The board, known as the take-off board, should measure 4

feet in length and be 8 inches wide. The landing area itself must be at least nine feet wide and thirty feet in length. For the jump to be valid the competitor must land within the area and the distance of the jump is measured from the scratch line to the nearest point, in the landing area, contacted by any part of the body. If, in the course of the jump, the athlete touches the ground outside the landing area, nearer to the scratch line than the mark within the area, the jump is disallowed. The athlete can touch the ground outside the area if the point of contact is further than that made within the area.

The final restriction, concerning the use of weights or grips, is indeed an interesting one. The very early leapers of the ancient Greek civilisations, and more recently the professional jumpers of the eighteenth century in Great Britain, carried weights in the hand to give them extra distance. While such weights could restrict the approach speed, if released at a convenient point during flight extra lift would be experienced. However, in this age of ultra-fast, artificial approach surfaces, and faster and stronger athletes, it is almost certain that their use would detract from the speed and hence the distance of the jump.

The long jumper requires a fast controlled approach run, an explosive take-off, a controlled flight and a sound landing position. For the convenience of description, the event can be analysed under similar subheadings to those mentioned above, but it must be remembered that they do not represent a series of isolated movements. All aspects of the total skill must be blended together to compose the complete jump.

The approach run

To the uninitiated the approach run would appear to be simplicity in itself. However, when one strives for excellence, even the simple things inevitably become complicated and this is certainly the case with the approach run for the top-class jumper. The athlete wishes to strike an eight inch wide board, as near to the scratch line as possible, without fouling, and at peak speed with sufficient control to provide the necessary action to give lift. When considered in these terms, it is quite obvious that the long jump is composed of a series of very precise movements which do not permit a very large margin for errors.

Most top-class jumpers require an approach run in excess of 100 feet to reach a fast controlled speed. It is difficult to give hard and fast rules but the majority adopt a stride pattern of between 19 and 21 full running strides before they strike the board. The long striding athlete will need a longer distance to acquire the necessary speed and the short, faster striding athlete, less distance. Some athletes start their approach run from a static position, toeing their start check-mark, others perform a rocking stride from the mark, while some utilise a rolling start to hit the check mark, in the form of a walk or a very relaxed run. The precise nature for starting the run is unimportant

Plate 16. R. Williams (U.S.A.) Winner of 1972 Olympic Long jump, shows poise in the air.

provided it is consistent each time. Inconsistency in the method of starting will affect the stride pattern and accuracy to the board. One thing is certain, concentration at the start of the run is essential in order to help channel all the resources available into combining together to produce a full effort attempt.

The long jumper does not rush at the board from the outset. The early strides are like those of the sprinter building up speed, but at about seven strides out from the board the running pattern must change. The accent will remain on speed but the emphasis on running action will change. The leg

action of the sprinter is one of a powerful movement behind the body, pushing it forwards and producing a degree of forward lean. Such an action, from the board, for the long jumper, would be fatal as it could not produce a significant amount of lift. During the strides immediately prior to the jump, the athlete must prepare for take-off. This period of preparation does not involve the athlete in slowing down, or "coasting", a term frequently used. The jumper must be correct, at take-off, in order to make full use of the take-off potential in the legs. For the leg action to be efficient they must work under the body, hence the running action changes over this preparatory phase. There is an attempt to increase the cadence, the knees are picked up higher and the movement is more concentrated about the hip joint. This action will automatically cause a gradual lowering of the bodyweight, that becomes quite apparent in the penultimate stride, and is often termed a "sink". Top-class jumpers emphasise that the sink is not deliberate as at this stage concentration has to be focused on *striking* the board. Such an action will cause a consistent variation in stride length which must not be considered significant. It is all part of a natural, controlled, approach run and any attempt to lengthen the penultimate stride or shorten the take-off stride can only lead to catastrophe.

A number of athletes use a check mark associated with the position on the runway, where this change of emphasis occurs. It is not a check mark in the true sense of the word where the foot must hit the mark to indicate accurate approach run. It is more a "cue" mark to encourage the shift of emphasis. True accuracy of the approach run, although considerably dependent upon the consistency of the running stride, is influenced by the visual feed-back, and the way the athlete reacts to this feed-back, from the board. This phase of the approach run is more of an instinct that can only be nurtured through the repetition of the precise movements involved.

In events of this nature, discussion can always be centred around the use of check marks placed alongside the runway. Some athletes use them, others find their use restrictive and inhibiting. There is no doubt that a starting check mark is essential and another mark three or four strides after this valuable, only to illustrate the accuracy of the most inconsistent strides. However, any precise check mark, after seven strides of the approach run, is certain to conflict with the concentration necessary during the final five strides. A "cue" mark, merely to focus attention or change of emphasis, is quite acceptable closer to the board.

Take-off

At take-off the jumper has two different ways in which to develop take-off force. The first is by using the elastic properties of the muscles, brought about by the stretch reflex mechanism (a mechanism which permits the fast, efficient contract of a muscle placed under stretch), and the second the extension of the leg about the knee and hip joint. At, or just prior

to take-off, the emphasis must be on the position of the hips, or in more accurate terms, the pelvis. For take-off to be efficient the pelvis must be tilted upwards, made possible only by the correct running action. The actual take-off leg power is derived from two sources and because of this is somewhat of a compromise. If the take-off leg is deliberately allowed to bend, in order to produce a greater range for extension, the leg could completely collapse or the subsequent movement, driving from deep flexion, would necessarily be slow and fairly inefficient. Also the more deliberate is the leg flexion, the less can be the effect produced by the natural stretch reflex system.

Experimental and observed evidence would suggest that the long jumper does not deliberately bend the take-off leg. It might flex because of the pattern of movements undertaken by the body, just prior to take-off. However, it is more likely to attain the take-off angle through a combination of the bodyweight, the speed of the body and the extra muscular force provided by the athlete when the foot is being planted. The good jumper does not merely allow the take-off foot to touch the board, it is planted with considerable force. This would place the leg in a natural position to produce an explosive extension and to make the full use of the stretch reflex mechanisms.

The power provided by the take-off leg is further aided by the free limbs, although they are more concerned with a balancing movement rather than one providing lift. However, if the pick-up of the free thigh is timed correctly, it can add slightly to the lift producing forces. At the moment of take-off it is true to assume that every part of the body should be directed upwards. The jumper should almost feel a sensation of a powerful force, pushing in the middle of the back, directed at about 45°. This will produce the effect of keeping the upper part of the body erect. The initial arm action is essentially a balancing movement, although in theory it can also aid the lifting forces. Since the free thigh has been pulled through to a fairly high position in front of the body, a similar high movement of the opposite arm is essential to keep body balance. As far as possible, all of the forces producing lift, and to keep equilibrium, should be directed in a straight line parallel to the long vertical axis of the body. By so doing they will add to those produced by the running action which has been directed down the runway towards the landing area. It is absolutely essential that the take-off movement should be fully completed. Many novice jumpers, who have been taught a mid-air action, tend to perform the movement prematurely before full lift has been obtained.

Controlled flight

To make full use of the speed provided at take-off, the jumper must be balanced during the flight, but the action of producing counterbalancing movements in the air is likely to detract from the essential position, just

prior to landing, where both legs are extended in front of the body. This presents the jumper with a degree of compromise, between producing balancing movements in the air and preparing efficiently for landing. Balancing movements, performed in the air, are only made necessary by the fact that the action at take-off is likely to provide the body with forward rotation. If this rotation is allowed to continue in the body, it will make an efficient landing position impossible and will place the legs, on landing, considerably behind the predicted landing position if the body could follow the normal flight curve. However, it is often wrongly assumed that the body will always possess a degree of forward rotation, making such balancing movements essential. It is possible for the action at take-off to produce backward rotation or no rotation at all, thus making the supporters of fancy mid-air actions seem rather ridiculous.

The duration of flight, of the long jumper, is very short and there is not the time to perform elaborate movements in the air and get into an effective landing position. The only essential, during flight, is that the athlete should make a long, thin "shape", at about the apex of the flight curve. This extended position of the body will offer great resistance to any form of rotation about a horizontal axis. Most top-class jumpers perform one, or a combination of two, movements to help balance the flight. They are commonly termed the "Hitch-kick" and the "Hang" and although a considerable amount of physical science has been applied to the movements, they still remain a simple and practical means of offering resistance to the tendency of the body to rotate about a horizontal axis.

The "hitch-kick", or "running in the air" style is well illustrated in the sequence series, see figs. 27-34. As the term suggests, the jumper performs a running action in the air continued from that at take-off. Once the free knee has been picked up, to coincide with the extension of the take-off leg, it is in a bent position in front of the body. If, from this position it is extended forwards and then the long, straight, leg rotated backwards about the hip joint, it will have the effect of forcing the upper part of the body erect and slightly backwards, producing a counter force to the forward rotation. The movement must be performed fairly quickly and with an extended lower limb on the backwards sweep. Some athletes perform a complete single leg cycle, others as many as a double leg cycle. Such a leg action is dependent upon the duration of flight and the speed of the leg cycle. The longer the flight the more time provided for elaborate leg movements. There are two very grave dangers in performing this type of movement. The first is that the athlete might be obsessed with the leg cycle and start the movement before full extension from the board has been achieved, so detracting from the lifting force. The second is, by performing the movement rapidly, the athlete can still be placed in the "tucked" position, ready for landing too early, allowing a chance for the rotation to continue, so permitting the legs to strike the ground behind their true landing position. Although most of the emphasis

has been placed on the legs, since their turning effect is greater, the arms do contribute to the movement by working in sympathy with the legs and can provide a turning effect when extended above the head.

The "hang", as the name suggests, calls for the body to hang extended in the air, at the high point. This stretching action slows down any form of rotation by increasing the body's moment of inertia. However, this style is not so popular with the jumpers as the "hitch kick", probably because of the difficult and strenuous "jack-knife" position the athlete must get into prior to landing. In the "hang" position both legs and arms will be trailing the trunk, meaning that both legs have to be brought through to the front in a single fast movement due to the speed at which the body is dropping towards the sand. With the "hitch-kick" action, only one leg will be required to move to the extended position in front of the body, as the normal leg cycle will have placed the other leg in a position of extension in front of the trunk.

The landing position is really one of extreme importance, as vital inches can be saved by positioning the body correctly just prior to striking the sand. Again the jumper is forced to make a compromise. The ideal position for the legs to be in, just prior to landing, is one where they are held high and extended in front of the trunk. Unfortunately this would certainly mean

Figs. 27   28   29   30

31   32   33   .   34

that on landing the athlete would fall backwards, so making a mark behind that of the heels. In practice, therefore, the best landing position is one where the legs are well extended, with the trunk "jack knifed", so that the head is almost between the legs, with the arms as far behind the hips as is possible. Such a position will permit a very fast pivoting action, where the bodyweight is forced over, and in front, of the heels, which form the fulcrum for the rotation. Even with the best executed "leg shoot" it is unlikely that the jumper's heels will contact the sand beyond that predicted by the flight curve, which is established at take-off and merely represents the path which the centre of gravity of the body will follow. Unless weights are carried, nothing can be done to increase the distance of the flight path. However, by remaining balanced during flight, and establishing an efficient "leg-shoot" position, one can more closely make full use of the potential provided by the take-off forces.

Long jumping is essentially a simple event and the benefits of a fast, accurate approach run, and a vigorous planting and striking action at take-off, cannot be over-emphasised. Indeed, this is where time must be spent during training as this combined action can add feet to a jump, whereas the balancing and landing movements can only save inches.

Teaching the long jump

As long jumping is an extremely natural event, the main emphasis during the early teaching stages must be on the natural skills of speed and spring. The first thing the teacher should do is to dispense with the very artificial skill of having to hit a take-off board. Many top-class athletes find this aspect of the skill very demanding and inhibiting, so the effect must surely be magnified considerably with the novice. The inspired teacher will provide artificial aids such as "beating boards", ramps, etc. in order to help give the novice some extra height. By providing a fairly large take-off area and permitting a degree of assistance at take-off, the novice can focus all attention on the speed-spring co-ordination. In the early stages, the length of the approach run must be limited. If it is too long the novice will be slowing, or have reached a speed which cannot be controlled for a take-off. Ideally it should be limited to about nine strides and this speed, together with an assisted take-off, will constitute a good platform for jumping a fair distance, which will provide the necessary motivation to practise the event.

The basic fundamental of the event is to be able to lift the body from the ground at speed. This will involve the powerful striking action of the take-off leg associated with the vigorous pick-up of the free knee. While learning this phase of the jumping action, a simple "sail" style is quite acceptable, to place the jumper in a position ready for landing. The "sail" style is descriptive of the position the athlete adopts just prior to landing. (See plate 17.) The complete emphasis must be on the powerful striking action of the take-off leg. If this is done in a class situation, enveloping the complete spectrum of

Plate 17. H. Rosendahl (W. Germany) prepares for landing on the way to winning the 1972 Olympic title.

ability, the natural jumpers will stand out. Following on from the powerful action necessary for take-off the novice should be encouraged to direct the upper part of the body upwards. It often helps to stress the importance of the chest and head which must not be allowed to drop, as this will reduce the efficiency of take-off and will promote an unstable flight. These simple instructions are best given to the novice during a number of competitive jumps, where the first emphasis is on jumping a long way. While trying to encourage other important factors, influencing the range of the jump, the teacher must be aware of the essential fundamental position of the take-off leg and hip. The hip must always be kept in an active position forwards of the take-off leg, with the trunk erect.

With teaching an event like the long jump it is very difficult for the teacher not to focus attention on aspects of the jump that are of relatively minor importance. Here I refer to mid-air styles such as the "Hitch-kick" and "Hang" which are often taught as gymnastic-type skills, because most teachers are more secure teaching a movement which can be based on a series of well-defined progressions. If the take-off position is correct the body will

Plate 18. A. Lerwill (G.B.) demonstrates the side pivot landing.

extend, almost vertically, in the air, and if possible this position should be held up to the apex of the jump when it is admissible to go into a landing position. The thing which must be avoided is to adopt the landing position, directly after take-off, before the peak height of the jump has been reached.

The idea of forcing the body to make an extended, thin, shape in the air, approaching the apex of the jump, is very sound.

Once the skills of take-off and flight control have been learnt the teacher's role becomes that of a motivator, as the skills have to be perfected at speed. Running fast and jumping is a fairly boring activity for most children *unless* the level of motivation is kept high. A series of competitive targets to encourage the idea that the jump is one for maximum distance, an occasional change of emphasis from the style of the approach run to the vigorous action of the take-off leg, to the erect position of the trunk at take-off, help to relieve the monotony, so making the practice worthwhile. The only problem the novice has is one of gaining the correct type of speed, which involves the modified sprinting action, and to be able to control this speed by placing the body in the correct position at take-off. The skills of long jumping are essentially speed directed ones, so the practising of the event in slow-motion is less likely to have a beneficial effect upon performance.

The simple fundamentals of the event can be summarised as follows:-

(a) A fast sprinting action with an upright carriage of the trunk, associated with a slightly exaggerated knee pick-up a few strides before take-off. The emphasis being on leg speed rather than stride length.

(b) The correct position at take-off, with the hips in an active position.

(c) The powerful striking action of the take-off leg.

(d) The control of flight by attempting to keep some form of extended position in the air before adopting the tucked position, with legs extended horizontally in front of the body ready for landing.

Coaching the top-class performers

The simple skills listed in the teaching section cannot be ignored when working with the elite of the event. The difference between the ways in which a novice performer interprets the skills of the event might be very slight when compared with that of the experienced performer. Indeed some novices might even perform the skills better, particularly the gifted novice. The difference lies in the speed and power factors of the event, which require tremendous strength and timing. Hence the long jumper must spend countless hours away from the pit developing both speed and strength. However, it is most important to realise that the advanced skills are strength/speed dependent. As the levels of strength and speed change, so too must the skill pattern change. Therefore, it is essential to develop the skill, strength and speed qualities together, throughout an entire year. Admittedly the emphasis must change with the seasons, but it is certain that one season,

completely lacking in one or more of the three essential qualities of jumping, i.e. skill, speed and strength, will not produce rewarding results.

From working with top-class jumpers it would appear, the more advanced they become, the harder it is for them to strike the relatively small area of the take-off board. While on the surface of it such a situation seems hard to understand it is quite logical, as the advanced performer is approaching faster and wishes to take full advantage of the width of the board in order to gain those extra inches. So it is essential for the good jumper to do many fast approach runs, without necessarily performing the vigorous act of jumping, in order to familiarise himself with the situation. When approaching take-off, the athlete is constantly receiving a feed back of information, through the visual senses, about the relative position of the board. The way the body interprets the information varies considerably, from person to person, but once the performer is aware of how he reacts to the board, then the situation starts to become constant. However, it is certainly the most difficult aspect of the jump and probably the most important one. For the novice it does not matter unduly if the stride pattern changes just prior to take-off, or if the take off foot is a few inches behind the board. However, at the other end of the scale a change in stride pattern could mean the loss of vital speed, hence distance jumped. In terms of accuracy to the board, every centimetre counts, as many competitions are won or lost by this distance. The complete performer, through hours of diligent practice, develops a consistent stride pattern so that as far as this is concerned little is left to chance. Through extreme concentration on the final strides of the approach run, the visual feedback, from the board to the athlete, becomes consistent again leaving less to chance, making last minute adjustments unnecessary, so that all energies can be directed into driving the body upwards. Because of the constantly changing situation in the approach run, and because of the high speed required for superlative performances, much of the work done by the long jumper has to be confined to the approach run.

The timing of the various movements at take-off are quite precise, hence, in the final analysis, this phase of the movement must be practised at peak speed. It is very uncertain whether or not movements of this nature, practised in isolation, at reduced speed, have any direct carry-over to the event itself. However, because of the very high energy requirements, for fast approach jumping, few full effort jumps can be experienced in a single session. Hence the athlete must practise certain of the movements, at reduced speed, from a shortened version of the approach run, so permitting a greater experience in performing the final explosive effort. During the take-off phase the athlete must be made aware of the vigorous "striking" action of the take-off leg. It is not just sufficient to allow the take-off foot to hit the board. It must be forced to strike the board so that the hip and the trunk are in an active position. During all of the short approach work the emphasis must be placed on the forward position of the hips.

Once the explosive take-off position is fully appreciated, some of the time can be spent perfecting the balancing movements and those necessary for an efficient landing. This can be performed from the short approach run, but essentially the movements will be hurried as less time is spent in the air when approach speed is reduced. It is a phase of the jump which can be perfected with assisted take-offs from a spring board, ramp or even a slightly raised platform. It can be done indoors, landing on foam cushions, as for the high jump, and as such can provide a little variety during the winter conditioning months.

The cine camera and associated projection equipment, video recorder, hundredth of a second stop watch and tape measure are all extremely valuable to the long jumper and his coach. The essential feature, the coach has to convey to the long jumper, is the correct running action over the final stages of the approach run, particularly the increase in cadence. The only way this can be done is for the coach to call for it during training sessions, show the athlete the result on film or video, until a clear appreciation of the movement is forthcoming from the athlete. The stop watch, capable of recording to one-hundredth of a second, is a valuable aid, as an accurate time taken, over the last 20 or 10 metres can be used to compare approach speed relative to proven sprinting speed. If the approach run speed does not approximately match the normal sprinting speed for the same distance, then the factors inhibiting runaway speed must be explored.

As mentioned earlier, the long jump is not a technically complex event, hence proportionally less time is spent perfecting an efficient technique, and more time devoted to developing speed and strength. In this event, the rewards for an improvement in these two qualities are immense.

Training the top-class jumper

It must be appreciated that the prerequisite of this event is speed. Hence most of the training routines, described in the sprint section, should be used by the long jumper in order to help develop this quality. However, it is a very specific quality, requiring the ability to generate a fairly considerable speed, over a distance of about 40 metres. Therefore, timed runs, over a distance approximately equal to the run-up distance, must form an integral part of the jumper's conditioning programme.

While the long jumper does require sprinting speed, it would be most unwise for him to train consistently with the sprinters, as their priority is quite different. The long jumper is only required to sprint fast for a period of 40 metres, which is then followed by a rest period, while fellow competitors are jumping. To satisfy these demands the jumper should do fast sprints over 40-60 metres allowing sufficient recovery for the quality to be kept high on each successive repetition. A weekly session of sprints over 150 metres, with again an adequate recovery between each repetition, enables the jumper to concentrate on the "flow" of the movement, something difficult

when working over distances of 60 metres or less. Extra fitness training is best done in the form of a "fartlek" run, over about 3 miles, to include sustained running, fast running, hopping, bounding, etc., all spaced with slow jogging or walking. The odd 400 metres, divided into 50 metre sections, composed of sprinting, hopping, "giant" strides, bounding, etc., adds variety to this aspect of conditioning.

Quite a large proportion of the work should be done in the winter, so permitting more time to be spent on actual long jumping as the season approaches. A considerable level of general fitness is required to perform the number of quality approach runs and full effort jumps, demanded of the good jumper during a single training session. Hence this rather mundane and often boring aspect of the jumper's routine cannot be neglected.

The other peripheral aspect of the jumper's training routine is development of strength, and this is best approached in two different ways: first, the level of pure, or animal strength; secondly, the specific strength element which could permit the jumper to utilise more of the general strength, possibly made available through an improvement in the first strength quality.

General strength is best developed through the various forms of weight lifting. The long jumper wishes to develop strong resilient legs, and in normal circumstances this presents the jumper with a number of problems, all associated with safeguarding his own personal well-being. Leg strengthening exercises, with the normal barbell, often place considerable strain on other parts of the anatomy, particularly the back. This is because the most widely used exercises, such as the various squatting movements, usually place the weight across the shoulders, hence the resistance is transmitted to the legs by a quite vulnerable structure. Therefore the jumper must take particular care when exercising with the barbell to avoid placing the back in a vulnerable position. It is a good idea if the athlete can secure the use of a well constructed "power-rack", leg-press machine, or better still one of the "multigym" units now appearing on the market (see plate 34).

It must also be remembered that during jumping events the leg does not flex more than about 30 degrees, hence the use of deep squatting movements must be questioned.

During long jumping, the ankle joint is an area that is subjected to considerable stress and special attention must be given to this region during strength training.

Although the legs, and in particular the ankle joint, have been highlighted, the jumper cannot ignore the middle and upper body. The general strength training routine must include exercises likely to have a specific effect upon these particular areas. However, the jumper's training schedule should contain at least two leg exercises to one arm or trunk exercise. For example, an eight item strength schedule might contain four leg, two trunk and two arm exercises.

The specific strength areas are best developed by performing sprinting,

bounding and leaping movements with or without resistance. I am an enthusiast of the leaping decathlon, shown in Appendix I. A considerable amount of explosive leg work can be done, especially if the tables are used to form the basis of a competitive training routine. It is my experience that most long jumpers in the United Kingdom use them and keep a written record of their best total and individual event score.

Box work forms a part of the training routine. Utilising the normal gymnastic vaulting box, the height can be varied to allow for performing bounding movements on and off the box. If two boxes are used then greater variety can be incorporated. Specific details can be found in the section on triple jumping.

Depth jumping, calling for the jumper to leap down from a height, controlling the movement of landing and subsequently leaping off again, helps to promote explosive leg strength.

Medicine balls can also be used effectively in the jumper's training routine (see plates 39 & 40).

Triple jump

The triple jump, as it is now more aptly termed, has been given two earlier names which have basically described the evolution of the event, although unfortunately one still hears the former titles mentioned. Early in its evolution, it was termed the "hop, skip and jump" which, with a reasonable degree of accuracy, described the actions involved in the event, but suggesting a short "skip" phase between the first and third phases. As the event developed technically, the "skip" was gradually replaced by a *step,* suggesting that the middle phase was a little more than a recovery between two successive bounding movements. The term "triple jump" more closely meets the definition the initiated would give it, in their attempts to convey the precise movement of three almost equal jumps joined together in a definite way. In historical terms the triple jump is a comparatively recent event, its precise origin remaining camouflaged in the annals of Gaelic sports and pastimes. However, many theoreticians believe that the jump accorded to one "Phayllus of Croton" in the ancient records, was in fact a triple jump, or better still, a series of jumps, as an unassisted jump would have been unlikely to have produced such an incredible performance. (See page 14).

In many respects, the triple jump resembles the long jump, in that the facilities required for each are basically the same, and the approach-run pattern is similar. However, the forward speed of the body is slowed only once by a take-off action in the long jump and by three successive take-offs in the triple jump. The two events combined together are termed the "horizontal jumps", suggesting that the speed required for performance is applied essentially in a horizontal direction, and the whole skill of the actual triple jumping action is associated with conserving as much of the approach speed as possible during all three phases of the jump.

Basically, the rules of the event are identical to the long jump with the addition of the imposed jumping sequence. This insists that the jumper should first land on the same foot as that from which the take-off was effected, then land on the other foot for the second phase and both feet, in the landing area, for the final phase. This gives a sequence of "same"— "other"—"both". During the three phases, up to the final landing, only one foot is permitted to strike the ground. This particular rule is known as the "sleeping leg rule"; the precise reason for its inclusion in present day competition, is, to say the least, obscure.

The pattern of approach run is very similar to that of the long jumper in terms of distance and basic running style. Triple jumping is very speed dependent, hence every effort must be made to take-off with the maximum amount of useable speed. It is difficult to stipulate precisely the distance an athlete requires for the approach run as this will vary considerably from athlete to athlete. However, the majority of jumpers have a run varying from between 120 feet-140 feet in total distance. A good method to determine the distance required is to sprint, from a standing start, on a clean, brushed cinder surface. This will enable the athlete/coach to study the stride pattern. If the stride length, for each successive stride, is measured, one arrives at a point where the stride length starts to become consistent. This will mean that almost peak speed is reached. If the total distance from the start line, to the point where the stride length starts to become consistent, is measured, this will serve as a guide to the total distance required. The distance has to be transferred to the runway, making slight variations to enable the athlete to be accurate to the board. Before the distance is finalised, a number of full effort jumps should be made, and also the time taken to cover the final 20 metres of the approach run should be obtained, using a watch capable of recording 1/100th second. This way ease of take-off and approach speed can be used to help decide the final distance. Once this has been determined only very slight variations will be found necessary, depending upon local conditions. For the final 20 metres of the approach run, most good athletes will record between 2.0 seconds and 2.20 seconds. This is useable speed, as some athletes can cover the final 20 metres in less than 2.0 seconds but find it impossible to execute an efficient take-off.

The running pattern, over the complete approach run, changes as the take-off board is approached. The early strides are those of the sprinter, with the associated leaning of the trunk, to aid acceleration. The trunk will naturally become erect as the final strides of the approach run are taken. These are the vital strides, the last five or six, where the emphasis must be on sustaining speed, or even increasing leg cadency. To help plan this stride pattern the athlete might well use two check marks. The first check mark, after about five strides, is an accuracy mark and the jumper should aim to hit this mark precisely. If the approach run is based on an odd number of strides, and the take-off leg leads the running action from the start mark,

then this foot will also correspond to the one striking the five stride check mark. However, some athletes like to take an even number of approach strides and prefer the check mark after four or six strides. It is unimportant, but the early strides must be accurate as this is where the greatest variation in stride-length occurs. A few inches out with the early strides can mean a few inches out at the board. The second "check" mark is much later in the run, between five and seven strides from the take-off board, and is more of a "cue" mark rather than an accuracy mark. At this point most jumpers attempt to increase leg-cadence. It is essential that any response should be relaxed, but there must not be any attempt to coast or reduce speed. The jumper must arrive at take-off, at maximum controlled speed, with the trunk erect and the take-off hip in an active position.

The triple jumper's main concern is to retain the maximum amount of forward speed, and to keep perfect body balance, once the take-off has been executed. These together form the skill of the event, and provide the "flow" which is characteristic of the good performer. The skills can be grouped under the following headings:-

    i) Efficient take-off.
    ii) Active landings.
    iii) Momentum transfer.
    iv) Body balance.

The first, and most important take-off is that from the board. The take-off here will be determined by the type of hop used by the jumper in question. The triple jump is an event for the fast athlete, so when I refer to "slower" and "faster" it is for comparison only. The faster athlete will certainly approach the board with more speed and the take-off will closely resemble that of the long jumper. This will produce a fairly low hop and an overall "flat" technique, characteristic of the Polish style, certainly made famous by Schmidt, in the early 1960s. The slower jumper will have to rely more upon leg strength, hence the hop will be higher. The high hop is more typical of the Russian jumpers, who have dominated the event since the passing of the Polish school. I favour the high hop and believe that the event will progress towards this, with improved strength training techniques, that will enable the athlete to withstand the stress of a fast, high, hop. As it is, the event is not one for the fragile; and the incidence of injury in this event is certainly higher than in any other track and field event. However, both types demand balanced movement from the board, with the associated opposite knee pick-up and balancing arm movements. The essential feature is that the hip must be kept tilted correctly to evoke the stretch reflex mechanism. The athlete should have the sensation of "stroking" the board away. The active position of the hips is a key feature of each subsequent take-off.

Directly after this take-off the athlete is faced with keeping the body balanced. Here the first essential is to keep the trunk erect and control any possible forward rotation by performing a "cycling-type" of movement with

the legs, which are balanced with a similar movement performed by the arms. The extent of the balancing movements will be determined by the type of take-off. The fast, flat, technique produces more problems associated with forward rotation. The movement is very similar to the balancing hitch-kick movement performed by many long jumpers.

As the landing from this phase is approached, the jumper is faced with conserving speed. The first method is to place the limbs so that they are a store of potential energy, using the transfer of momentum principle. This means, that just prior to landing from each of the early phases, the thighs must be well "split" with the free leg trailing. Upon landing, the trailing leg must be brought through vigorously, to transfer the momentum, given to the limb, to the body as a whole.

The only time the triple jumper can exert a force, which can add considerably to the distance jumped, is when in contact with the ground. During the jump, the contact time is relatively small, hence all movements during contact must be very efficient. For this to be so all landings must be active. For a landing to be active the foot must strike the ground under the body and be moving in a direction opposite to the direction of the jump, at the time of contact. For this to be effective the foot must land flat, otherwise balance will be lost. The timing of the foot placement is very precise. If contact is made with the foot in front of the body, then it will act as a brake to forward speed. If contact with the ground is made too far behind the body, then the effective work period is considerably reduced.

The transfer of momentum and active landing action is common for each phase of the jump.

The real key to success in triple jumping is the way the step phase is controlled. The novice often treats this as a recovery movement between the two more powerful phases of the total leap. However, the skilled performer works on this phase and extracts as much from it as speed and technique will allow. During the step phase, the athlete must essentially feel the sensation of floating. This sensation cannot be experienced unless the leading limb is prevented from striking the ground prematurely. This means a positive attempt to keep the thigh of the leading leg high and near parallel to the approach surface. However, it is not sufficient for the advanced performer to do this action alone, although it will add considerably to the performance of the novice. Although the high thigh action of the leading leg will provide the floating sensation and will extend the step, the knee is placed in a position that encourages a "poking" action of the lower leg, causing the foot to strike the ground too far in front of the body, thus retarding speed, and producing an inactive landing. If during the high thigh position the lower limb is squeezed towards the buttocks, it will help to produce a very natural leg cycle about the hip joint. This will prevent the "poking" action.

It is important, during this phase particularly, to keep the trunk erect. The novice, when learning the high thigh action of the leading leg, will find it

41   40   39   38   37   36   Figs. 35

45   44   43   42

51   50   49   48   47   46

Fig. 52

Fig. 53

Fig. 54

Fig. 55

much easier to lower the trunk to the thigh, than to raise the thigh high to the chest. Unless corrected this will remain a feature of the jump as the body finds it difficult, in this case, to distinguish between the two positions.

Just prior to landing for the final take-off, the thighs must be split. On landing, the free thigh must be brought forwards very quickly to help give lift for the final phase. The actual take-off leg must extend vigorously, and the take-off side hip must be kept forward and active. Again the trunk must remain erect. By the time this phase has been reached the forward speed will be considerably reduced, hence a very efficient position for the final landing, in the sand, must be achieved. Often the speed remaining in the body does not permit a very sophisticated mid-air action. Admittedly some jumpers attempt a reduced "hitch-kick" or "hang", while others settle for a simple "sail" position in order to get the legs out in front of the body. Due to lack of speed, the pivot over the feet is difficult and the possibility of falling backwards, towards the take-off board, a real hazard. If the pivot can be achieved it will be identical to that performed in the long jump. However, with some athletes the "skid-through" landing might merit experimentation. Here, the leg shoot is pronounced, and on impact the hips skid through under the body, dragging with them the trunk. The buttocks strike the sand, behind the heels, but the advantage of the longer leg shoot might permit a slightly longer jump.

As a complete movement, the event is a series of rhythmic jumps, each

having a direct relationship with each other. Indeed, the novice performer should always try to keep the distance of the first and final phases the same, with only a slight drop-off in distance for the second phase. The most commonly recommended ratio is 10:8:10 and this does seem to be supported by the "splits" recorded by most jumpers. To illustrate the true meaning of this ratio, it might be easier to consider the following specific jumps.

"SPLITS"

Total Jump	Hop	Step	Jump
28 feet	10 feet	8 feet	10 feet
37 feet	15 feet	12 feet	15 feet
56 feet	20 feet	16 feet	20 feet

Plate 19a. R. Kirk (W. Germany) demonstrates a good step phase.

Plate 19b. D. Johnson. G.B. shows double arm shift at take-off.

The "splits" are usually measured from the toe of the first landing, to the heel of the second and the heel of the third. However, some coaches measure toe-toe-toe, or heel-heel-heel. It must be realised that they are only used to serve as a guide to technical efficiency during training. A good triple jump can be instantly recognised by merely listening to the landing rhythm, as the time spent in the air, during each phase, should be approximately equal.

Teaching the triple jump

Triple jumping is an event best taught by the "whole" method. While it is possible to split it down for analysis into three phases, the skill of the event is the continuity of movement. The event lends itself to using a competitive approach to learning, with the aid of a grid (see page 136).

			LANE 1
			" 2
			" 3
			" 4
			" 5

All pupils should start in lane 1 of the grid and be allowed to progress up a lane, provided they can land beyond each of the phase markers. The position of the markers should be chosen to develop, automatically, a good rhythm. Initially, the event should be done from a standing start and later with a short approach run. The landing sequence can be taught by insisting on "same—other—both" landings. At any level of jumping the "hop" should be made from the dominant leg, thus permitting two phases to be completed from this leg. This places the athlete in the situation where the final jumping movement has to be made from the weak leg. However, with practice this never presents a problem and within a short space of time the dominant to weak leg differential approaches zero.

As confidence and technique improve, a faster approach speed can be encouraged. Once the rhythm of the event has been learnt, it should be practised at the pit in the competitive situation. It is wise to place phase markers, alongside the runway, until the "floating" step phase becomes a natural movement. This will avoid any tendency to return to the hop-skip and jump of the absolute novice. During all practice sessions the pupils must be encouraged to keep the head and the trunk erect, as this is the key feature of a balanced movement.

Coaching the top-class performer

While the long jump is a technical event, it does not capture the interest and the imagination of the jump's coach in quite the same way as the triple jump does. It is an event requiring all of the natural qualities of the long jump, together with the technical expertise involved in conserving momentum for three successive jumps. The triple jump event is certainly the one that responds most readily to coaching and an improvement of several feet is not unusual, as the jumper makes the transition from novice to advanced ranks. However, once this initial spurt is over, progress can only be made with diligent practice, but here the jumper's task is made easier by the tremendous variety of conditioning work which the imaginative coach can invent.

When dealing with the coaching aspect of the sport, many writers resort to listing faults together with possible corrections. This is a very negative approach as it presupposes that a fault exists. My own philosophy is one to

work from a series of essential aspects of the skill which must be present with all jumpers, and if these aspects of skill are absent then positive efforts must be made to acquire them.

1. *The approach run must be accurate and fast.* Without a fast controlled, approach run even the strongest, "springiest" person will be inefficient. While on the surface it might seem a very simple task to establish an approach run pattern, in practice it is most difficult. In fact a novice might find this aspect of the jump easier than the accomplished, because the advanced performer is attempting to stretch every aspect of it to the absolute limit. The coach must observe many jumps taking note of stop watch timing, impressions of leg cadency and fluidity. Any attempt to reach for the board, "chop" for the board or "stutter" during the run must be corrected instantly before it becomes an ingrained fault. Good jumpers do not require check marks, other than one quite early in the approach run, to check the accuracy of the early strides. The jumper must be free to concentrate on the board and take-off action.

2. *The step phase must be in reasonable proportion to the rest of the jump.* This is a simple basic, but its importance cannot be overstated. During the step phase the trunk must be kept fairly erect, the free thigh must be picked up high, at least parallel to the runway, and the athlete must sense the feeling of "floating" through the air. When approaching the landing from the phase, it is most important for the lower leg to remain under the knee and not reach out to anticipate the landing. An anticipation of landing in this way will produce a retarding force. The expert jumper is well advised to squeeze the calf of the leg, about to accept the landing, towards the thigh of the same leg. This squeezing action sets up a rotational movement of the leg causing it to reach out, and back so that it strikes the ground in an active position.

3. *All landings must be flat footed.* Actually it would be more accurate to say that they must not be on the toes, as with some jumpers there is a pronounced heel strike. If the landing is made on the ball of the foot the body will be placed in an unstable position, which will place excessive strain on the supporting leg, probably causing it to collapse. A flat-footed landing will provide a stable platform for a subsequent jump, and will give the athlete sufficient time, with the foot in contact with the ground, to exert force before the take-off is effected from the toes.

4. *The hip must be in an "active" position at take-off.* Again this is a simple fundamental of jumping which is frequently ignored by coaches. As the take-off leg is about to make its final strike the hip must be rotated forwards and in advance of the take-off foot. This will also mean that the trunk must be erect.

5. *The take-off movement must be a dynamic one.* The jumper can only exert force while in contact with the ground. This means that the trailing leg must be pulled through very fast. To achieve this successfully, the timing

must be precise, and as such presents a most difficult part of the jump. A key feature of triple jumping is the apparently effortless "floating" position while in the air. Hence it is very difficult suddenly to switch from what appears to be an effortless position to one requiring extreme effort over a very short space of time. Similarly the explosive action of the take-off leg must be performed at peak speed and effort.

6. *The ground must come to the athlete and not vice-versa.* This means that the athlete must never reach for the ground with the legs. This is very common during the first phase, where the jumper hurries the balancing movement of the free leg, in order to get into the landing position quickly. This will produce loss of balance on landing, usually characterised by forward rotation of the top part of the body. There is also a tendency to reach out for the ground at the end of the step phase.

7. *The arms must help balance the movement.* I am personally an enthusiast of the "high hop" type of triple jump associated with a double-arm shift during all phases. However, I would not attempt to inflict this personal opinion on all jumpers and their coaches. Nevertheless the arms can aid lift and certainly help in keeping the body balanced. If they are used to help provide lift, they must be moved fast and in co-ordination with the leg movement.

8. The legs must move about the hip joint while the trunk remains erect.

Training the top-class triple jumper

I find devising training schemes for triple jumpers the most rewarding of all, in that it is possible to include a tremendous variety of truly purposeful work. Many training schemes are made varied and at times the variety chosen has no application at all to the event in question. Hence variety is given just for the sake of it and often the activity performed is a waste of valuable training time. With the triple jump the tremendous variety of bounding and hopping exercises all have a most beneficial effect upon the jumper.

Training for the triple jumper can be grouped into four different categories:- Speed Training, General Strength Training, Specific Strength Training, Technical Event Training.

1. Speed

In general terms, it is hoped that the strength training and specific strength training will have an effect upon improving speed. Nevertheless the triple jumper will have to do a fair amount of flat-out running. I find that there are two suitable distances for this type of work:-

(i) A fast, timed sprint, over the distance of the approach run. This should be repeated about ten times with sufficient recovery to permit fast running for each of the repetitions.

(ii) Quality striding over a distance of 150 metres where there is a chance to place emphasis on running form, and peak speed is only sustained for a

short distance of the total run. These should be repeated six times, again with a fair recovery period.

Both of these sessions should be included at least once a week during the winter with some extra quality work, with the sprinters or hurdlers, during the summer.

2. General strength work

Basically this means concentrated work using conventional weight-lifting techniques and work with multigyms (see plate 34) if available. Readers should refer to chapter 17 on strength training for specific ideas. In terms of exercises I find the following most suitable:-

1. Legs:- half squats, heel raise (both in rack with heavy weight across the shoulders).
   Leg press (with leg press machine). Step-ups-15 inch bench.
   If a machine is available leg flexion and extension exercises are very worthwhile.
2. Trunk:- Inclined sit-ups, back hyperextension with twist. Single and double leg raising with the body suspended from a hanging position from gymnasium wall bars, beams or ropes. The actual triple jumping leg action is also a good exercise using the suspended position.
3. Arms:- Sprinting arm action using dumb-bells, concentration curls and bench press.

If these exercises are done using one of the conventional systems, with heavy weights, then a good level of general strength will be assured.

3. Specific strength

(i) 1 x 400 metres, timed with the distance broken down into 8 x 60 metre segments, doing the following activity for each segment.

Segment 1. Left leg hop.
2. Giant strides.
3. Right leg hop.
4. Relaxed jog.
5. Hop—step—step—Hop—step—step sequence.
6. Relaxed jog.
7. Double foot bounds.
8. Giant strides.

When a time standard of sub 2 minutes is imposed, it becomes an excellent conditioning exercise and times of approximately 95 seconds have been recorded for a single lap performed this way.

(ii) *Bounding activities from a standing position.* These are excellent strength promoting and conditioning exercises and can be used in the competitive situation to add an extra incentive during training. The table listed in Appendix I gives the jumps which I have combined together to compile the "jumping decathlon", and each series of jumps can be converted

to points. Ideally a jumper should attempt three of each jump, converting only the best effort to points, and keep a points total for five or ten events, in a single training session. The first five events can usually be fitted in to most gymnasia; hence it can form part of the winter conditioning work during the dark evenings or when the outside weather prevents training. All of the events listed in the jumping decathlon can be performed from a short approach run of five or seven strides.

(iii) *Bounding activities with a short approach run.* Here the variety is almost endless. They can be performed in sports halls or outside on the track and as such they form a very enjoyable part of winter conditioning work. The ones which I frequently use are:- 4 hops and a jump; 3 hops, step and a jump; Hop—step—step—Hop—step—step; Hop—step Hop—step Hop—step. All of the jumps should be measured as it provides a focal point for effort. Good jumpers will cover between 20 metres and 30 metres for these combinations.

(iv) *Bounding activities using a raised platform.* Some of the recommended activities can be seen in the illustrations on pages 132 & 133. Ideally they should be done indoors, with a short approach run and a slightly assisted take-off. The training task can be made harder by increasing the height of the platform(s) and (or) the spacing of the equipment. The simplest, and most obvious activity using this equipment, is the triple jump itself, placing the raised platform for the step-up phase.

(v) *Depth jumping.* The platforms used in the previous section can be used to raise the performer, who should jump down from the elevated position and instantly leap up again on to another raised platform. This activity can be done with a weighted belt placed round the waist. (See figs. 54-55.)

4. Technical event training

The amount of technical training done, will vary according to the time of the year. However, I insist that at least one session a week, throughout the year, be devoted to the practice of the event. There is a tendency to neglect this during the winter in order to concentrate on strength promoting activities. I believe that technique and strength should be developed hand-in-hand so that the technique is adapted to cater for increased levels of strength.

The technical work will be of two sorts: that performed from a short approach run of about seven strides, and work from the full flat-out approach run. During each technical session the coach should isolate the fundamental he intends to concentrate on and all work should be directed towards this. It is most unwise to concentrate on more than one important aspect at a single time.

Chapter 11

High Jumping

It would appear that jumping for height is part of both the natural development of man and animal. Logically barriers placed in man's way would have to be cleared by a combination of speed and spring and it follows that such barriers would more likely have been ones calling for a horizontal jump rather than a vertical jump. It is, therefore, not surprising to find only horizontal jumping documented as part of the ancient Olympic Games.

The first records of competitions involving jumping for height date back to 1830 and in the years following this it was popularised in the universities of both Oxford and Cambridge. However, the most interesting historical survey is one centred around the development of styles, the terminology of which will be very familiar to the high jumping enthusiasts.

In the early days of high jumping the method of bar clearance used was the tucked jump, which was quite inefficient, and jumpers frequently covered a horizontal distance of sixteen feet and more in clearing heights below six feet. The next development in technique came with the introduction of the "scissors" style of high jumping. This permitted the athlete to be more efficient about the bar and make more use of the legs to perform a vertical lifting movement. This style remained the favourite of the jumpers until 1895 when an American jumper, from the east coast of the United States, set a new world record with what then appeared the strangest of styles and was aptly termed the "Sweeney twist" after its originator Michael Sweeney. At a later date the style was rechristened the Eastern Cut-Off to distinguish it from the Western Roll.

The Western Roll was first developed by an Irish/American, George Horine, in about 1912. The style was forced on him by a restricted approach run when using the "scissors" style, while an approach from the other side was unrestricted. This produced a take-off from the foot nearest to the bar and placed the jumper in a side on position while crossing the bar. It really produced quite an efficient jump in that it placed the bar much closer to the performer's centre of gravity.

During the period 1912-1936 jumpers became technique conscious, some experimenting with various forms of "scissors" jumps incorporating a "layout" position about the bar, some persevering with the Eastern-Cut-Off while

others really perfected the Western Roll. But in 1936 Dave Albritton of the U.S.A. cleared 6'9¾'' with the now common straddle technique. This technique enabled the jumper to drape about the bar, in a face down position, producing the most efficient clearance permitted by the rules. The straddle jump might have come a number of years earlier had it not been for the rules of the day that prevented the head from dropping below the level of the hips. So, in terms of bar clearance, the ultimate in efficiency has been reached unless someone can perfect a dive forward roll from a single leg take-off.

With such an advanced style as the straddle it left the inventive jumper little else to do except experiment with increasing the lift at take-off. This

Plate 20. A. Wilson (G.B.) demonstrates the dated Western Roll style.

phase attracted the attention of the Iron Curtain countries, particularly Russia, and their work on approach run, use of the free limbs, etc. brought the epitome of perfection in Valeri Brumel who won a silver in the 1960 Olympics, the Gold Medal in the 1964 only to be struck down, at the peak of his career, during a motor cycle accident soon after. With the Russian intervention came the built-up shoe for jumping, causing a sensation when in 1957 Yuri Stepanov took the world record away from the U.S.A., where it had remained for over seventy years.

During the early 1960's the attention of high jumping was centred around the changes in the world record as it went from Russia to the United States and back again. The period produced some very classic high jumpers like John Thomas, U.S.A. and his characteristic free leg swing. But leading up to

the Olympic Games of 1968, one heard of yet another new style being developed in the U.S.A. by Dick Fosbury, who was later to triumph in the Games with his simple, yet spectacular, jump. Since then this style has captured the attention of most jumping enthusiasts. It has made essential the complete redesigning of landing areas, which must now be able to accept full back landings, hence the areas of artificial foam, air cushions and the like are now the essential prerequisite for safety. But above all, it has permitted the natural jumper to make full use of his ability to spring, by removing from the jump the very precise approach strides and timing associated with the straddle style.

So the event has moved from the Western Roll dominance of the 1948 Olympics to the complete straddle dominance in 1960, 1964 and 1968 on to the quite mixed straddle—Fosbury situation of 1972. The women's version of the sport has, quite naturally, followed the same evolutionary pattern as their male counterparts, only in some cases a full Olympiad removed, although the women have taken more favourably to the Fosbury innovation.

In high jumping one aims to project the centre of gravity of the body as high as possible, in a vertical direction, and then, by the careful manipulation of body levers, clear a bar as close as possible to this predetermined vertical height. I emphasise the word "predetermined", because once the body has left the ground there is nothing the body can do to increase vertical lift. So, what the body does while it is in contact with the ground is of paramount importance.

In many respects the high jumper is faced with a compromise similar to that encountered by the long jumper. The high jumper requires speed to help the crossing of the bar and to position the body favourably for take-off. Unfortunately speed and vertical lift are not completely compatible. If the high jumper approached at peak speed, the bodyweight would pass over the take-off leg so quickly, making it impossible to generate maximum vertical lift. A very slow approach run would not favour any aspect of the jump. Therefore, the high jumper has to get the correct blend of speed and spring in order to produce an efficient take-off.

Spring is an innate quality possessed by relatively few people. Those who have this quality will, through careful nurturing, make high jumpers. Those who lack this vital quality essentially have to do other athletic events. While leg strength is a contributing factor there is not a significant correlation between this and the ability to jump high. Hence there is a neuro-muscular factor, associated with the speed of contraction, that plays the dominant role.

The lift, given to the body at take-off, is derived from two main sources. The first, and most obvious, is the vigorous extension of the take-off leg. This provides most of the power. However, a lifting force can be transferred to the body by performing an upward swinging movement of the free leg and arms, but the lift produced this way must be co-ordinated with that

produced by the take-off leg so that the lifting force reaches a maximum at one and the same point. If this is executed correctly maximum vertical lift will be given to the body.

The performer then has to make the best use of this lift to clear the bar. Here he has three main considerations:-

(a) To make sure that his high point is directly above the bar.

(b) To make sure that the trail leg passes the low point of the bar.

(c) To effect the best lay out according to the style being used.

The high point of the jump is determined by the position of take-off relative to the bar and this in turn is influenced by the speed of approach, direction of approach and the intended lay-out style. The position at which the trail leg clears the bar is also influenced by the same factors, only the final consideration must be the centre of the bar. These points will be discussed, in full, later in the text, when the various layout styles are considered.

Although a considerable influence, on all aspects of the jump, is exerted by the lay out style, there are a number of essential factors common to all forms of jumping for height. These are:-

i) Maximum vertical lift must be given to the body by the extension of the take-off leg.

ii) This lift must be aided by the free limbs.

iii) The trail leg must cross the low point of the bar, thus placing the take-off close to the uprights.

iv) The final approach strides must not be on the toes.

All other factors must be considered relative to the bar clearance style. Current top-class jumpers only exhibit two styles, the straddle and the Fosbury, hence these are the only two which will be discussed in this section of the book.

THE STRADDLE

Crossing the bar from the *left* foot take-off.

1. The approach run

(a) Angle. Straddle jumpers approach the bar at an angle of approximately 30° to the plane of the uprights. This will permit a fast approach run, a relatively short period of time over the bar and enable the athlete to perform a long swinging movement of the free leg without forcing the take-off point too far away from the bar. A deviation of 5° either side of the 30° norm is quite acceptable.

(b) Distance. This varies considerably from jumper to jumper; although the majority of jumpers, both men and women, take nine strides it is always difficult, as an observer, to determine the precise distance. This does not suggest that the approach run of a high jumper is a haphazard one. Quite the reverse, as they can only arrive at their precise take-off position after

countless hours of practice. Many high jumpers take a few easy jogging strides before striking the check mark to indicate the start of the approach run proper. However, the problem of listing a precise measurement does exist because few, if any, high jumpers measure the distance of the run along the line of approach and for the Fosbury jumper, using a curve, this would be almost impossible. Most jumpers use the stands as a datum point and measure their marks, with a tape measure, either parallel to the line of the uprights or at right angles to it. But even with the accurate distances, using a tape measure, the approach run must be checked on the day as it is always liable to slight variations, depending upon external conditions and the "feeling" of the athlete. The essential aspect is that the run up should be long enough to enable speed to be built up without tension.

(c) Speed. Ideally the jumper should use the maximum amount of speed that will permit an efficient take-off. There is no doubt that a fast speed of approach is conducive to a good take-off. Research work from Russia suggests that their best performers approach at 7–7.5 m/second.

(d) The running technique. Without doubt this is the most important aspect of the straddle jump. Failure to adopt the correct running rhythm will always lessen the efficiency of take-off. In fact, many straddle jumpers resorted to the Fosbury style because they could not accept the very disciplined, precise, running action essential for the straddle-type clearance. The essential part of the approach run is the final three strides, during which the jumper makes all of the necessary preparations for the take-off. During the early strides the jumper is faced with two possible lines of action. The first is to build up the speed gradually and then accelerate during the final three strides. This will assure a high horizontal speed at take-off but could produce tension and remove the emphasis of preparing for the jump. The other alternative is to build up the speed quickly, but maintain it until take-off, thus leaving the important preparatory strides free from the tension of having to increase speed. Most good jumpers favour the second method.

The running action of the final strides is of paramount importance. They must be flat footed; they must increase in length. Both actions are forced on the athlete by the changing position of the body during this phase. The early strides are similar, in some respect, to sprinting strides in that there must be a noticeable forward lean. This forward lean changes to a backward lean during the final strides. For an efficient take-off the pelvic girdle must be rotated forwards and upwards. This movement will force a running action to pivot essentially about the hips, increasing the swinging action of the legs and forcing a flat-footed landing. Because these strides are so very important many jumpers use check marks to help their accuracy. As the final strides progress, the body sinks lower and lower, there is a greater flexion of the legs at the knee joint, the thigh is picked up higher with a swinging action, and the feet contact the ground further in front of the body, forcing a heel contact. It is for this reason that high jumpers must use heel spikes. The

knee flexion is very important otherwise the braking force of a straight leg would be excessive.

While the legs and trunk are being carefully positioned, the arms are being gathered behind the body, so that they can be thrown upwards to aid the lifting force. On the penultimate stride, as the right leg is coming forward, the normal backward movement of the right arm is inhibited, while the compensating left arm comes forward in a relaxed manner and slightly across the body. With the right foot only in contact, a situation is produced where both arms are forward. As the left leg swings forward for the final stride the arms swing together, outwards, and backwards, so that as the left foot contacts they can be swept vigorously forwards. At this position the backward lean will not be pronounced and the shoulders should be pushed forwards. (See figs. 57-59).

2. The take-off

(a) The position. This will vary slightly from jumper to jumper. It must be fairly close to the stands and most good jumpers could almost touch the upright with their left hand. The precise point can only be arrived at by trial and error to place the high point of the jump directly over the bar.

(b) The arm action. The final swinging movement of the arms is allowed to take on a "scissors-like" action. The right arm swings across the body and is held high to reach over the bar. The left arm also swings across the body, towards the right arm-pit and there it remains, across the chest during the early stages of the flight.

(c) The free leg action. The exact free leg movement can only be executed if the hips are in the right position (see fig. 58). The free

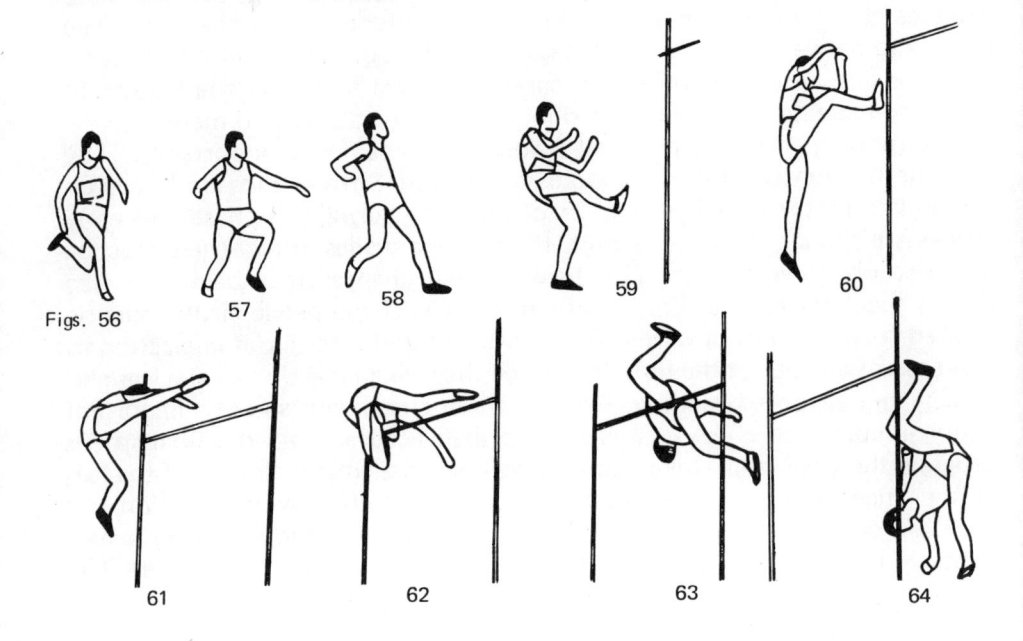

Figs. 56   57   58   59   60   61   62   63   64

knee is swung through, initially flexed, so that it does not strike the ground and then straightened so that it is "athletically" straight as it swings up to a horizontal position. The swing through of the free leg is slightly aided by a built up shoe on the take-off foot. As the leg approaches bar height it must bend.

(d) The take-off leg action. Again the position of the pelvis is of paramount importance. If all of the other actions have been done correctly it only remains for the take-off leg to extend vigorously, when the weight is over it, to produce the lift. Unfortunately the movements leading up to this point are very precise and often the take-off leg is called upon to do a rescue act and "muscle" the body out of trouble. This it can do, but superlative performances will never be registered.

Plate 21. A fine mid-air position in the straddle.

3. Bar clearance

While this is the aspect of high jumping that seems to capture the interest and imagination of most high jump coaches, it cannot be emphasised enough, "That you cannot make up in the air for what you failed to put in on the ground." At low heights the bar clearance is no problem. Only when the jumper is attempting to clear a bar very close to the highest possible point of the centre of gravity does it become a problem. At this point the jumper must manipulate his limbs with tender efficiency.

Once the high point has been reached the jumper must attempt to lower the complete right side of the body towards the landing area. This will not be too difficult as there will be a certain amount of rotation, about a long

axis, in the body, due to the eccentric movements at take-off. This is important as the body relies upon this rotation to clear the trailing leg. At the high point of the jump, the jumper will be in a "frog-like" position, face down to the bar. Both legs must be bent. As the rotation carries the right side of the body towards the pit, the left elbow reaches almost vertically upwards. This has an effect of slowing the rotation of the upper part of the body, thus automatically speeding up the rotation of the lower part of the body. The rotation continues, forcing the body almost back under the bar so that the landing is virtually effected on the back, with the right forearm acting as a break-fall. This form of rotation will automatically lift the trail leg up and clear of the bar. There must not be any attempt to straighten the trailing leg, although some actually rotate the leg upwards and outwards, aiding the rotation of the body as a whole, and giving a wider split of the thighs. (See figs. 56-64.)

From here it is, one hopes, a happy *safe* landing.

THE FOSBURY STYLE

Compared with the straddle style the Fosbury is very recent, hence it has not, as yet, been subjected to the same degree of experimentation. Even so there are several varieties of the jump already in existence. Some athletes have experimented with variations in the curve of approach, others have experimented with the use of the free limbs and some have even attempted to perfect the bar-clearance. One thing is certain, the technique has revolutioned high jumping, for the present moment, and as far as the United Kingdom is concerned it has given the event a "kiss of life". Many enthusiasts argue that it produces uninhibited jumping because at one very important point, the bar is obscured from view. However, the relative merits of the jumps will be discussed at the end of the section.

Again I must emphasise that while the straddle form of high jumping is close to the ultimate in its performance technique, the Fosbury is still in its evolutionary stages.

i) The approach run

Since the Fosbury style of jumping demands a certain amount of rotation about a vertical axis, it is generally accepted that the approach run should curve. At the moment, the position and the extent of the curve are subject to considerable experimentation. Fosbury, himself, used a gradual curve over the complete duration of the run-up, which consisted of eight fast strides. The run started from a position almost in line with the right-hand side upright, but at right angles to the plane of the uprights and swept well outside a line at right angles to the left upright, curving in to take-off fairly close to it. The curve was fairly symmetrical, with the apex of the curve approximately opposite the centre of a line joining the start of the run and the take-off. The current vogue seems to be departing from this type of run

in favour of an initial straight part, followed by a fairly late curve. My early observations suggest that this move is correct.

Most athletes take a very fast approach run and this would seem to be one of the greatest assets the style has. The number of strides vary, but is usually in excess of eight. The final direction of the run presents the body in a position parallel to the plane of the uprights.

ii) The take-off

Here the essential difference between the straddle and the Fosbury must be emphasised. Whereas the take-off leg for the straddle is the one nearest the bar, the Fosbury is from the leg furthermost from it. It must also be remembered that the Fosbury jump is not a backwards take-off.

(a) Position. This should be in an almost identical position to the straddle, in that the legs must cross the low point of the bar. However, as the jump often involves greater approach speeds, the take-off will be slightly further away from the bar. (See figs. 68-72.)

(b) Free limb action. The present situation with the jump is that the take-off action is very similar to that of the long jump. This essentially means that the free knee must be picked up high. In this respect it is completely different from the straddle, although it is not beyond the realms of possibility for a jumper to perfect the Fosbury layout after having performed a straight free leg swing. The lift is aided by the vigorous pick-up of the free knee and in this case a moderate single arm shift. Here again, jumpers are experimenting with the arm action and already many are employing a double arm shift.

(c) Body position. Whereas the approach run is of vital importance in the straddle jump, the most important aspect of the Fosbury is the position of the body just prior to take-off. As the final approach strides are not extended, hence the lean back considerably reduced, the bodyweight arrives over the take-off leg more quickly. Because of this, the lift producing levers have to act faster. The fast curving approach run has the tendency to force the bodyweight outside the take-off leg. In order to take the bodyweight over the take-off leg the Fosbury jumper performs a slight side step on the last stride. As the extension of the take-off leg is faster, the hips must be in an active position, with the pelvis tilted forwards and upwards. It is essential for the body to be side-on to the bar at take-off and not back-on to the bar. The rotation to turn "back-on" for the bar clearance, takes place once the body is in the air, and is derived from the curved approach run and a slightly eccentric movement at take-off. It is also essential for the inside shoulder, the one nearest the bar, to lift high and remain high during the take-off. This action, combined with a knee pick-up that curves slightly across the body, presents the hips in the correct position for the back lay out.

(d) The layout position. As in all layout styles, the problem is always one of clearing the trailing leg. In this case both legs are together, and for an

efficient clearance they must hang limp until the seat has crossed the bar. The back must be kept arched and some very good exponents of the jump suggest that they attempt to lift the hips at the high point of the jump. This will have the effect of forcing the shoulders, already clear, towards the landing area, so making the clearance of the legs easier. The arms also play a very active part in the clearance. Until the hips are clear, the arms remain close to the body, then they have to be taken to a position above the head and wide of the body. Once the hips have cleared the bar, the legs must be lifted by pulling the knees to the chest and at a later stage straightening them. Although the latter points do help in bar clearance, they also prevent over-rotation, so that the landing is effected on the shoulders and not on the head.

Whenever a new style is introduced, discussion is always centred around the advantages and disadvantages of one style over another. The argument always presented after Mexico was that the Fosbury style was a winning one.

Plate 22. A fine mid-air position in the Fosbury.

It then continued to have further success in European championships and the Munich Olympic Games, particularly with the women. Hence, with an Olympic victory, it has gained the greatest possible support from both men and women. As a person who believes that motivation is the greatest aid to superb performance, it is in this area where the Fosbury style has made its most significant contribution. The Fosbury style rapidly caught the imagination and interest of the younger generation. This is the age group which counts, as the sport of track and field athletics is the domain of the young. It lifted the restrictions of the fairly complicated straddle approach and enabled athletes to use fully the qualities of speed and spring. Furthermore it is a jump for jumping high and not just for clearing a bar, because at the most critical time the bar is removed from the sight of the performer. However, one of its greatest attributes is that it makes it extremely difficult for the jumper to drop the inside shoulder, the main reason for failure in the straddle jump. As a purist, I believe that the jump is less mechanically efficient than the straddle, which is also still enjoying Olympic success. However, the seemingly uninhibited approach, which the Fosbury encourages, more than offsets any slight mechanical disadvantage. It is my opinion that the styles will continue to exist side by side, and produce

success for the various exponents, for many years to come. The passing of time will certainly see minor changes to both techniques and the modifications of the rules could again revolutionise the event.

Teaching the novice

In recent years the over-analytical approach to track and field athletics has cultivated groups of coaches who are obsessed with the intricacies of performance techniques. This situation has been allowed to carry over to the teaching profession and in high jumping it has manifested itself with teachers paying undue attention to layout styles. The essential aspect of high jumping is to jump high. To a large extent these qualities are innate and the novice with natural ability immediately stands out. The successful teaching of high jumping must be centred around fostering this natural ability and the realisation that all of the pupils, in every class, will not make high jumpers.

High jumping requires confidence as well as the ability to spring. A painful experience associated with a hard landing, or the knocking of a rigid bar with a tender part of the body, can soon destroy this essential quality. The teacher/coach must make sure that the safety of the pupils is safeguarded and that all conceivable danger points are removed. High jumping should no longer be taught at the conventional sand-pit. The only safe area is one of a raised, solid, block of foam, or foam-like material, covering the total area of the stands and bar. The height of the landing area will depend upon the density of the material from which it is constructed, and the falling momentum of the body. The area must be sufficient to cushion the heaviest possible person in the group, falling from the highest possible height. Only by considering these factors can an area be deemed safe.

In the very early stages, the fear of striking the bar is quite a formidable one. It is wise to replace it with a taut length of one inch wide elastic. Here, the essential prerequisite is that the stands must be weighted down, otherwise they could fall on the performer and cause injury. Without doubt the elastic is a teaching aid.

Once the facility is considered safe the thrill of jumping for height can be experienced. This is best done in the competitive situation with a running, frontal, tucked jump. This is the simplest form of jump where the actual skill in the air is minimal. Hence it can focus all of the attention on developing a vigorous lifting action at take-off. The distance of the approach run should be restricted, and the single-footed take-off emphasised. At this stage deviation from the tucked jump should be prohibited. At low heights a bar can be cleared by performing a scissors or straddle-type jump without the body being given any lifting sensation. The "tucked" jump emphasises the need for an explosive take-off.

High jumping is then best developed along the lines of fostering spring as opposed to perfecting layout positions. It should be done through controlled experimentation rather than through imposed stereotyped movements.

However, there are a number of basic essentials that must be emphasised. These are:-

1. Irrespective of style the take-off position must be such that the legs cross the low point of the bar. For all progressive styles this will place the take-off close to the upright. Many coaches and teachers believe that the take-off point should be in line with the centre of the bar. This is wrong and could also prove very dangerous. A jumper, with a high horizontal speed, who takes off in this position, would almost certainly land off the cushion. Therefore, for safety alone this must be emphasised.

2. The approach must be accurate. Initially five good running strides are sufficient to produce the required amount of speed. The distance of the approach run must be restricted for the novice, although there is no need to restrict the speed as this is imposed by the short run.

3. The final strides of the approach run must *not* be on the toes. If these strides are performed on the toes it encourages a dive rather than a jump.

4. The free limbs must aid the jumping movement. The action of the free leg is best emphasised and will, of course, depend upon the experimented style.

Initially most novice jumpers will feel more confident with a scissors-type of jump. There is nothing wrong with this as it can help develop an efficient take-off. Once confidence has been achieved, the rudiments of both straddle and Fosbury can be encouraged, particularly with those who show an aptitude for high jumping. Experimentation with assisted take-offs using ramps, beating boards, etc. all form an enjoyable and valid part in encouraging leaping for height.

Coaching the top-class performer

High jump coaching is probably the most frustrating one of all of the track and field events, and certainly the one demanding the greatest amount of patience. The true development of the technique can only take place when attempting heights close to a jumper's personal best. Hence there will certainly be times when the bar is continually dislodged. This must be accepted and recognised as an essential part of the development of the skills of the event.

The advent of the Fosbury style has forced the high jump coach to consider the event as one of two styles leading to a single purpose. While there are certain similarities between the straddle and the Fosbury, in that they both demand one to jump high, the advanced technicalities of each are quite different.

Sound high jump coaching is based on, and around, the appreciation of certain essentials of technique which, if not present in the athlete's performance, must be nurtured. When considering the following essential features of high jumping, one must assume that the top-class jumper has, through his training, all of the necessary physical attributes to produce spring. Without this vital quality all else is lacking in purpose.

1. The approach run must be accurate and rhythmical. The jumper must arrive at the precise spot, at speed, with the body levers in the correct position to apply a lifting force. The straddle approach run is fairly easy to mark out initially, using the upright as a datum point. In the first case the jumper should experiment using a seven or nine stride approach, from a static starting position. This will help in the development of a consistent stride pattern. The aim of this is to try to establish the amount of speed necessary for a successful jump. As experience and strength develop, the precise starting point for the run might change and the static starting position could well give way to a jog or walk-on approach. These final factors are determined by the feel of the athlete. Once the basic distance and speed have been determined the rhythm of the run-up has to be developed. Herein lies the secret of an efficient take-off. It is essential for the jumper to master the correct rhythm and action of the final two strides. Their precise nature is described in the technique section. "The spring must be coiled ready for extension."

The Fosbury jumper has greater initial problems in marking out the approach run, because of its curving nature, but these are considerably reduced once the distance has been determined. The nature of the curve will depend upon the philosophy of the coach and the feeling of the athlete. The point of issue is the gradual or the late curve. The approach speed must be kept high.

2. The take-off position must be such that the legs cross the low point of the bar.

3. The inside shoulder must not drop at take-off. This is probably the most common error with all jumpers striving to beat the two metre barrier. In the straddle event the dropping shoulder is characterised by a "pouring" motion about the bar. An advantage which the Fosbury jumper has is that it is more difficult to drop the shoulder with this type of jump.

4. The pelvis must be tilted upwards to place it in the correct position to produce maximum lift. Many athletes are unaware of this and its importance cannot be over-emphasised. Its positioning must also feature as part of the approach run style.

5. The timing of the free limb movement must be perfected. In the straddle it means the correct gathering of the arms and the swinging action of the free leg; in the Fosbury, the long-jump type action.

6. During flight the correct arm and leg action must be developed in order to control the rotation which helps in bar clearance. Again these are detailed in the section describing the techniques of the two styles.

Training the top-class jumper

The high jumper will be required to spend countless hours with the barbells and dumb-bells in order to strengthen the whole body, so that it is able to get maximum efficiency from a single contraction. It is fairly safe to say that a large number of jumpers and coaches only pay "lip service" to the

essential conditioning aspects for the event. The natural quality of spring will only take a jumper partway along the road to success. The high jumper requires vast resources of muscular energy that can only be developed through sensible conditioning.

The conditioning of the high jumper can be broken down into four different categories:-
1. Running movements. 2. Bounding and leaping movements. 3. General strength promoting movements. 4. Specific strength promoting movements.

1. Running movements play a dual role in the complete conditioning of the athlete. In the first case sustained runs, or fartlek runs, over 2 miles or 3,000 metres can be used to develop basic endurance, a foundation of which is required for the development of all other aspects of the event. Secondly, short sprints, over a distance of about 40 metres, are ideal for helping to develop the speed necessary for the approach run. In the sprinting movements the emphasis must be on relaxation, because this is the essential feature of the high jumper's approach to the bar.

2. All of the bounding activities, leaping decathlon, box work, etc. detailed in the sections on the horizontal jumping events, are also ideal for the high jumper and should be a regular feature in the conditioning work for this event.

3. Before any athlete attempts to develop a high degree of specific strength, a basic reservoir of general strength is required. In this area there is a tendency for high jumpers to concentrate on the "lower body". While one accepts that the legs form the "power-house", they are aided by the arms and must be secured to a strong body. The common arm, trunk and leg exercises, outlined in the strength section of the book, are suitable for the high jumper.

4. The area of specific strength is one which cannot be ignored. The ingenious coach, given time, will develop a vast repertoire of these activities. The essential feature of them is that they must be purposeful and likely to have a carry over to the event. The activities are best considered under three different headings:-

(a) Running and bounding exercises, with weights or some other form of resistance, aimed at developing the power necessary for producing maximum lift, with particular emphasis on the take-off leg. Here running and bounding activities with weights across the shoulders, or a weighted belt secured to the body, immediately come to mind. As the approach run is fairly restricted, the complete pattern can be rehearsed with some form of resistance.

(b) Fairly static exercises using medicine balls as the means of applying resistance (see page 255).

(c) Exercises which are more of a suppling nature. These include high kicking and leg swinging movements both with and without an active partner (see page 255).

Chapter 12

Pole Vaulting

The pole vault is probably the most spectacular of all athletic events. It more closely fulfils man's most early dream; that of unaided flight. Present day technologists, with their fibre-glass rods, have created a different event, far removed from the days of hedge hopping and river crossing. The history of pole vaulting is indeed an interesting one. It would appear that the event developed in this country along diverse lines; on the one hand for height in the professional arenas in Northern England, and on the other hand as a means for crossing dykes in the fenlands of East Anglia. Other authorities on the history of the sport claim that pole vaulting, as an athletic activity, is of Gaelic or Celtic origin.

A very important landmark in the history of the event, and indeed one which is reflected in the rules of the event today, is the incident of the Ulveston climbers about the middle of the nineteenth century. Vaulting was a popular activity in the professional meetings centred in the Lake District of England. The vault was one for height where the take-off and landing were on grass, and the hickory poles had spikes in the end to help the planting action. The poles were heavy and so the speed of approach and the rise of the pole to the vertical position were very slow, which permitted the hand-over-hand climbing action. This form of vaulting was outlawed in 1889 as a result of some "orthodox" vaulters in the U.S.A. being beaten by the "climbers".

The recent history of the event is really one of technological interference. The old hickory poles of the early twentieth century gave way to bamboo versions, then came the introduction of metal and alloy poles until finally the fibre-glass rod appeared, which is with us today. Unfortunately the intervention of the technologist has turned vaulting into a rich nation's sport, the cost of the fibre-glass poles being very high. Experiments have been made with gas filled poles, poles with special fibres, all of which culminated in a colossal misunderstanding in the 1972 Olympic Games in Munich.

The event, as we know it today, is one where a long leap is converted to a high leap by means of a flexible rod, and this simple definition is descriptive of the actions necessary to perform the event. From time to time, particularly at school level, one occasionally sees the rigid pole version of the sport, but I am certain that as the plastics' industry develops this will be a relic of the past. However, the administrators of the sport could stand firm

and ban the flexible pole in which case the skills involved in rigid pole vaulting will be pardoned.

The advanced mechanics of the event, involving the compound pendulum effect, and the storing of energy, is really only understood by the physicist/ mathematician. However, the practical mechanics of the event is best understood by referring to the tree chart on page 158.

The height of a vault is determined by three major factors. They are:- (a) The grip height, (b) The speed of the pole to the vertical position, (c) The ability to lift the centre of gravity above the hands. The factors are at times influenced by outside elements such as run-up surface, wind, etc. but as they are outside the control of the athlete they will not be dealt with here.

(a) *Grip height.* The first thing which influences this is the standing height of the athlete. The taller the athlete the higher the grip. The most significant factor is the speed of approach. The faster the approach the higher can the athlete grip. In recent years the material from which the pole is constructed has had a great bearing on grip height. With a flexible pole it is possible to increase the grip height by a foot, or more, compared with a rigid pole.

(b) *The speed of the pole to the vertical.* The factors influencing this are very similar to those affecting the grip height and again the most significant factor is speed. However, this time it is take-off speed which is the resultant of the approach speed and the lift given to the body during the take-off. The grip height and stature of the athlete influence the speed of the pole to the vertical but in a negative way. The higher the grip, the taller and heavier the athlete, the slower is the pole to the vertical. Hence, in this respect, pole vaulting is a compromise and automatically provides the event with the ideal somatotype. For example, the average height of the vaulters in Munich 1972 was 6' 0'' and the average weight was 165 lbs.

Once the athlete has left the ground he must rely upon his skill as a vaulter to keep the pole moving to the vertical. A vaulter using a rigid pole must hang close to its long axis during the early swinging action. The fibre-glass vaulter has to rock back quickly to concentrate as much of the bodyweight as possible towards the free end of the pole.

(c) *Ability to lift the centre of gravity above the hands.* In the early stages of vaulting, the novice should be content merely to clear a bar level with the top hand. However, as vaulting expertise is achieved the skilful vaulter will manipulate the complete body, well above the grip height. In gymnastic terms, the vaulter performs a "hand-stand" on the top of the pole. This is the most intricate part of the whole movement and demands great strength, skill and co-ordination, first, to pull the bodyweight up to the hands and then push it above the hands, often to clear a bar several feet above the gripping point on the pole.

All good vaults are predetermined at take-off, hence the athlete must make full use of the time he is in contact with the ground, which includes the final approach strides and the actual take-off movement. The vaulter

requires all of the accuracy of the long jumper, without having a board to aid the qualities of perception. His task is made even more difficult in that the running action is restricted by the action of carrying a pole, and the focus of attention is directed towards planting the pole. This only in part determines the accuracy of take-off.

The approach run of the good vaulter is similar to that of the long jumper. The total length of it will vary considerably from vaulter to vaulter, although the majority of them favour a distance of between 100' and 120' or 17 strides to 21 strides. The early strides form a build up of speed with probably an accuracy check mark after five strides. Peak speed is reached about four strides from take-off, which is sustained until the final foot plant. The final approach strides are critical and there is quite a noticeable change in the running action. The vaulter, like the long jumper, picks the knees up higher, and attempts to increase the rate of striding. The preparation for take-off causes the final strides to be fairly flat-footed and slightly shorter in length than the normal running stride. Most vaulters toe out slightly on the final strides. This is certainly not a deliberate movement, but rather one forced on the athlete by the action of planting the pole.

The good vaulter has to give a tremendous amount of time and energy towards perfecting the approach run. Unfortunately the final aspects of the run-up can only be rehearsed during full effort vaults, as any different situation calls for a slightly different sequence of movements. The vaulter, going for heights above, or close to, the personal best vault, naturally increases the approach speed slightly and drives in much harder. So the true situation can only be reproduced during actual vaulting sessions. This does

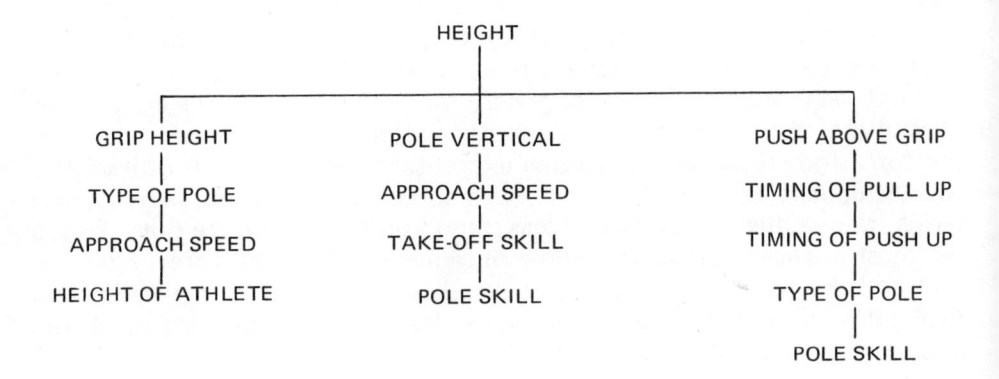

FACTORS AFFECTING THE HEIGHT OF VAULT

not mean that the vaulter avoids working on the approach run in any other situation. If this was the case very few approach runs would be performed, as the energy demand for high level vaulting is very exhausting. Hence the vaulter has to practise a tremendous number of dummy runs in the hope that a proportion of the skills learnt carry over to the full vaulting situation.

Success or failure of a given vault is often determined by the planting action. A smooth, efficient, pole plant will pave the way for an efficient vault. Many texts devote a tremendous amount of space to the specific action, grouping them under specific headings of overhead, underarm and side-arm plants. From my observations of the top vaulters, it is difficult to see how such confusing terminology arose as I can see a little of all of them in the way current pole vaulters plant the pole. However, irrespective of the various methods for planting the pole, there are several essential features about this phase of the vault. They are:-

(a) *The grip must remain secure.* Most vaulters carry the pole with about a two foot hand spacing, with the dominant hand to the top of the pole. During the plant the fibre-glass vaulter hardly permits any shifting of the hands. The metal vaulter must allow a certain closing of the bottom hand, towards the top, in order to aid control on the pole. But once this slight shift has occurred, the grip must then remain completely firm. Indeed, all vaulters use some form of adhesive to prevent any slipping of the hand hold.

(b) *The plant must be early.* This feature is of particular importance to the fibre-glass vaulter. The pole must be led into the box by the bottom hand and should start two strides out from take-off.

(c) *The plant must be active.* Again, this is of particular significance to the fibre-glass vaulter. Although the momentum of the athlete will do much to direct the pole towards the end of the box, the driving action of the arms is of particular importance. The more forceful the plant, the greater the bend.

It is my opinion that this is a very natural phase of pole vaulting, and although it is a very important one, too much time should not be spent isolating and concentrating on this aspect of the vault. The vaulter will develop a co-ordinated, natural, movement and provided it permits an efficient take-off, that is all that is required.

The take-off is not just a movement where the vaulter loses contact with the ground to swing on a pole. The act of take-off is a co-ordinated, springing movement executed with great force. The actual movement is almost identical to a long jump, or a traditional Fosbury high jump take-off. The free knee has to be picked up vigorously and co-ordinated with the powerful extension of the take-off leg. The accent of the movement must be on the "power" factor; during this phase the athlete is only in contact with the ground for a split second, hence considerable speed and strength is required.

A most important factor is the place of take-off relative to the hands. In theory it would appear that the most efficient place for take-off is directly

under the top hand, as this would position the bodyweight directly over the take-off foot, and might apply with a rigid pole. However, with a flexible pole the action is closer to that of the long jumper where the bodyweight must be in advance of the take-off leg in order to produce a greater horizontal component. This will make the position of take-off closer to the bottom hand, but with a take-off in this position considerable force is exerted on the grip, about the shoulder joint and the lower back, to which the performer must be conditioned. (See fig. 79.)

With all jumping movements the position of the hip-joint, relative to the take-off leg, is of paramount importance. The hips must be in an active position so that valuable force is not dissipated in merely extending the body. When the take-off leg is applying its final force, the pelvis must be tilted slightly upwards.

Once contact with the ground is broken, the athlete has to work very quickly to make full use of the speed given at take-off to clear a high bar. In basic terms this will mean getting the hips above the hands; but here a compromise has to be made in order to keep the pole moving to the vertical and the sequence of movements is essentially different for the rigid and flexible pole. The rigid pole vaulter must hang close to the long axis of the pole during its early swing to the vertical, followed by a very fast lifting movement of the hips. The fibre-glass pole vaulter, who wishes to charge the pole with as much energy as possible, has quickly to centre most of the body mass about the end of the pole furthermost from the pivot. The action produced by the vaulter using the rigid pole is termed the "hang" and that by the fibre-glass vaulter the "rock back". The "rock back" is a very active position, where the athlete attempts to get the legs up so that they become parallel to the pole, so placing the athlete in a tucked position. During the whole phase the vaulter should attempt to stay away from the pole and resist any forward movement of the body alone. This is effected by a pushing action with the bottom arm and a pulling action with the top arm. This, in effect, would produce a bending moment about the bottom arm, but as the lever is very short its influence over the total bending action is very small. There is no attempt to pull the whole body vertically up the pole. Some coaches advise a forcing back of the head at this stage of the vault. I am not in favour of this as it creates an artificial sense of "rocking back" and produces undue tension in the arm and shoulder girdle, so restricting their subsequent movements.

With a rigid pole the whole action is over very quickly. The "hang" phase is followed by a rapid pull-up in an attempt to get the feet as high above the hands as possible; in other words, a "hand stand" on the end of the pole. Once the "rock back" is complete, with the fibre-glass pole, there follows a fairly passive stage of the vault while the athlete waits for the pole to perform its catapulting action and returns to a straight, vertical, position. During this phase the vaulter attempts to remain on his back, with the

buttocks approaching the bar. As the pole approaches the vertical, the athlete is forced to perform a very fast pull-up movement to get the feet above the hands. This action must be performed with the legs close to the pole, otherwise the muscular effort involved is likely to be beyond that of the vaulter. With the body close to the axis of the pole, and a very fast pull-up, the body weight will pass quickly above the hands making the push phase easier. (See figs. 78-83.)

The spiralling, twisting, action, characteristic of all good vaulting, is something that follows on quite naturally from a pushing action with vertically spaced hands. Some vaulters interpret the movement as a scissoring action with the legs, although I would not advocate this.

The theorist would believe that once the hips are above the bar it should not be dislodged. While in theory this might be correct, too many vaults are lost at the top of the pole. Once the hips have cleared the bar there still remains the arms and shoulders to clear. The novice placed in this situation might believe that the arms could be cleared by throwing them up and back. This is the action, but if it is not timed correctly the chest or the arms will dislodge the bar. The legs must be allowed to drop below the level of the bar before the arms are thrown up and back as part of the arch-flyaway clearance. If this is timed correctly, the upper body will lift up and away from the bar and force the performer to land on the back. Because of this a safe landing area is essential.

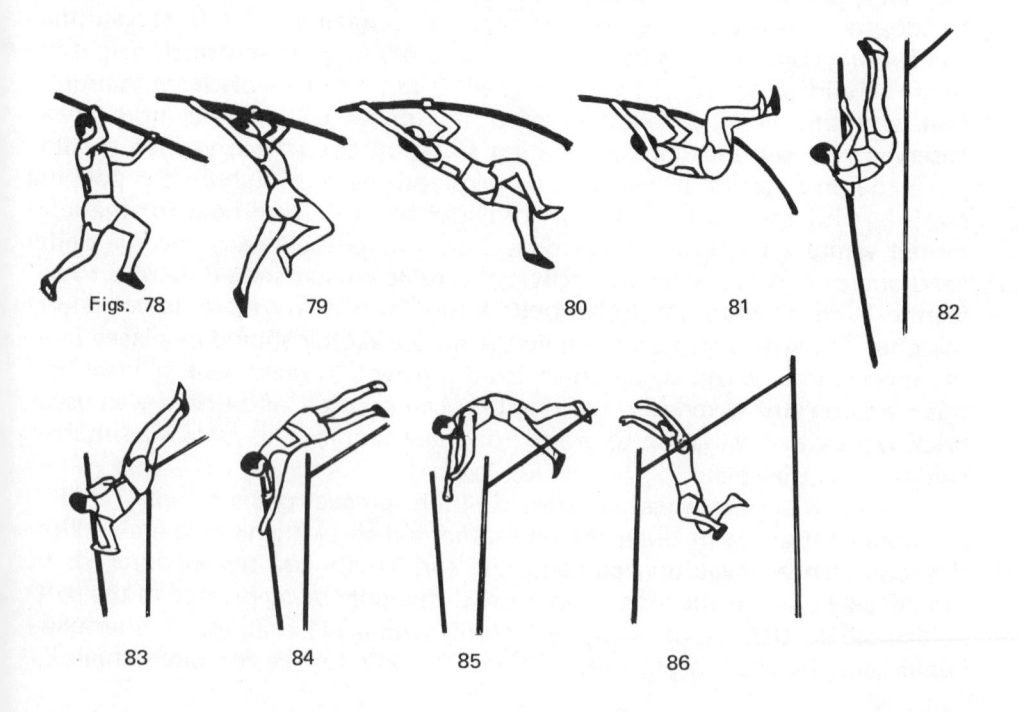

Figs. 78   79   80   81   82

83   84   85   86

Teaching pole vaulting

Pole vaulting, in the competitive form, is one of the few track and field events that does not lend itself well to a "whole" class approach for teaching. However, very enjoyable vaulting-type activities can be introduced to a full class and those showing the necessary aptitude, encouraged to take part in the more restricted skills as used in the vault for competition.

The vaulting skills, suitable for children, can be divided into two groups; the first "indoor" skills requiring suspended ropes and a certain amount of gymnastics apparatus, and the second "outdoor" skills requiring only a pole.

The indoor skills are fairly gymnastic by nature and encourage the performer, by means of carefully placed gymnastics equipment, to swing across gaps in apparatus, to swing from high situations to low situations and from low situations to high situations. Initially a suspended rope is the most suitable "swinging" aid, and as confidence improves ash or bamboo poles can be used. For example the challenge might be to take-off from ground level and swing up, with the aid of a rope, to land on a box top. These activities will certainly indicate an aptitude for the event.

Most boys enjoy the simple vaulting skills outside, provided the situation is made safe for them. The first thing the novice vaulter must be made aware of is that the pole is a means of support, and provided it is held correctly it can be an aid to jumping for height or length. Hence from the very outset the novice must be taught to grip the pole correctly and securely. As all of the early vaulting skills are to build confidence the learning situation must be adopted to suit this. The first essential is to use fairly short, light, vaulting poles. For young children bamboo poles, slightly more than stretch height in length, are ideal. Initially, I encourage all children to take-off from their left foot and this is only modified after a number of attempts have been observed. To get the correct vaulting situation the novice vaulter should place the pole vertically, between the legs and reach as high up the pole as possible with the right hand. This provides the top hand hold for the left footed vaulter. The base of the pole should be pushed away and the right hand and pole dropped to the right hip. The left hand should then form an identical grip to the right, only about a foot, or slightly more, lower down the pole. Using this grip on the pole the novice vaulter should be placed in a situation where he can swing down from a height. A grass bank is ideal for this situation, the gymnastic vaulting box can be used, and I have even used brick walls which verge on to grass. For these simple skills grass is a suitable landing area. (See plate 23.)

The swinging activities, outlined in the preceding paragraph, rapidly promote confidence in using the pole as an aid to swinging in the air. With this confidence a vaulting competition for length can be encouraged. It should take place at the long jump pit, with the pole being planted in the soft sand close to the run-up and the landing taking place at the further end. Pupils must be encouraged to hold on to the pole for the complete "flight".

A short approach run should be used, and the pole should be carried naturally on the right-hand side of the body, with a left foot take off, and a swing to the right hand side of the pole. The carry position, the take-off foot and the side of the swing should be emphasised, and careful observation made of those who find extreme difficulty in using the right side orientated method, and changed over if necessary. Again this activity rapidly promotes interest and confidence.

At this stage the activity can be returned to the bank where the pupils can approach, plant the pole at the bottom of the bank and swing to land up the bank (see plate 23). The "boy scout" vault, using soft grass and a vault for height at a sand pit, are quite natural progressions. During the early stages of all of these activities the pole should not be released but held firmly throughout. In vaulting for height this soon becomes a restriction and it then indicates a time when the turn on the pole and the release of the pole should be introduced. This phase should not be introduced prematurely as it can lead to quite serious accidents and injury to the spine. The hand hold should also be kept at about stretch height.

It must be accepted that pole vaulting requires great confidence and the very nervous child is unlikely to accept the event as a challenge. Hence, by the time the preliminary vaulting activities have been completed, it will be quite obvious who can be encouraged to adapt to the more demanding skills of the competitive vault. These will be very few in number, hence the event is best continued as a group, rather than whole-class, activity or better still removed to the out-of-school situation.

With those pupils who have adapted to the situation, the vault must now be taken to the proper area. I carefully omit using the term "pit" as this suggests a hole, and the vault landing area must essentially be raised and made of a soft foam-like substance. Sand pits are no longer adequate for this event. At the vaulting area the novice should be encouraged to raise the grip height slightly, approach faster, plant the pole in the box and swing the legs high. Because the concentration is on swinging the legs high, and not on a landing position, a raised, soft, landing area is essential. At this stage I find it better to encourage the pupil to swing the legs high, to kick a suspended football with the soles of both feet, rather than attempt to clear a bar for height. However, the preliminary practices must not be allowed to develop into a skill in themselves; the whole purpose of them must be realised and the true vaulting situation introduced as soon as possible.

Once the bar is placed at a height, the novice rapidly progresses from the ranks of the learner, who requires teaching, to the individual requiring coaching, and apart from words of encouragement from the teacher/coach, should be allowed to experiment and gain confidence without having to concentrate on finer points of technique. A valuable aid to the novice, vaulting for height, is the replacement of bar with a length of inch wide elastic. Provided the stands are securely weighted down, this gives a target

Plate 23. Swinging down from a bank to learn the vault.

over which one's body can be projected and avoids the wastage of time spent replacing the bar after each unsuccessful attempt. For the young novice it also avoids the discomfort of bruising tender flesh with the impact of a rigid bar.

Progress to a vault of three metres is quite rapid and this can and should be achieved with a minimum amount of coaching. Of course the teacher/ coach must be ready to observe and instantly correct any divergence from a fundamental aspect of technique, that might prove difficult to correct if allowed to become part of an established pattern of movement.

In the very early days of competitive vaulting, the focus of attention should be directed towards developing a consistent fast approach run. The novice vaulter must be made aware of the old adage in the sport "You cannot make up in the air for what you left out on the ground."

Coaching the good performer

Failure to clear a given height, by a top-class vaulter, seldom stems from the lack of observation of any intricate aspect of skill. It is nearly always attributable to the failure to observe a simple aspect of the fundamental techniques of vaulting for height. Like all other athletic disciplines, it is unwise to regard the event as a series of well-established faults and their correction. The positive approach is to consider that all good vaults must be composed of certain essential characteristics around which the vaulter has latitude for personal interpretation. Should a vaulter fail to interpret an essential aspect of technique then the coach must recognise this, make the athlete aware of it, and try to repattern the sequence of movements until they come in line with the essential characteristics of the event.

Although pole vaulting must be regarded as a fairly complex event, the essential aspects of technique can be simplified and brought well within the powers of concentration of the athlete during both training and competition. While in discussion the intricate aspects of techniques can be appreciated; during training the event must be returned to simple fundamentals.

I consider the following to be essential aspects of technique, but I must insist that they are not placed in any order of priority as this must change with the individual:-

(a) The approach run must be fast and controlled. This aspect calls for a tremendous amount of controlled experimentation upon the partnership. It is an aspect of the event which will be constantly changing until full maturity, and even then is subject to the fluctuations made necessary by external conditions beyond the vaulter's control. The best way to establish this phase of the vault is to determine the speed potential of the vaulter. Initially the vaulter should be timed over a 40 metres sprint without the pole. He should then be carefully observed sprinting over the same distance with the pole, to establish the point at which the stride length becomes consistent. This will give the approximate distance of approach run required

by the athlete. With this distance in mind the approach run must be taken to the pole vaulting runway. With the pole at the back of the box, in the take-off position, the point of take-off can be established as one slightly in front of the top hand hold. Taking this point as a starting mark for the approach run, the vaulter, carrying the pole, can run in the reverse direction to that which he would use during a normal vault, for the approximate distance determined by the first sprinting movement with the pole. The position of the take-off foot, nearest to this mark, is established. Using this new mark as a starting point for the run, and commencing the run-up with the take-off leg, the approach run and plant can be rehearsed with the coach, carefully observing the final position of the take-off foot and the general fluency of the run, relying also upon feed back from the athlete. This way the starting check mark can be moved forwards or backwards depending upon the final positioning of the take-off foot. This position established, full effort vaulting must follow, with the coach accurately timing the final twenty metres of the approach run, comparing the times taken with the initial free sprint time and attempting to relate the times to the performance of the vault. With the statistics obtained from this experimentation, valuable work can be done on the approach run at subsequent dates.

This work only provides the basic approach pattern. The vaulter might decide that he requires a number of walking, or slow jogging, steps before striking the approach run check mark. He might also decide that he requires an accuracy check mark after four or five strides, and a "cue" mark six or seven strides out from plant. The idiosyncracies of the vaulter can be catered for here, and the basic pattern established. It must always be remembered that the full competition approach run is speed dependent and that adjustments must never be made during slow-motion rehearsals.

(b) The plant must be active. It is no longer sufficient to allow the pole to drop into the box at the end of the approach run. The fibre-glass pole demands an early vigorous plant with the arms playing a very dominant role. Once the pole is in the entrance to the box, the final drive is one coming from the arms, with great care placed upon the position of the elbow of the bottom hand. The vaulter attempts to keep this flexed at ninety degrees and great effort is required to prevent the body from going past the point of support. (See plate 24.)

(c) The rock-back must be fast and controlled. Once in the air the vaulter must concentrate his body mass about the free end of the pole. This will mean that once the legs have provided all of their latent take-off power, they have to be brought up to a position close to the head and almost parallel to the pole. This movement is initiated by the powerful contraction of the abdominal muscles.

(d) The pull up must be delayed. If the pull up is premature it will work against the natural tendency of the bending pole. The vaulter must remain on his back, almost passive, until the pull can be effected straight down the

Plate 24. Soon after take-off with R. Seagren (U.S.A.)

long axis of the pole. Because, at this stage, the pole will be approaching the vertical very rapidly, the pulling-pushing action has to be performed at speed.

(e) The release of the pole must be timed carefully. If the release of the pole, followed by the throwing back of the arms is not timed correctly, the chest or the bottom arm will knock the bar. The point here is that the legs must have started to drop below the level of the bar so that the centre of gravity is close to the bar.

(f) The positioning of the stands is crucial. The precise position of the stands can only be established by trial and error, and careful observation on the part of the coach to see where the high point of the hips is positioned. In fibre-glass vaulting the stands will be essentially further away from the vertical face of the box, in a direction towards the landing area. N.B. The term 'vertical' is used in a descriptive sense. Modern boxes do not have the rear face vertical.

Training for the good vaulter

The vaulter has a tremendous amount of basic conditioning work to do.

He requires the speed and spring of the horizontal jumper, hence all of the conditioning work outlined for this group of events will not be out of place for the vaulter. However, the conditioning work necessary for the correct execution of the flight phase can only be performed in an equipped gymnasium and to a certain extent the weight training room. Here I refer to the conditioning and not the skill training aspect of the vault, which is essentially completed at the vaulting area, although one hopes there will be a high degree of carry-over.

Like all other athletic events, the strengthening work necessary can be considered under two headings, general strength and specific strength.

1. General Strength

Here I would like to make specific reference to the pure animal strength that is best developed through some form of progressive resistance training, using the overload principle. The most common and easy form to obtain is weight training. Chapter 17 is devoted entirely to this aspect of the sport, and to avoid duplication here reference will only be made to a number of suitable exercises. The reader is advised to study the special section to decide the form the exercises will take.

The vaulter requires quite a tremendous all round strength, although one might highlight the arm and shoulder girdle that plays such an important part in the plant and the pull-push phase, and also the abdominal and lower back which help to execute the rock-back. The arms have to be capable of handling the bodyweight, hence this can serve as a guide to the poundages used.

I recommend the following arm exercises which should form part of a balanced strength training schedule:-

High cleans, inclined dumb-bell press, bench press, bent over rowing, weighted dips and behind neck press seated.

For the abdominals and lower back the choice is considerably restricted with inclined sit-ups and back hyperextensions being the most suitable.

2. Specific strength

Here the variety is considerable and it is only limited by what the imaginative mind can think up. However, one should keep in mind that training time is at a premium and all activities must be purposeful. The common gymnastic activities, well documented in books on vaulting and agility, are very suitable. They help to promote strength, co-ordination, balance as well as the orientation of the body when the feet go above the level of the hands. The rope exercises and beam work also described in many similar texts on gymnastics are also worthy of mention. For the specific strength work I would like to group the activities under three different apparatus headings, i.e. gymnasium beam or horizontal bar, suspended ropes and wall bars.

Plate 25. The "hand stand" on the pole.

(a) Beam or horizontal bar work, all performed with the body in the hanging position

  i) Leg swinging and circling movements, pivoting about the hips, with a weight held between the feet. A medicine ball is ideal as the weighted agent.
  ii) Upward circling movements around the beam or bar. Again it can be done with a weight held between the legs.
  iii) Horizontal arm travelling movements along the beam.
  iv) Kicking a medicine ball, thrown by a partner, on a trajectory that calls for the athlete to lift the legs above the head. (See plates 39a/b.)

(b) Suspended rope work

Items (i) and (iv) of the horizontal beam/bar can be performed very effectively on the ropes. The suspended rope can also be used for vaulting-type activities, where the legs can be raised above the head. If a target can be placed high, towards the extremity of the rope swing, then the activity is made even more purposeful.

(c) Wall bars

Items (i) and (iv) of the horizontal beam/bar can be performed effectively using the wall bars.

Upward circling movements of the body, using a vertically spaced handhold, are also a very worthwhile activity.

If these strength promoting activities are dovetailed into a programme of work, which also includes sprinting, horizontal jump training and specialised technique training at the vaulting area, a measure of success will be assured.

Section 4

Throwing events

Chapter 13

Shot Putting

Shot putting is the domain of the big, strong person and although it is one of the technical events, it can be enjoyed, and success achieved, at a fairly low skill level, provided there is a high speed-strength level. Although the history of the event, as we know it today, only dates back a hundred years or so, it does not require a very vivid imagination to conjure up pictures of early man casting heavy rocks for distance as a measure of strength. Basically, this is still the event today—a means of measuring explosive strength, although ultimately technical expertise will play its part.

The event involves pushing a round, cannonball-shaped object, the weight of which varies according to age and sex, from a position close to the neck and in front of the shoulders, for maximum distance. The recent evolution of the event has placed certain other restrictions on the performer in order to standardise the event throughout the world. According to the rules of today the performer must start and finish the movements involved from within the confine of a 7 feet (2.135 metres) circle and for the put to be valid the shot must land within a sector measuring 45° at the centre of the circle.

In technical terms the performer is concerned with two fundamental mechanical principles: the speed of release, and the angle of release, although to a certain extent the height at which the shot is released will have some influence on distance achieved. Easily the most important single factor is the speed of release and it is towards this end that all significant advances in performance techniques have been directed. Of course, when the athlete is striving to gain the final extra inches, the height of release and angle of release become a consideration. However, provided the athlete directs the shot at about 40° and releases it at around stretch height, all concentration can be directed towards the fast, explosive action necessary to produce the high speed of release.

The ultimate values of the three main variables are really dependent upon a skill factor which has to be developed through years of constant practice. However, speed, strength and aggression all play a most valuable role.

In shot putting, the version known by all competent athletes, the performer first puts a high speed in the body by adopting a form of shift, which will take it from a stationary balance position at the rear of the circle

172

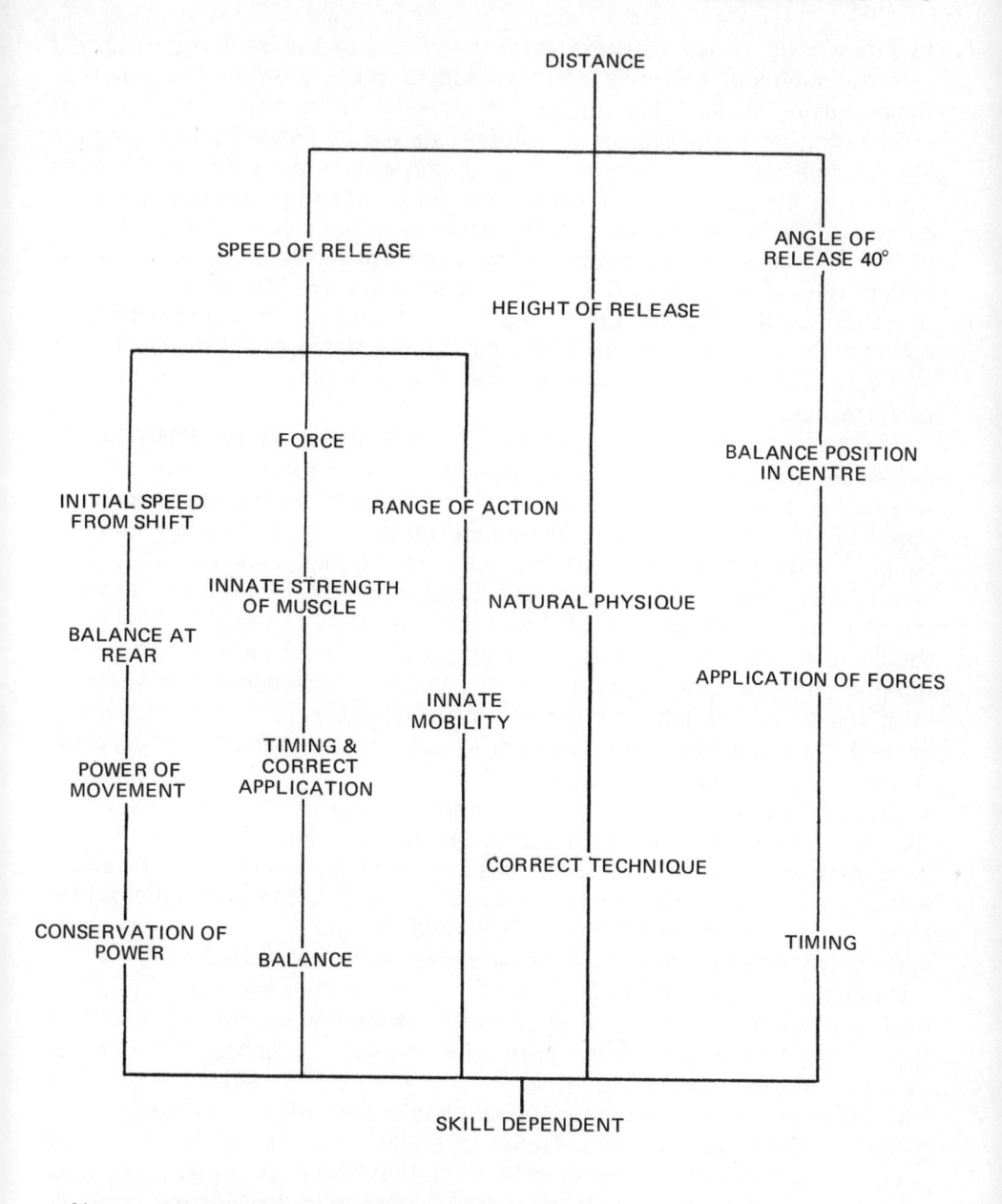

Note:- All descriptive sections and diagrams refer to the most common right-side orientated performer. The sections should be transposed, in the normal way, for the left-handed person.

to a powerful balance position, with the weight of the body more centred over the middle of the circle, and then adding to this speed by the powerful, final, putting action. The important thing is to try to keep the shot accelerating from the instant the shift is started. If balance and timing are lost the movement of the shot will slow, and will certainly detract from the distance of the put. The shift is merely an attempt, within the very restricted confine of the circle, to gain a little extra speed, but a very large proportion of the final speed is generated by the explosive movements, made by the athlete, once landing from the shift has been achieved. The final position is often termed the "standing put" and most athletes can record to within ten per cent of their maximum from this almost static position. Hence the perfection of this final pushing movement is essential for any level of performance.

The key feature of the final movement is the pushing action of the propelling arm. While there is a mechanically sound position for the arm, when the shot is being accelerated, to a large extent the degree of acceleration will depend upon the innate speed of the contracting muscles, coupled with their combined strength and timing. As the shot is a comparatively heavy object, strength is very important, and most throwers spend a considerable amount of their time developing this quality. The event should really be thought of in terms of a pushing movement, as this term is more descriptive of the type of action involved, particularly from the arm. With the trained athlete, the levers that combine together to form the arm anatomy, are capable of producing a fast, powerful, movement provided the structure is correctly positioned.

The key feature of almost every accomplished performer is the position of the elbow joint relative to the shot. As far as I am concerned, it is of paramount importance for the elbow to be behind the shot while the arm is working on it. So *elbow up and behind the shot* is the cardinal coaching point for this event (see plate 26). Should the elbow drop to a position underneath the shot, then the lever mechanics will be less efficient.

Compared with the other levers which combine together to make up this final movement, the arm is a relatively weak one, while the legs and back form a very strong, yet slower, propulsive mechanism. Hence, the contribution that can be made by these areas of the body is considerable but they must be timed, so that they supplement the movement of the arm and not detract from it. The essential factor to understand here is that the more powerful, but slower moving muscles of the leg and back, must make their contribution before the arm is brought into the action. If this basic principle is observed, the shot will accelerate throughout the entire movement. So the various levers combining together to produce the final effort must be poised correctly. This involves carefully balancing the bodyweight over the rear leg and transferring it to the front leg by a fast explosive action, coming mainly from the rear leg and applying its force through the trunk and the arm, via

Plate 26. The "Great" Komar (Poland) wins the 1972 Olympics. Note the high elbow position.

the hip joint. While I know that it is the leg which provides the power, I feel that the focal point of this phase of the movement should be centred around the hips. The movement produced by the rear leg will have an associated lifting component, in an almost vertical direction, but the main emphasis should be on producing rotation in one side of the body, about a vertical axis, while the other side of the body does its utmost to prevent this rotation from being carried over to its side. Such an action will cause the rotating side to speed up considerably and this is the side transporting the shot. For the right-handed shot putter, this will mean that the left leg and hip form a brace which helps to speed up the rotation of the right hip.

Before the rotational movement starts, the body must be correctly poised with the weight over the rear leg. The very basic position, which one attempts to get with the average performer, is one where the chin and the knee and toes of the rear leg, are in approximate vertical alignment (see

fig. 89). This is a very basic position and one which is fundamental for the novice performer. However, as far as the very accomplished, rotational performer is concerned, it has one disadvantage in that it can place the hips in a "tucked" inactive position. For the hips to be fast acting they must not be allowed to tuck back in so that they are at 90° to the line of put. To be active they must be, at the very least, parallel to the line of put. If the hips are tucked the right leg can only produce a lifting movement and it would appear that most putters now aim to rotate first and then vigorously lift behind the shot. Such an action seems quite logical for the speed of movement involved. The advanced thrower would tend to have the chin and the toes of the rear foot in vertical alignment, with the hips forced to a position in advance of this plane. However the novice performer should not attempt this position as it is one which requires great expertise to achieve. It is yet another instance of where the novice should not be allowed to copy the advanced performer until he is technically and physically able to execute the necessary movements involved.

The balance position in the centre of the circle is not a static one, it is essentially an active position, which the athlete passes through momentarily, although initially the novice performer might have to make it a fairly static position in order to develop the correct awareness. However, with experience it should be made as active and dynamic as possible. When practising the standing put, some athletes start from the static balance position and initiate the complete movement from it. Others start from an erect position and step either towards the centre of the circle or towards the stop board, with the appropriate foot, and then pass through the active balance position. From

Figs.   87   88   89   90

91   92   93   94

this poised position the rear leg forces the hips round square to the front; associated with this is a slight lifting action. For the right orientated athlete, the weight will be over the right leg and the action will cause the heel of the right foot to rotate anti-clockwise, taking with it the right hip and shoulders. As the athlete can really only work against the ground, the heel turns in advance of the hips and the hips well in advance of the shoulder. The arm action should not really start until the chest is square to the front. If the arm enters into the movement early, the elbow will almost certainly be low and the right arm *will* have to work against the unnecessary resistance of the left shoulder. For the arm to have a fast, clear, easy, movement, the chest must be square to the front. It is possible to open the chest by sweeping the left arm away from the line of put, but this should be avoided as it is essential for the action to come from the right leg. The whole action of the left side should be one of preventing the left side from rotating anti-clockwise.

While one must admit that the most important aspect of shot putting is what the athlete does with the shot, from the moment contact with the centre of the circle is established, until final release, the method of shift is important because if balance is lost during this phase, it is unlikely to be regained. In very simple terms, it is unimportant how the athlete moves from a position at the rear of the circle, to one in the centre, provided as much of the circle as possible is used and that the shot continues to accelerate from the furthermost position at the rear to a similar position at the front. In their efforts to increase performance levels, athletes have invented many methods of traversing the diameter of the circle. These range from simple side shuffling steps to backward hopping movements, and even rotational movements similar to those employed by the discus thrower. Through the years most styles have enjoyed a vogue often influenced by the one used by the Olympic Champion or World Record Holder. The current favourite is one which has been in use since about 1952, and is known as an O'Brien glide, being that it was first used by the very famous American shot putter, Parry O'Brien, whose presence was felt in four Olympics during the 1950s and 60s. Although other methods of shifting across the circle have been used with varying degrees of success, during the current era, most performers rely upon a modified O'Brien shift.

The O'Brien shift is a very adaptable movement and can be used equally well by athletes who rely upon a long rangy movement, at reduced speed, and those who use a much faster "stabbing-type" movement to drive across the circle. Basically the movement is a hop, in that the body weight is driven across the circle and received in the centre by the same leg. The athlete who uses the right arm performs the hop with the right leg. However, the term "hop" could convey entirely the wrong impression of the movement, as the term "hop" suggests not only a horizontal displacement of the body weight but also a vertical one. So the term "glide" is more commonly accepted because the movement is essentially one where the body weight is forced fairly low

across the circle. During the shift, the performer attempts to keep the shoulders square to the rear while trying to force the hips ahead of them. Those who use the short, stabbing shift across achieve a very active position at the centre of the circle, with the right foot turning to a position parallel to the centre line, and some even go beyond this position, with the foot even pointing further round to the front (see plate 27). Athletes who rely upon this style perform a very rotational movement at the front of the circle. It is often suggested that such a movement is more suitable for the smaller shot putter, but of course the term is quite comparative, as in essence there will never be a small performer in this event.

The athletes who try for an increased range of movement go into the "T" position before shifting across the circle. The "T" position, which is quite a delicate balance position, enables the shot to be lowered outside the rear of the circle, with the ground contact still remaining within. This can increase the range of movement quite considerably. Most athletes who use this method of "shift" cover less of the circle with the drive leg, so making it difficult for them to get the right leg under the body for a very fast explosive movement. However, some athletes use a "T" shift and still achieve a very active position in the centre of the circle.

The athletes who fail to get the right foot into the front half of the circle have to rely upon a slightly different action from the right leg and hips. The right leg can only be fast and active to produce rotation, if the leg is directly under the body mass. If the legs are well spaced, the hips have to be allowed to drift towards the front at 180° to the line of put, until the right hip is in front of the driving right leg. This system appears to be the one favoured by the real giants of the circle.

The power for the movement across the circle is derived from a co-ordinated pushing action of the supporting leg, and a kicking in the air action of the free leg. Those who pass through the classic "T" position have to use a more vigorous kicking action of the free leg, than those who merely fold over the driving leg before performing a "stabbing" like movement. With the latter group the free leg must kick directly towards the stop board, in order to brace the left side of the body, ready to take the fast rotation of the right hip.

However, all of these are merely styles which athletes employ to give their body and the shot some initial speed. The essential thing is that they should arrive in an active position in order to keep the shot accelerating.

Once the shift has started, the athlete should continue to work on the shot, for as long as is physically possible and the shot should finally leave the finger tips, which perform a very fast "flipping" type of action, well in front of the stop board. If this action is carried to the extreme, it will present the athlete with considerable problems to remain in the circle which is essential for the rules of the event. The recovery movement, known as a reverse, should be an integral part of the movement and not just performed as a rescue act. Once

the shot has left the finger tips the advancing body weight has to be checked. The bracing action of the left leg will do much to control it, but if the final action is a lifting one, behind the shot, the forward movement of the body mass has to be rapidly checked and reversed. This will involve a rapid transference of weight from a braced front leg to a very bent rear leg which, in the process of the movement, overtakes the front leg. During a correctly timed movement, the athlete will feel the sensation of leaning on the shot. It must be emphasised that the reverse is neither a premature movement, nor an afterthought. It is a natural reaction to contain a fast explosive movement in order to comply with the rules.

It is possible to give the body its initial speed by performing either a step back movement or a rotational movement similar to that of the discus thrower. The step back, while probably an aid to teaching, is never used in top-class competition, and the rotational style, although seen in the Olympic stadium, requires some perfection and modifications before it can rival the various forms of O'Brien shifts, as it seems to produce an unstable position in the centre, and is difficult to contain in a 7 feet circle.

Teaching shot putting

It must be remembered that this is an event which must be introduced to the novice performer in such a way that it keeps his interest, satisfies his innate competitive desires and at the same time conveys to the performer the essential fundamentals of technique. Most athletes will want to "run before they can walk" and others will wish to emulate the Olympic performer without possessing his degree of strength and co-ordination. The teacher is, therefore, faced with the problem of suppressing this desire and implanting in its place the simple, but nevertheless enjoyable, fundamental skills involved.

The first fundamental to learn is the correct pushing action of the arm. For this the shot must be placed firmly, in the dominant hand, in such a way that the second joint of the first, second and third fingers rest against the shot. The thumb and little finger secure the grip by providing lateral support. The shot is placed at the base of the jowl, and the pushing elbow raised so that the upper arm forms an approximate right angle with the trunk. The feet, hips and chest should be placed square to the front. The pushing action is started with a slight turn away, from the square position, of the right shoulder and hip, with them instantly returning to the square position and the arm continuing to push the shot on its way. During the entire movement, the head should be held erect and the shoulders kept square. Most novice performers drop the free shoulder and the head. This must be avoided by encouraging the performer to push the chest up after the shot, followed by an attempt to see it leave the hand. With this modicum amount of skill, competition is possible, and should be encouraged in order to inspire the aggressive speed of the movement.

Once the arm action is learnt, the more powerful muscles of the legs and

trunk can be employed in the movement. This will mean placing the performer in a position of torque and then forcing the unwinding movement to proceed the pushing action of the arm. It is best to rock back to the twisted position of the trunk from the basic starting position. With both feet, about hip width apart, the right leg, hip and shoulder are withdrawn by a stepping back movement. This will place the "chin" right knee and toes of the right foot in vertical alignment (see fig. 89). Once the right side is withdrawn, the right leg forces the hips and then the shoulders square to the front, when the arm again takes up the pushing action. This skill should be quickly placed in the competitive situation.

With these two fundamentals learnt, a simple side shuffle should be encouraged to give extra speed, provided the performer arrives in the balanced "chin-knee-toe" position, opens the chest out with the hips and continues to push with the elbow up.

These simple, yet fundamental, skills form the essence of shot putting and around these can be moulded the more advanced shifting and twisting movements of the sophisticated athlete. Care should be taken ònly to introduce the advanced skills when the novice is ready to receive them and this can only be judged by the intuition of the teacher.

The teacher, faced with introducing this event to the novice, does not require Olympic-type equipment and facilities, because the novice will not be performing the same sort of movement. I have seen an inspired and gifted teacher enthuse a class in this event with stones gathered from a nearby wall. The good teacher will improvise because the aim, in the early stages, is one piece of equipment for each person. Under normal circumstances this would be beyond the budget of any school which has to support large classes, as is the case with the majority of state schools in the United Kingdom. For the young novice, sampling the event for the first time, an improvised shot made from a plastic ball, filled with concrete, is ideal. It is more likely to be the correct size and weight as it is not governed by any technical specification necessary for competition. A novice performer cannot learn the event with an implement which is too heavy to handle efficiently. Many of the mistakes that I see, with novice performers, stem from learning the event with a weight beyond the strength level of the performer.

In the initial stages a grass surface is quite suitable, progressing, if possible, to an asphalt surface. But remember, only about one per cent is ever likely to require a concrete circle complete with stop board, and to impose restrictions such as this early in the learning situation can only inhibit the performer. There will be plenty of time for Olympic-type equipment and facilities once the novice is enthused and wishes to take part in the sport.

While shot putting is the least dangerous of the throwing events, people have been seriously injured while carelessly observing or taking part in the event. When working with groups of athletes strict safety precautions must be observed. The golden rules are:-

1. Look before you throw, the area must be completely clear.
2. Only throw, and above all else, only *retrieve* the shot when told to do so.
3. Never throw the shot to a person.

If these simple safety regulations are followed during the learning process, they are likely to remain for one's complete career.

All sports are dangerous, some more so than others, but many injuries can be avoided by a little careful thought.

Coaching the advanced performer

With the correct motivation the novice will rapidly progress to the level where coaching supersedes teaching. Once this level has been reached greater gains in distance can be achieved by adopting more sophisticated training techniques detailed later in the chapter. However, the advanced performer is a delight to coach as a true partnership has to develop with both athlete and coach learning together. While the coach might know and understand the positions and actions he requires from his protégé, the method of communication by which the skills are taught and perfected is a constantly changing one, and all of the time the coach is searching for the correct combination of words, personal demonstrations, etc., etc., to bring about the desired results. The interesting thing about coaching is that all athletes are different and they will all react differently to the "verbal patter" adopted by the coach. So all of the time there is an interesting field of experimental communication.

Most coaches like to look for faults in their athletes and then try to seek the remedy. I find this negative approach very frustrating and unsuited to my personality. I rather favour a repertoire of essential fundamental positions which the athlete is encouraged to adopt, allowing ample facility around these fundamentals for personal style.

(a) Elbow behind shot coming into delivery. The correct pushing position for the arm is the top of the list as far as I am concerned. Failure to get this arm in the correct position will prevent the correct use of this fast and powerful lever. Athletes who drop the elbow must be made aware of the weakness of the position and then a remedy explored. An athlete who starts with the elbow in the correct place at the rear of the circle, yet pushes the shot from underneath, will almost certainly have brought the hips and shoulders round as one unit. If the hips are brought round square to the front, in advance of the shoulders, it is almost impossible for the elbow to drop.

(b) An active right leg is essential for all good throwers. It is the right leg, acting through the hips and then shoulders, which provides most of the early "putting power" before the shot is moving sufficiently fast for the arm to strike. An inactive right leg can be caused by a number of things, but the most common is the loss of balance, particularly in the centre of the circle.

However, this is a feature in its own right and will be discussed later. In order for the right leg to be active, the knee of this leg must start to turn towards the front, almost as soon as the foot has broken contact at the rear of the circle. With the right knee must follow the right hip so that once contact with the centre of the circle is established, the hips can continue to the front in advance of the shoulders.

(c) *The right hip must be kept open.* This really follows on from point (b). It is fatal in this event, if the shoulders and hips are parallel with each other, and square to the rear, when landing in the centre. Many, quite good athletes keep the hips tucked in because they are not aware of the position, and to be made aware of it will often provide an automatic solution to the problem. However, a closed hip often results from a poor shift due to an unstable position at the rear. If the shift is balanced, a closed hip can be caused by a "sagging" upper body. Once the shift has started, the upper body must be kept on an "even keel" with the head up and the back fairly straight. This does not mean an upright position, as the head must be kept approximately over the driving foot. A sagging position could be caused through too great a vertical displacement of the bodyweight, so that it falls beyond a controllable position on landing. With big athletes, who have a fair proportion of their bodyweight in the arm and shoulder region, a sagging upper body can result from the dropping of the free arm during the shift. I am a person who favours a fairly high carriage of the free arm. It must not be a tense position, but rather a draped one carried slightly across the chest. A glance on the part of the athlete, to see the time on a wristlet watch on the left arm, often conveys the correct position for the free arm.

A "tucked" hip will always result in a considerable loss of balance once the right leg has completed its drive. A falling away to the athlete's left is fairly typical of the final position resulting from the right hip being tucked fairly well back.

(d) *A shot putter must be perfectly poised at the rear and centre of the circle.* As the drive across the circle, and the landing in the centre, is executed from a single leg, balance must be a key factor. It is fairly safe to say that if balance at the rear of the circle is not achieved, balance at the centre will be most unlikely. If the weight is not correctly positioned over the drive leg, excessive force is required to perform the shift, or to attempt to keep balance through muscular tension. Only through experience can the athlete find out if he is going too low, or allowing too much of bodyweight, than can be controlled, to pass outside the boundary of the circle. Admittedly, the experienced coach can suggest that balance might be wrong, but by and large the feed back in this situation must come from the athlete. Once balanced, an excessive and poorly timed kick of the left leg can soon create instability. Again, through experience, the athlete learns to combine the left leg kick back, with the right leg drive, to bring about a co-ordinated movement across the circle. This phase is most difficult to coach as there is often very little

concrete evidence for the coach to work on. In this situation the coach can get the general impression of a smooth co-ordinated movement but this impression must be confirmed by a feeling which the athlete gets.

It is fairly true to say that the head acts like a rudder. If it is allowed to drop, instability almost always results. The coach soon learns to place key markers, at set distances away from the circle, to attract the focus of the athlete, in an effort to keep the head in the correct position. For example, a marker placed about four metres away from the circle, at 2 o'clock, often puts the head in the correct position, just prior to landing in the centre of the circle.

(e) At release the chest must be square. In the main, only novice performers allow the free shoulder to drop coming up to release. However, accomplished performers can be forced to drop the free shoulder because of loss of balance, or a closed left hip, which will prevent rotation taking place about a vertical axis, but will encourage rotation about a short horizontal axis through the centre of gravity.

(f) The feet must be slightly offset in the pushing position. Ideally the left toe, firm against the stop board, should be in line with the right heel (see fig. 95). If the left foot is in line with the right toe, or further across to the same side, the situation is known as "blocking". This position will prevent the hips from acting quickly, as the left hip will be on the wrong side of the rotating axis. If the left foot is outside the line of the right heel (as shown in diagram) the term used is *"In the bucket"* and this will force a premature right hip movement.

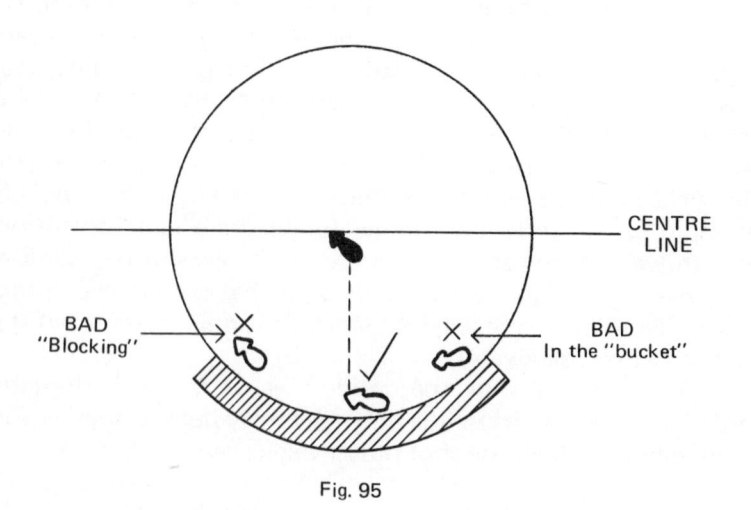

Fig. 95

(g) The movement must be fast. True shot putting is essentially a fast movement, and when the athlete is away from competition, the coach will

have to provide the necessary motivation and encouragement to keep the movement fast. At times it might be necessary to isolate a certain aspect of the skill, develop it slowly with less emphasis on the speed of the movement, and at a later stage return it to the full skill. However, it must be remembered that the only test for skills learnt in "slow-motion" is to subject the skill to the level of speed which will be required in competition. All technique training sessions must contain a number of full effort puts observing the necessary rules of competition.

Training for shot putters

Training for a shot putter is both simple and logical but very time consuming, and there is no short cut to success, even with numerous ergogenic aids now permeating the strong-man's domain. The shot putter must be fast, and very strong, and towards this end about eighty per cent of training time must be directed, so leaving about twenty per cent for technique and other peripheral, but worthwhile, training activities. As far as the shot putter is concerned, it is difficult to separate the speed factor from the strength one as they go "hand in hand" to produce an explosive effort.

Strength

The shot putter requires two forms of strength: a general, pure "animal" strength and a specific strength. Most of the athletes gain the former by working with barbells, and the latter by merely performing the shot putting movement. This system, over the years, has proved successful, in that world and Olympic records continue to improve. However, with each successive record man approaches the ultimate, and the margin by which records are broken gets smaller as progress is made. The shot putter is now looking for inches, and when all else has been tried he could resort to a different approach to the development of strength, particularly the field of specific strength. At the present time shot putters train so much with weighted discs, and gain such expertise in handling them, that many could hold their own with Olympic lifters. Indeed a number forget the original intention behind training with weights and are often forced to change sports in "mid-stream". But an interesting factor often emerges, and that is that the strongest man seldom wins. This does not mean that strength is unimportant but it is not so important as to exclude all else.

Chapter 17 will deal with the various ways in which strength can be developed. To avoid repetition it is only necessary here to suggest the various avenues for training which the shot putter might care to explore.

(a) Weight training

This must rank highest on the list of training priorities because around this activity all shot putters, and this does not exclude women, must centre a large proportion of their training time. A part of the male shot putter's

philosophy is that he must look big and feel strong, and weight training goes a long way to help the shot putter feel secure with the basic ideal. The only way to become really strong is to exercise the various muscles against a large resistance. This type of training will develop the animal strength around which the event must be nurtured. In this area the heavy thrower does not require the variety of exercises, which other athletes find necessary, to help relieve the boredom of training with weights. Indeed, the heavy thrower often scorns variety and frequently selects about six standard exercises, or less, at which he can frequently measure progress and so satisfy the strength-ego associated with the personality of the heavy thrower. Many good shot putters warm up with a simple Olympic routine, before embarking upon a few carefully selected exercises, that form part of the almost daily programme. They all observe the simple lifting precautions necessary to avoid injury and most wear the stout leather lifting belts or corsets to prevent injury to the back. Often, the shot putter lifts very heavy weights in a vertical direction and this places considerable pressure on the lower vertebrae. Hence the safeguard of adopting sound lifting techniques and support for the pressurised area.

Probably, the most common lift used by shot putters is the bench press, and a number can lift in excess of 500 lbs. for a single repetition. It can always be argued that the bench press has little to offer the shot putter in that the muscles used for executing the lift operate in a different manner from when performing the putting movement. This fact is beyond argument, as the shot is not pushed from the supine position. But I feel that psychologically this lift has everything to offer the shot putter in that very heavy weights can be handled safely and progress is quite easily measureable. The lift really needs "spotters" (two other strong people ready to take the strain of the weight should the lifter experience trouble), but this seldom presents problems as most throwers do their routines in groups, often with "weightlifters".

Other favourites for the putter include the inclined press, weighted dips, tricep curls, sit-ups, squats and leg press. All should be done using a relatively heavy weight, with a low number of repetitions.

(b) Specific strength training

Most throwers are reluctant to forsake one of their weight training sessions for other forms of resistance training. I am an enthusiast of attempting to perform strength promoting activities which may have a carry-over to the event. Associated with these activities, is a form of strength-mobility work essential for those likely to build up large bulks of muscle. Such activities will include work with friction pulleys, standard pulleys using weights, exercises against the resistance of, or with the aid of, a partner, dynamic work with medicine balls, etc. However, these must only be considered as a supplement to training with weights.

(c) Speed training

The speed required by the shot putter is a very specific one and quite far removed from the speed involved in sprinting. The shot putter, during his event, has only 2.135 metres in which to generate speed. Basically it involves the ability to suddenly promote speed and almost instantly stop again. While I believe that throwers should include a little short sprinting in their training programmes, I would place a greater importance upon bounding activities, like those listed in Appendix I. Bounding activities call for the athlete to shift the body weight in a most controlled manner, at times very similar to the movement employed in the actual event.

(d) Technique training

The performance technique must be developed hand in hand with all of the other facets of the event. Many athletes have made the fatal mistake of concentrating on strength training during the winter conditioning period, only to find that performance standards, at the end of it, are below what could have been expected. Undoubtedly athletes raise strength levels to such a degree that a complete re-education of technique becomes necessary. Hence technique training sessions must be an all year-round activity.

Each technique session should start with a number of easy standing puts, building up the level of speed as the sessions progress. The area should be marked so that both athlete and coach have a quick measure of standards. Once the body is accustomed to the explosive effort of the standing put, a few easy shifting puts should be performed before the main session starts.

During such a training session the coach can either work to a pre-arranged plan or coach from what the situation produces. Both have their merits, but whichever is chosen it is wise to work only on just one fundamental aspect during a single session, otherwise confusion can result. It must be accepted that coaching is a series of predetermined focal points. When concentration is focused on a certain aspect of skill other aspects might deteriorate. This must be accepted as part of the drive towards perfection, only by accepting a temporary deterioration in one aspect of a skill can the "whole" be perfected.

Like the athlete, the coach never ceases to learn. Almost every top level coaching session, with good athletes, will provide the coach with educative experiences which contribute to the coach's total expertise. Coaching cannot be learnt from a book. It is the practical experience gained from working in many different situations which help to produce coaching expertise.

Diet

As a coach, I am always totally at conflict with myself on this topic. An analytical mind encourages the coach to seek the advice of the expert. Coaching is a massive field which covers not only ideas on performance techniques, but also those relating to applied psychology, kinesiology,

physiology, etc. and diet is just one facet that must be considered if physical perfection is to be achieved. The coach cannot hope to become expert at all of the applied arts. By attempting to be so he might become a "jack of all trades" and "master of none". Hence the wise coach counsels the advice of dieticians. Here there appears to be some conflict between what an expert says are the dietary requirements of an athlete and the natural feed-back one obtains from having been with throwers. While I admit in theory, the dieticians are likely to be correct. there is a psychological factor which the coach must consider. The shot putter has to be big and strong, and associated with this he develops an enormous appetite, he enjoys eating, and when eating he feels good. Although the dietician can calculate for us the quantity of food that a healthy shot putter requires, those I have been associated with are far from happy on such small amounts.

The problem, as seen by a layman, is threefold. The shot putter needs food to provide the vast amount of energy he expends in training. For example, in a single weight training session the shot putter will probably displace several tons of weight, and this requires a vast amount of fuel. The shot putter requires mass to exert force against the shot; so apart from merely maintaining bodyweight many, in fact, require to increase it. For the very active person the only way to increase body bulk is to increase food intake.

During strength training the action involved causes a breakdown of muscle protein. For the muscle to rebuild stronger, a fairly large intake of protein and vitamins is required. So although the immediate demands of energy are likely to be supplied by a breakdown of carbohydrates, tissue rebuilding requires protein.

Again, the dieticians inform us that the normal diet contains all that a person requires in terms of carbohydrates, lipids, proteins, vitamins, mineral salts, etc. I cannot help feeling that the athlete is a special person, requiring considerably more than the man in the street and that it is wiser to insure against any likely deficit by consuming a certain amount of artificial foods.

As far as the shot putter is concerned, the protein intake is one of the prime considerations. While the athlete might enjoy the pleasures of eating vast amounts of juicy steaks, and as such should not be prevented from doing so, they are not the most efficient means for obtaining protein. I am very much in favour of the artificial proteins, usually in powder form, and manufactured by the leading firms who produce foods for the pharmaceutical trade. Natural foods, particularly those of pollen derivation and the wheat germ extracts, can all play a very important role in the physical well-being of the shot putter. If one adds to this the normal diet including fresh vegetables, eggs and fairly high quantities of milk, then the athlete should have no fears of lacking the vital raw materials.

Ergogenic aids

There seems to be increasing evidence that athletes, particularly those

involved in the heavy throwing events, are taking drugs which will help them work harder, make them stronger and probably make them more able to channel more of their resources, into a single attempt in the competitive arena. The International Amateur Athletic Federation have very strict laws banning the use of drugs. However, it is interesting to note that prior to 1972 precise details of the banned drugs were not listed in their handbook. In 1972 the hormone group of anabolic steroids was singled out, suggesting that the Federation was aware of the practice of using hormones.

The anabolic group of steroids are derived from testosterone, the male sex hormone. To quote from *Medindex*: "Anabolic Agents—The male sex hormones are androgenic and also affect protein metabolism and calcium retention promoting nitrogen anabolism muscle and skeletal growth." It is suggested that athletes use the drug, in fairly large doses, to increase muscle and skeletal growth. However, a number of experimenters suggest that the anabolic effect is relatively small. Other researchers suggest that taken in large quantities there could be a gluco-corticoid action which could vastly speed up the recovery process from training, thus permitting more frequent and more intense training programmes.

Rule number 144 is quite precise and athletes who take such aids are breaking a rule as well as endangering themselves, as the hormone balance of the body cannot be disturbed too frequently without the risk of side effects. The precise nature of the side effects are unknown with the fit, healthy adult, as these are likely to be delayed. There is ample evidence of the side effects with aged patients when they are used to rebuild the body to prolong life, or in treatment for an illness. The side effects with women are well established and are certain to produce masculinity and its associated characteristics.

It has been suggested that this particular group of drugs was first used in the 1950s by sportsmen. It is a pity that documentary evidence, over twenty years later, is not available to examine any long-term side effects when taken by healthy adults.

The situation in the world of sport today is such that success in the Olympic arena is all-important, and it is likely that drugs such as these will be taken until detectable, by which time the pharmacologist will have found something to take their place.

There are also rumours suggesting that drugs affecting the sympathetic nervous system are being employed in order to produce an "aggressive animal" effect, enabling all of the athlete's resources to be channelled into a single, unimpaired, explosive effort, that could win a gold medal. However, it is hoped that the rumours are without foundation as the possible side effects in this area are frightening.

The use of drugs in sport must be condemned, but the athlete/coach must be made aware of their existence, and this very brief summary of the situation may help him to widen his knowledge on the subject.

DANGER—THROWING IN PROGRESS

In recent years a number of deaths, particularly in the 13 years to 17 years age group, have been attributed to the throwing events. The throwing events are dangerous unless the strictest safety precautions are observed. The teacher/coach must insist on a high standard of safety precautions all of the time and hope that this will cause the throwers to take extra care. However, the whole athletic population must be educated to the fact that the events are dangerous. But I must stress that they are only dangerous if one strays into the area where the missiles are likely to land.

Please take care, always look before you throw, and always look before entering a throwing area.

Plate 27. M. Winch (G.B.) demonstrates an active landing in the shot.

Chapter 14

Discus Throwing

Like shot putting, discus throwing is the domain of the big strong man, but if anything the discus thrower must be faster, as the weight of the implement thrown is less than half that of the shot. This is not suggesting that the shot putter can be slow, quite the reverse, but it does suggest that the discus thrower must be capable of great speed. Most discus throwers are also good shot putters and the incidence of this is far higher than the opposite situation. Although the shot put event is always considered as a straight line throw, and the discus a rotational throw, the performance techniques include many similar, if not identical, qualities of movement.

Discus throwing is the classic of all athletic events and its origin is steeped in the history of ancient Greek cultures. From the evidence contained in the arts of the ancient Greeks, more has been written about the discus thrower than almost any other athletic performer and he has been made the subject of many a sculptor's chisel. The most famous is the "discobolus" by Myron which depicts the thrower in a most unusual pose and is most probably the artist's impression of the throw, rather than an historical record of how the ancient throwers performed. However, it is fairly certain that this statue influenced the early development of the event, and the Olympic Games of [1906] * 1908 contained two versions of discus throwing—the free style similar to that which is in existence today, and the "classic" style where the discus was thrown from a "balbis" (raised pedestal) after having adopted a stance similar to that depicted by Myron. The following is quoted from the rules of 1908 Olympic Games held in London:

"Throwing the discus as at Athens. The discus is thrown from a rectangular pedestal 80 centimetres (31½ inches) long 70 centimetres (27½ inches) broad sloping forward from a height of 15 centimetres (6 inches) at the back to 5 centimetres (2 inches) at the front. The thrower places himself on the pedestal, feet apart, and holding the discus in either hand. He then grasps it with both hands and raises it without letting go the discus with either, extending the rest of the body at the same time in the same direction. After that he turns the trunk to the right and bends sharply, so as to bring the left hand, which has now left hold of the discus to the right knee, and the right hand still holding the discus as far back as possible. At this moment

*1906 Interim Olympic Games held in Athens.

190

the right foot should be forward and both legs bent; the right foot rests full on the sole and the left toes only. Then by a sharp and simultaneous extension of the whole body the thrower throws the discus forward. The thrower may leave the pedestal at the moment of throwing. The measurement of the throw shall be from the point at which the discus first strikes the ground to the centre of the front side of the pedestal."

The dual event was short lived as the Olympic motto "Citius altius fortius" (Swifter Higher Stronger) has always been the athletes' inspiration and the classic technique imposed considerable restrictions which limited the distance thrown.

Many athletic historians have tried to compare the performance techniques in the ancient events with those of their modern counterparts. Although in certain instances the documentation is fairly good, direct comparisons have always been made impossible for one reason or another. In the discus event the precise weight of the discus is unknown. Although there are a number of ancient implements which have withstood the pressure of time, those that have been preserved all differ in weight and size, and the passing of time has obviously had an effect. It would appear that the ancient discus had no set dimensions but was merely fashioned from a convenient piece of stone or bronze.

The event, as we know it today, is obviously restricted to force the standardisation of rules and to impose certain safety factors. As always it is a competition for distance, and the thrower who records the longest throw, in a competition, where it is permitted to have between three and six attempts, is declared the winner, provided the throw lands within a 45° sector and that the thrower remains within a circle whose diameter is 8' 2½" (2.50 metres) for the entire duration of the throw. Once the movement is complete the exit from the circle must be through the rear half. There are, of course, other restrictions but this is sufficient to give a sound understanding of what the performer must do in order to comply with the rules.

In terms of simple mechanics, the discus thrower is concerned with three important principles: the speed of release, the angle of release and an aerodynamics factor, necessary to keep the discus flowing efficiently through the air. The most important factor is the speed of release, (see page 193) but if the discus leaves the hand in such a way that it presents a large surface to the air, then the true value of the throw will be lost because of the air resistance considerably reducing the effect of release speed.

Fig. 96 should help readers understand the three simple mechanical principles, and how the throwers adapt the technique to keep all values at a significant level.

The expert discus thrower first of all puts a high speed in his own body, and hence the discus, by using some form of running rotational movement across the circle, and then adding to this initial speed by performing a powerful, long arm, slinging movement. While this final flinging position does

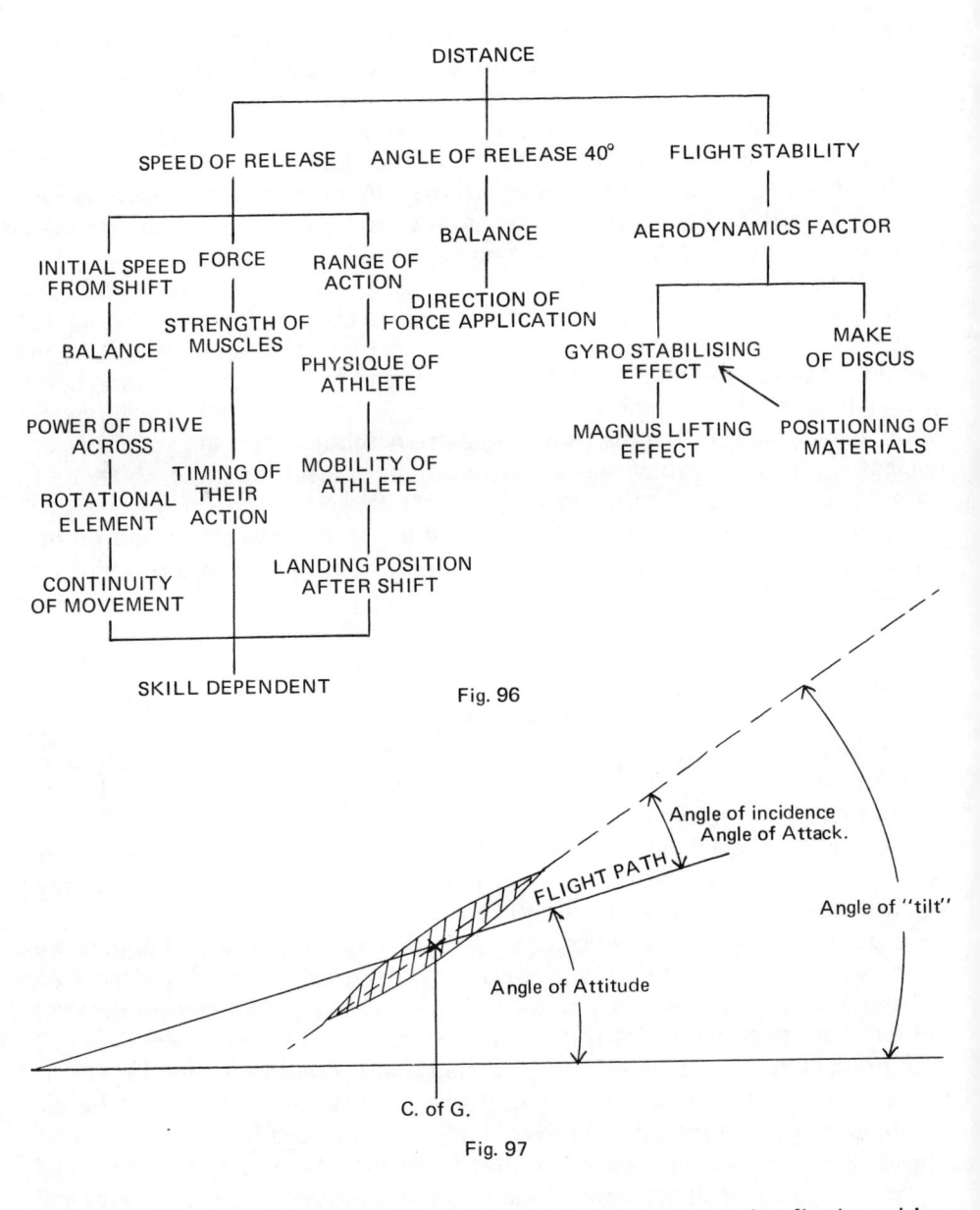

DISTANCE

SPEED OF RELEASE   ANGLE OF RELEASE 40°   FLIGHT STABILITY

BALANCE   AERODYNAMICS FACTOR

INITIAL SPEED FORCE   RANGE OF
FROM SHIFT   ACTION
                DIRECTION OF
      STRENGTH OF   FORCE APPLICATION
BALANCE MUSCLES   GYRO STABILISING   MAKE
      PHYSIQUE OF   EFFECT   OF DISCUS
        ATHLETE
POWER OF DRIVE   MAGNUS LIFTING   POSITIONING OF
   ACROSS   EFFECT   MATERIALS
      TIMING OF MOBILITY OF
ROTATIONAL THEIR   ATHLETE
 ELEMENT   ACTION

CONTINUITY   LANDING POSITION
OF MOVEMENT   AFTER SHIFT

SKILL DEPENDENT   Fig. 96

Angle of incidence
Angle of Attack.

FLIGHT PATH

Angle of "tilt"

Angle of Attitude

C. of G.

Fig. 97

not provide quite the same proportion of the throw as the final pushing
movement in the shot, it is nevertheless an extremely significant part of the
whole action and most throwers spend quite a lot of their technique training
time trying to achieve a powerful final position.

As the section of the mechanics chart suggests, the speed of release, in the

Discus Table—Showing theoretical range of flight at a release angle of 45°.

Release Speed	Approximate Flight Distance
60 feet per second	112 feet
70 feet per second	153 feet
80 feet per second	200 feet
90 feet per second	253 feet

Note: In these calculations the other variables such as aerodynamic factors have been ignored. They are perfect release conditions. An increase of 10 f/p/s in release speed provides about fifty feet improvement in flight range.

final flinging action, is dependent upon the force and the range over which the force is made to act. In this aspect the thrower often has to make a compromise. It is possible for the thrower to get an extremely long range of movement, but to achieve this he might have to place the slinging arm in a very unnatural, tense, position, requiring muscular effort to sustain it, and this will ultimately detract from the speed with which the movement can be executed. The withdrawn position, which must be as far behind the right shoulder as mobility will allow, has to be a relaxed one. It is difficult to obtain a good "wind up" position when just performing the final part of the movement, or the standing throw, because in the running position the body can move ahead of the discus, leaving it trailing and the arm fairly relaxed. However, as far as range of movement is concerned, the essential point to observe is that the throwing arm remains as long as possible and any flexion about the elbow joint will ultimately detract from the speed of release. It must be remembered that the discus is not gripped or held by the fingers in any way; it is merely kept pressed against the end pads of the fingers by the centrifugal force, set up by the rotational aspect of the movement. Therefore, if the arm is kept long, and the discus is not held, it will spin from the hand at the correct tangent to the circle made by the arm. So, to a large extent, the release is a natural thing provided the arm is straight.

The ultimate value of the forces propelling the discus will depend upon the power which the athlete can produce. Power is, of course, strength and time dependent, so provided the movement is performed at peak speed, strength is the only other variable factor. The "strength" of the movement is dependent upon the innate strength of the individual muscle groups concerned with the movement, and their correct application. The "animal" strength of the muscles concerned is one of the focal points of the thrower's training programme and provided this can be improved without any retarding effect upon speed, or decrease in the range of action, the total

force will be greater, and therefore the net speed of release greater. However, the timing of the various muscle actions is of concern. The movement must be executed in such a way that the slower muscles of the legs and trunk add their power first, and the faster acting muscles of the shoulder and arm follow on, so that the various forces combine to produce the accumulated effort at the point of release.

The angle of release is not quite such an important factor, provided that it is kept in the region of 30°-40°. This will need to be varied slightly, depending upon the prevailing wind, and quite naturally discus throwers prefer a head-on breeze, quartering from the right, as this will give the discus added lift. Wind is such an important factor in this event, that all modern stadia have more than one circle, so that throwers can take advantage of it. In certain countries, major competitions are held in centres where there is frequently a favourable wind, and this is often the case when a new world record is established. The world record is such that without some assistance from the wind it is unlikely to be improved under less favourable conditions. Provided the thrower is well balanced in the circle, and can time the leg and hip drive correctly, the angle of release will always be of a reasonable order. Many coaches confuse the angle of attitude (attack) with the angle of release and this will be dealt with under the section covering the aerodynamics.

Any missile which is aimed for either accuracy or distance must have a stable flight path. For example, a bullet leaving the muzzle of a gun is forced to spin about its long axis by the rifling (spiral grooves) running the length of the barrel. To make full use of the release speed, the discus must not present a large surface to the air. This will mean that it must travel along its flight path with a "flying saucer-type" motion, spinning about a vertical axis through its centre. This gyroscopic action has one very positive, and one other possible effect. The positive one is that the gyroscopic action makes it difficult for the discus to rotate about a horizontal axis, thus changing its attitude in the air. So, provided the discus can spin the correct way it will remain stable in flight. Unfortunately, for very long throws, the spin imparted by the athlete runs out before the flight is complete, hence the near edge drops, causing the leading edge to lift, so presenting a large surface to the air. The discus leaves the hand, spinning in a clockwise direction, from the end pad of the first finger. The athlete has to dig this finger in to put that little extra friction on the rim which causes the gyrating effect. The spin can be aided by the action of a slight adhesive material such as venice turpentine, resin, friars balsam, etc., but the greatest aid is a well manufactured implement. With the desire for nations to succeed in sport scientists have been encouraged to take an interest and, with this situation, it was only a matter of time before the technically loose specifications were exploited to produce a better discus. The first significant "aerodynamic" discus was the *Obol,* and this, quite naturally, placed most of the weight to the rim so that it could perform somewhat like a flywheel. Of course such a discus

requires a greater effort to set the gyroscopic action in motion, but once spinning it will continue to do so for a longer period of time.

Photographic evidence suggests that a discus spins through the air at over 300 r.p.m., and it is theoretically possible for it to disturb the air currents producing a "magnus" lifting effect. However, this is most unlikely, but nevertheless a consideration.

In pure aerodynamic terms, the athlete has only one consideration, other than the release angle and the gyroscopic stabilising effect, and that is the angle of incidence of the discus, or the angle of attack as it is more frequently termed. Unlike the shot and hammer, the discus is an aerofoil and once released will behave quite differently from either of them, and is considerably influenced by wind conditions which can produce forces aiding lift or drag. The athlete's concern is to keep the drag force to a minimum, hence the interest in aerodynamic factors. However, it must be emphasised that the athlete should seldom be aware of them during throwing, but the coach must be conscious of them when striving for perfection.

The angle of release, which has been mentioned earlier, is the angle between the horizontal and the path of the centre of gravity of the discus commencing its flight (see fig. 97). The angle of incidence (attack) is that between the line drawn through the long axis of the discus and the path of the centre of gravity (see fig. 97). If this angle has a high positive value (i.e. above the plane of the long axis) the drag forces will be excessive. One could assume that in theory the angle of incidence should be zero, but the effect of flight is one that gradually increases the positive value of this angle so there might be some advantage in releasing with a negative angle of attack, somewhere between zero and ten degrees. However, this angle is impossible for the coach to observe, so it is possible to derive a third angle often known as angle of inclination or tilt (see fig. 97). This is the angle between the plane of the discus and the horizontal and it is this angle which can give the coach the impressions of a correct release or otherwise. It is considerably affected by the way the discus rests in the hand, and in particular the relationship of the thumb and the first finger.

The speed of release, the most important single factor affecting flight range, can be increased if the discus is released from a moving body. Hence the discus thrower adopts a movement across the circle that will produce the maximum amount of speed in such a confined area. All top-class throwers use a running rotational movement, where the body rotates about a vertical axis. Most of them have a fairly standard movement in that they take up a stance at the rear of the circle, facing in the opposite direction to the line of throw. They then turn through 360°, to arrive in the standing throw position, rotating a further 180° to release. Indeed, the evolution of discus techniques has been mostly centred around turning through a greater range, and the "back-towards" style is something which is comparatively recent.

The whole purpose of the shift is to give the body some initial speed, but

Figs.   98   99   100   101

102   103   104   105

106   107   108

this will be of little value unless it also provides a sound launching platform. The essence of a well executed turn is perfect balance. Balance must be obtained at the rear of the circle before a shift is contemplated, and again the body must arrive in a balanced position close to the centre of the circle, before the final effort.

In their movements across the circle there appear to be two fairly distinct groups of throwers. In the first category there are those who use a wide sweeping free leg—in the case of the right handed thrower this is the right leg. Once the thrower has the bodyweight fairly well in advance of the supporting leg, the free leg is swept out wide and fairly close to the ground. However, just before landing in the centre it must be "clipped" in to make the hips active. This method produces considerable rotation, thus making the balance position in the centre more difficult to achieve. There is also the danger that the left leg will follow the same sweeping action as the right leg on its journey to the front of the circle. The wide sweeping left leg has two great disadvantages and must be avoided. The first is that it takes longer to

form the brace, ready for the fast acting right leg, hence speed is lost, and also it takes the leg into a position, out of alignment, opening the hips prematurely.

The second group of throwers rotate considerably more on the supporting leg at the rear of the circle and they do not shift their body weight so far in advance of the supporting leg. The movement is then more of a simple running action, but again the right leg must be "clipped in" fast and the left leg, moving to the front of the circle, must pass very close to the right leg.

In very simple terms, it helps the coach to understand the action better if they consider the role of the right leg as one to produce rotation, and the left to produce the linear drive to move across the circle in a straight line.

I am personally an enthusiast of the wider sweeping free leg, but it does demand tremendous concentration to hit the correct balance at the rear of the circle, and sufficient confidence to place the weight well over the supporting leg. However, once learnt it is a beautiful, flowing, symmetrical, movement that can give the body considerable speed.

As mentioned earlier, the key position for the discus thrower is the one achieved in the centre of the circle. Basically, for the novice, this is a "chin-knee-toes" position with the chin, and the knee and toes of the supporting leg in vertical alignment. This is a simple position and will give the athlete a well balanced position. The mature athlete, attempting to get greater torque, will stray only slightly from this position. Ideally the thrower is attempting to get the hips far enough in front of the shoulders so that the lines marking their respective planes almost form a cross. The shoulders should trail the hips by some 90°. The arm should be as far to the rear as mobility will allow.

To describe the chain of movements that follow from this tremendously "coiled", but powerful position, I will explain the sequence from the centre out, almost as if it were a standing throw. But it must be emphasised that the balance position is an extremely active one which has been mentioned earlier.

The aim, just prior to landing in the centre of the circle, is to keep the hips in advance of the shoulders. Once the right leg has made contact, the left leg should follow in quick succession to the front of the circle. The feet should be slightly offset from a line directly across the circle in the direction of the throw. The right foot should be pointing to 10 o'clock, and the left toes should be in line with the right heel (see fig. 109).

From this position the right leg can drive the hips firmly to the square frontal position, bringing with them the shoulders, aided by the back muscles; but leaving the arm trailing. The action of the left leg and hip at this stage, is to prevent the left side from rotating backwards, anti-clockwise. As in the shot, this action will speed up the right side which is carrying the discus. Once the shoulders are square to the front, the legs contribute very little. The throw is completed with a very fast vigorous slinging action from the

Plate 28. Faina Melnik 1972 Olympic Champion from U.S.S.R. demonstrates a wide leg sweep.

arm that sends the discus into orbit. During the slinging phase the head must remain erect and the shoulders square, to the front. The novice might tend to drop the left shoulder; this must be avoided.

Once the discus has left the hand, the body will still have a considerable amount of speed making it difficult to contain it within the circle. Here again there seems to be two fairly distinct schools of thought. At one end of the scale is the method often associated with the East German throwers, who hold the left leg down very firm to offer a considerable resistance to forward speed, but providing the tendency to release behind the front leg. At the other end of the scale are the group whose front leg hardly makes contact with the ground before the thrower rotates past it into a reverse recovery.

I am in favour of holding the left leg down firm until the discus has gone, but with an effort to "chase" the discus out with the arm, so giving a release over the front leg, and then allowing rotation to continue about the front leg to remain in the circle.

However, it must be emphasised again that discus throwing is not a series of parts, or static positions, that can be rehearsed in isolation. It is essentially a fast, symmetrical, movement which if performed correctly will automatically flow from one part to the next, presenting the athlete with few problems. Only when the balance and timing are out does the coach really earn his keep.

Teaching the discus throw

The discus throw is probably the most difficult and dangerous of the throwing events commonly taught in schools and clubs. However, if introduced correctly it can be performed in complete safety and in such a way that the novice is inspired to practise the event.

The teacher working in a full class situation, with a group of thirty or more, will have to introduce the event quite differently to the club coach who might work with two or three performers. The young novice has to be inspired and involved, otherwise boredom takes over, so making learning more difficult. A large class must be drilled in safety regulations, and so positioned that they can all throw in complete safety, remembering that the discus can slip from the hand in any direction. For complete safety the event should be performed from within a cage, with all observers positioned outside. However, this would not be practicable for the class-teacher as involvement would be so restricted.

In the very early stages of the learning situation, I recommend the use of a light, improvised, wooden discus, or the rubber equivalent. To keep a large group in a manageable area, I find that only about ten people can throw, and so gain experience, at one time. The remainder must stand away at a safe distance to watch the throwing carefully and then become involved directly after the preceding group has thrown. In this way, all of the discus are thrown and then recovered in a single operation. For the standing throws, a

gap of about two yards between one thrower and the next is sufficient, provided the slinging skill is correctly taught.

In technical terms, the first thing the instructor has to convey is that the event is a long arm slinging movement. However, before this action can be experienced by the performer a most difficult concept of the movement has to be emphasised. It involves the method by which the discus is held in the hand. All novice throwers become insecure when they find that the discus must not be gripped, or supported from the underneath, but merely held in a position against the end pads of the fingers by the centrifugal force, set up by the rotational aspect of the slinging movement. However, this insecurity can easily be overcome provided the learner is correctly positioned.

The ideal situation is to have the performer toe a straight line, with both feet, placed about hip width apart. The right-handed thrower should place the left hand under the discus so that it acts like a "tee" for the golf ball, or an "egg-cup" for an egg. The right hand must be placed on top of the discus with the fingers just curling over the edge. With the hands in this position the discus should be placed close to the left shoulder in order to permit a stable and long "take back".

From this position the discus should be withdrawn to the long arm position by a single, fast moving action, of the right arm. Preliminary swings should be avoided as this leads to greater insecurity. As the arm goes to the rear the trunk can follow it a little, but the feet must remain firm. From the withdrawal position the arm should propel the discus forward at great speed. The arm must be kept long, and the chest square to the front, with level shoulders. The skill can be placed in the competitive situation directly.

Only a very limited amount of time should be spent practising this aspect of the skill, even if the discus does not spin through the air correctly. At this stage preliminary swings should be avoided as they will encourage the bending of the arm. Provided the arm is kept straight the discus should spin from the hand correctly. Progress should be very quickly made to the position which encourages the use of the hips. From the basic starting position, with the feet toeing a line and pointing in the direction of the throw, the right leg should step away from the starting position, as the discus is withdrawn, to establish a "chin-knee-toes" position. This will place the feet as in fig. 109. The moment the discus is finally withdrawn, the right leg must force the hips rapidly to the fore, allowing the arm to trail slightly. The movement is then completed, as in the first practice, with a powerful slinging movement by the arm. Performers should be encouraged to use the right hip to aid the movement, keep the arm long and the head and chest erect. The comment, "See the discus leave the hand" will, in most cases, prevent the characteristic dropping of the free shoulder, which turns the movement into a "bowling" rather than a "slinging" action.

The preceding practice is the foundation for all good throwing and it requires both time and concentration to perfect. However, the novice

performer should be encouraged to perfect it using some form of shifting movement. Experimentation here seldom produces results; hence I am in favour of teaching a frontal, facing, running turn. To achieve this the performer should toe a line, about eight feet from the throwing line with both feet pointing in the direction of the throw. The discus should hang by the side at a full arms length. Ideally the movement should be started with an upward, underarm, bowling action of the discus until it reaches the long arm position at 90° to the trunk. This should be followed by a very fast running rotational movement to place the body ahead of the discus. The right leg must move first, the performer should arrive in the "chin-knee-toes" position and complete the throw as explained earlier. The dedicated novice can then be encouraged to position the feet side on to the direction of the throw, and ultimately back towards the direction of throw, using exactly the same running technique.

THE DISCUS

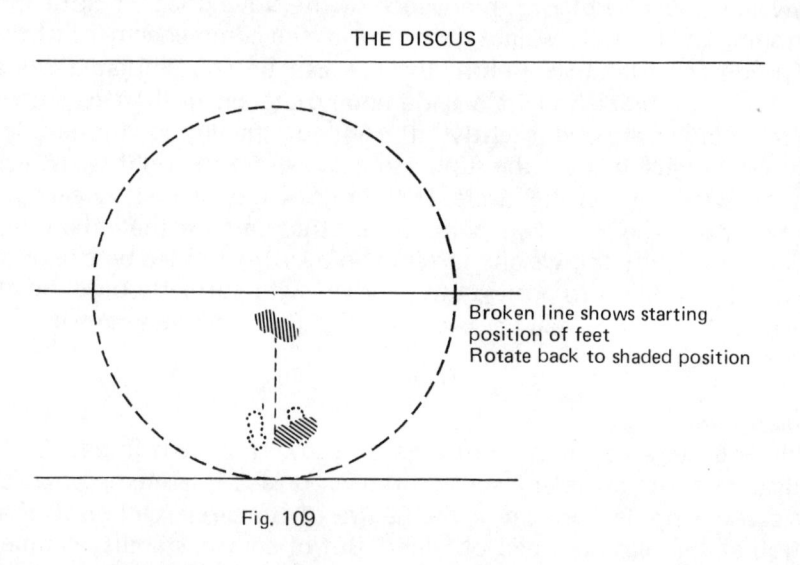

Broken line shows starting position of feet
Rotate back to shaded position

Fig. 109

It must be appreciated that very few, of a large group of beginners, will ever achieve any form of competent turn.

Coaching the mature performer

As in shot putting, the discus throw is best considered as a series of positive movements that aid a good throwing technique. So the coach should be encouraged, through his teaching, to insist on the positive actions rather than approach the event as a series of faults and their corrections.

For the mature performer the essential feature of any throw is balance. The athlete must be balanced before shifting across the circle, and again balanced in the centre of the circle before completing the final flinging action.

A. Balance at rear of the circle

A relaxed stance at the rear of the circle is essential and this can be aided by one or more preliminary swings, allowing the body weight to shift laterally in harmony with the swings. Large, vigorous, preliminary swings should not be encouraged as they will force a large countering movement from the rest of the body, so making the transference of weight, just prior to the shift, more difficult. Many coaches and athletes believe that the further the discus is withdrawn, before the shift, the further it will be behind the plane of the hips on arrival in the centre. This is only a part truism and often leads to an extremely tense position which does not aid the balance.

The movement across the circle is essentially a running action with only a very slight elevation or depression of the centre of gravity during it. Any tendency to jump must be discouraged and can only result from a poor balance position. To run smoothly and efficiently a good proportion of the bodyweight must be placed in advance of the driving leg. It is the incorrect positioning of the body weight, just prior to the commencement of the turn, that produces instability. Before the run can be contemplated, the athlete must lower the body weight a little and rotate on both feet, shifting the weight across over, and slightly in front, of the supporting left leg. The body weight must be over the supporting leg before the right leg is picked up ready to sweep across the circle. If the right leg is picked up early, balance will be lost. The problem with most throwers is that they lack the confidence to shift the weight far enough over the left leg before picking up the right leg. Failure to position the body weight correctly over the drive leg will cause the body to fall backwards across the circle, making balance in the centre impossible.

B. Balance in the centre

This is again a key feature of a good throw since it is impossible to give the discus all of the latent speed from an unstable launching platform. In most cases, a stable position in the centre of the circle will result if a stable position at the rear has been obtained. But of course, stability can be lost in the transition period between the two balanced positions.

The landing position of balance must not be confused with a situation which directly follows on, where balance is lost due to the incorrect timing of the hip drive.

My experience would suggest that provided all preceding movements have flowed correctly, balance at the centre is only lost through a stamping movement of the right leg and foot, or a slow wide sweeping left leg on its way to a position at the front of the circle. In order to produce an active right leg, the knee and foot must start to turn to the front even before contact is made. There is a tendency, with some throwers, to bend the right leg, about the knee joint, more than the desired amount. This will place the leg in the wrong position of flexion to receive the body weight, hence it has

to be straightened just before landing, causing a "stamping" action, which produces instability.

If the left leg sweeps wide on its journey to the front of the circle, it will take with it a proportion of the body weight, across to the athlete's left, so preventing most of the mass from remaining over the right leg, which is a prerequisite for balance.

So to aid balance it is essential for the left leg to move in an almost straight line across the circle, keeping it fairly close to the right leg. This is not easy to achieve, particularly for the throwers who use a wide sweeping right leg, as it means using a different pattern of movement for each leg. Once the right leg has left contact with the ground, there is no need to change its degree of flexion, otherwise the "stamping" action becomes apparent. The position set by the legs at the rear of the circle is almost the position of flexion they should arrive in, once contact with the throwing surface is regained. The legs merely help the body rotate about a vertical axis.

C. An active right leg/hip

Once the discus has been set in motion at the rear of the circle it should continue to accelerate until the moment of release. A common feature with the throwing of the novice athlete is that the movement is almost split into two halves—a movement to the centre of the circle, followed by a slight pause for the various parts of the body to become positioned for a final flinging movement. Hence a lot of the initial speed, built up in the shift, is lost during the pause. The only way to avoid this is to make sure that the legs move quickly into position, and start to act the instant contact with the ground is established. The action of the right leg is to help produce considerable rotation about a vertical axis. For the right leg to be efficient it must continually force the hips ahead of the shoulders. If the plane of the hips, on arrival, is parallel to the true direction of throw (i.e. at right angles to the centre line) they cannot start to produce a fast rotational movement until they get ahead of this line. Using the clock-face terminology, the right foot, knee and hip should arrive in the centre of the circle pointing to ten o'clock. This feature is fairly recent in that the more powerful athletes of today are quite rightly seeking increased distances through speed of movement, rather than range of movement. It is possible to increase the range of movement by landing with the plane of the hips pointing towards two o'clock, but such a position must be fairly slow to produce its action.

I use the hips, as the focal point for this action, although I accept that the power must come from the legs. With the throwers I coach, I encourage them to think of forcing the hips to the front all of the time. If the right hip is allowed to become "tucked", then an inactive, slow position will result.

D. The left leg must act as a brace

The complete emphasis of the discus throw is one of controlled speed. If

Plate 29. Faina Melnik (U.S.S.R.) A braced front leg delivery.

the right leg is made more active, so that it can produce a faster movement, the left leg must be even faster so that it can take up the action of the right leg. The action of the left leg, and indeed the whole of the left side, is one of preventing the rotation in the right side, carrying over to the left side. This does not mean to say that the left leg is kept rigidly straight, but it must present a firm brace for the right side to work against.

E. The body must possess torque in the centre

Many good throws are lost because the athlete has failed to keep the hips in advance of the shoulders, so loosing torque or "wind-up" as it is known in throwing circles. However, torque is not produced through the action of the hips alone. The head serves as a rudder and the throwing arm must be held back.

If the head is brought round to the front with the hips, it can create considerable tension in the neck and shoulder muscles so producing a resistance to a fast movement; or the head can bring the shoulders round with it. In either case it does not lead to good throwing. Extremely sound advice to the thrower is "keep the head up and back". If the head is kept erect, in natural alignment, it will keep the back straight and prevent a "sagging", inactive situation in the centre of the circle. A marker, for the thrower to view, placed at two o'clock, and about five metres from the thrower, is a good aid.

It is fatal if the thrower allows the throwing arm to creep in with the hips. It must be held back, but not through great muscular effort; rather by allowing the arm to be carried fairly low and relaxed in the preliminary swings and then by a very fast hip action, the arm is naturally raised and forced back. I believe that extensive preliminary swings can do exactly the reverse of their intention, by placing the shoulder muscles under such tension that the instant contact with the ground is broken, the body starts to unwind.

F. The throw must be finished with the arm

Many inexperienced throwers think that the movement is complete once the hips and shoulders are square to the front. Unfortunately such a belief misses out the fastest and most efficient lever in the body. Once the hips and shoulders are square to the front, they can no longer contribute to the throw. If the hips have been fast the shoulders will trail the hips and the arm will trail the shoulder. Hence, when the early levers have completed their action, the arm can still have about one hundred degrees of movement left in it. The final arm movement is a most significant part of the throw. However, it must be very fast acting and be timed correctly. The athlete should get the sensation of "chasing" the discus out.

There are, of course, many other minor situations that might arise during the coaching of a mature thrower. However, one thing is certain, if the

thrower is strong enough and fast enough the fundamentals outlined above will assure a very good standard of performance.

Training for discus throwers

Like the shot putter, the discus thrower requires speed, strength, skill and mobility and must include all of these facets into the training programme. To avoid repetition the reader is advised to read the section on training for the shot putter and the section on development of strength.

However, it must be recognised that the discus thrower needs to be faster and possess a greater degree of flexibility. Hence more of his training time should be directed towards developing these qualities. This will probably mean using slightly lighter weights with more emphasis on speed of movement. It will certainly mean more suppling exercises, using either a partner to manipulate gradually the "torque" producing levers, or to perform twisting movements with weights which can increase the range of movement in a joint due to their inertia.

Technique training sessions should be included in the programme for the whole of the year. Each technique session should start with a few dynamic flexibility exercises, followed by a few easy throws building up to full effort. Discus throwing is a speed movement and the number of throws, where the emphasis is on speed, that can be completed in a single session, are relatively few. Hence the coach must be very aware of what he is working for, so that valuable effort-throws are not wasted without correctly focusing the attention of the athlete to an important fundamental.

The coach must vary his position, about the circle, in order to observe the complete movement and to make sure that the fundamental point highlighted for a particular session, is the most significant one. By and large this will mean observing the throw from four major positions (see illustration below).

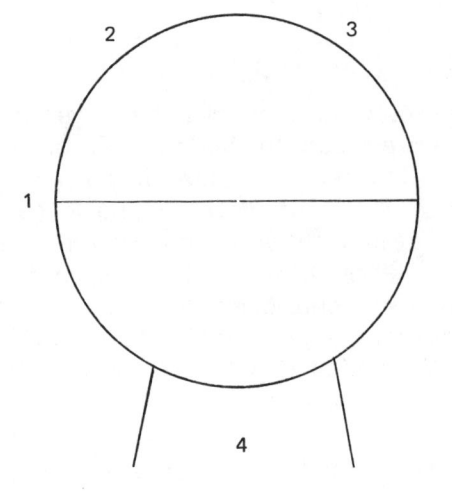

Position four must only be used when coaching one solitary athlete, whose performance is reliable. The position should be beyond the range of the thrower's ability. But it is a position from which a complete impression of the throw can be obtained. Position three is more frequently used to focus the attention of the athlete, rather than for the coach to observe a particular pattern of movement.

Chapter 15

Javelin Throwing

Of the four throwing events, the javelin is certainly the odd one out, for a number of reasons. The shot, discus and hammer throwers are frequently termed the "heavies" whereas the javelin thrower is always of a more slender build. The javelin thrower, in most cases, has a completely different personality and philosophy from the heavy thrower and could be placed in a category alongside the vaulters, jumpers and decathletes. Indeed, the javelin thrower is more the "complete athlete" than any of the other groups, and many world-class throwers have also been extremely good decathletes.

The other throwing events put considerable restrictions on the thrower, as they must stay within the confines of a relatively small circle. The javelin thrower has an almost unrestricted approach run in that its total distance cannot exceed 120 feet (36.5 metres), and the width variation cannot exceed 13 feet 1.5 inches (4 metres). Such an area permits tremendous variations in the initial part of the movement. The javelin must be released from behind an arc, joining the approach run sides, measuring a radius of 26 feet 3 inches (8 metres) and for the throw to be valid it must land within the fan-like extension of this arc. The javelin must be held about the cord grip, with the little finger nearest to the point and this, together with the rule which prohibits a person turning back towards the direction of throw, prevents the use of a rotational style, developed in Spain during the 1950s. This style, while improving records, put all but the thrower in a dangerous position, as its direction could not be guaranteed. The thrower, who records the greatest distance with from three to six efforts, wins the competition. The actual dimensions of the javelin vary according to age and sex. The basic weights are 600 gms for women and 800 gms for adult men.

In technical terms the performer is concerned with three fundamental mechanical principles. (A complete breakdown of these is shown on page 209.) They are:- The speed of release, the angle of release and an aerodynamics factor mainly associated with flight stability. Far and away the most important single factor is the speed of release. Varying the angle of release and the angle of incidence of the javelin, several degrees, only brings about marginal differences in flight range. However, an increase in release speed of one foot per second can bring about a six feet improvement in flight range.

The ultimate values of the three main variables are, in part, strength-speed

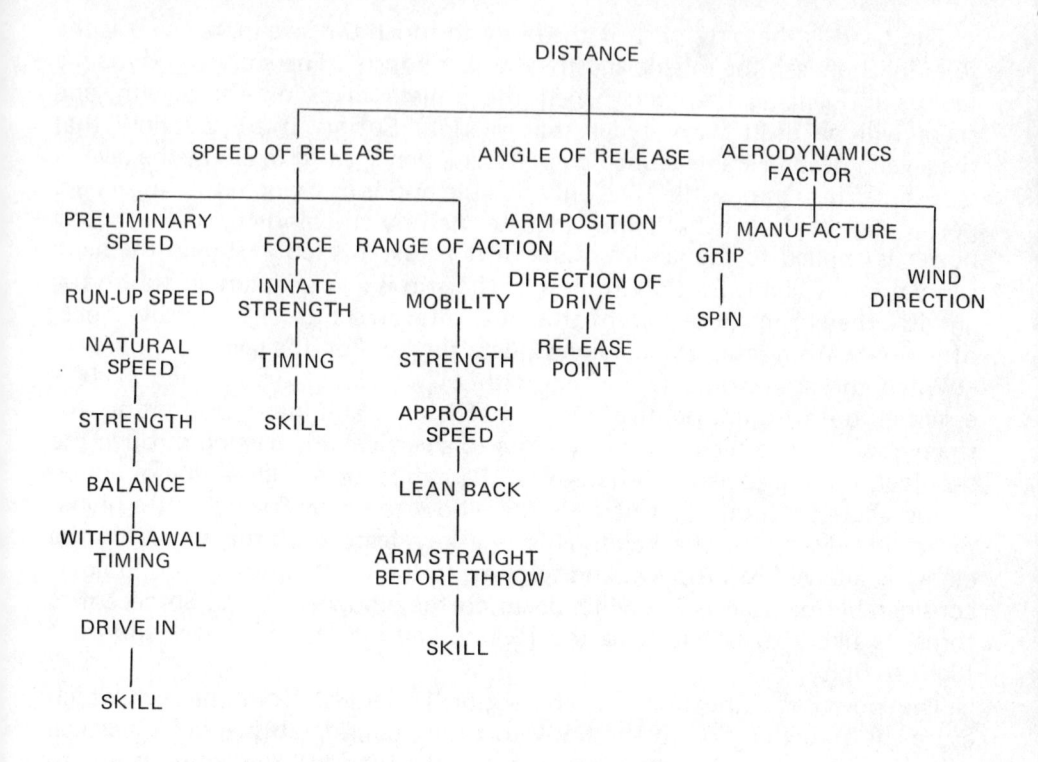

FACTORS INFLUENCING JAVELIN RANGE

dependent, but there is a tremendously high skill factor involved. The basic natural attribute is a fast arm and evidence suggests that such a quality is more an act of "nature" than "nurture".

The throw, as performed by all accomplished athletes, first of all calls for the performer to put a high speed in the body through executing a preliminary approach run, and then by adding to this speed with a final flinging action. To blend together all of the facets of the approach run and the final flinging action, split-second timing and co-ordination are required.

However, as mentioned earlier, the essential prerequisite of the javelin thrower is a fast arm. But it is important to understand that it is the arm which completes the fastest part of the movement, and that the co-ordinated power of several other lever combinations merely transmit their speed, to the javelin, via the arm. The key feature of the throw is the rotational power developed by the hip joint, but unless the arm can convey the power to the javelin, and still keep the javelin accelerating under its own power, then success will never be enjoyed.

The hand is the only part of the body to touch the javelin, hence it is the sole link between the missile and the "power-house". There are aerodynamic factors influencing the hold which the athlete takes on the javelin, and these will be dealt with under that section. Suffice it to say now that the javelin needs a stable launching platform, hence the grip about the javelin must be as firm as possible. The only reliable grip is one where the fingers are positioned securely behind the ledge formed by the binding, so that when power is applied to the javelin, none of it is lost in friction should the hand slip down the shaft. So the firmness of the grip is a key feature of the throw and in order to make certain of this, many throwers use a tacky substance, often made from resin, to help consolidate the hold on the javelin.

When the arm strikes it does so with a "whiplash" type of action. It is essential, both from a point of view of efficiency and injury prevention, for the elbow to keep high and fairly close to a vertical line passing through the shoulder. For this to happen effectively, there must be a rolling-type of action in the shoulder joint, that permits the elbow to come through on a higher plane, in advance of the hand. This is a key feature of the throw. If the elbow is allowed to drop low, and to come to the front wide of the shoulder, considerable damage is likely to occur to the elbow joint and an eccentric thrust is likely to be given to the javelin, causing loss of power and poor flight stability.

The power for the final flinging action is derived from the legs, which cause the throwing side of the body to rotate considerably about a vertical axis. The focal point for this movement is the hips, and the action is one to encourage rotation in the throwing side and to prevent rotation in the non-throwing side. However, the skill of the event is to arrive in a position, at speed, where this powerful rotation can be exploited. This will mean performing a controlled approach run that gradually builds up in speed, reaching a maximum at the time of release.

With world-class throwers, the total length of the approach run varies considerably. Wolfermann (W.G.), the 1972 Olympic champion, utilised almost the maximum permitted length of 120 feet, and Sittonen (Finland) used about two thirds of this distance. The early part of the run, covered by the majority of throwers in about twelve strides, is a relaxed build up of speed, with the javelin carried above the shoulder and both arms moving in balanced sympathy with the legs. It must be emphasised that this section of the run is not a full effort sprint. The preliminary approach run is followed by a transition phase, which can last anywhere between four and six strides in total. During the transition phase the javelin is taken to a position of a full arm's length behind the body, in preparation for the final throwing action. The body is also placed in its most advantageous position for the final effort. The majority of throwers start the withdrawal of the javelin five strides before the throwing position. The withdrawal mark is not one chosen at random, but one worked out very carefully and precisely to make sure that

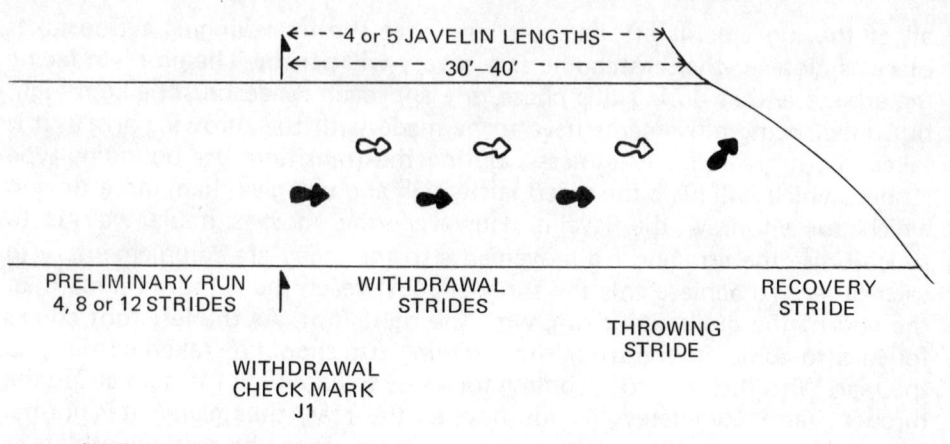

Fig. 110

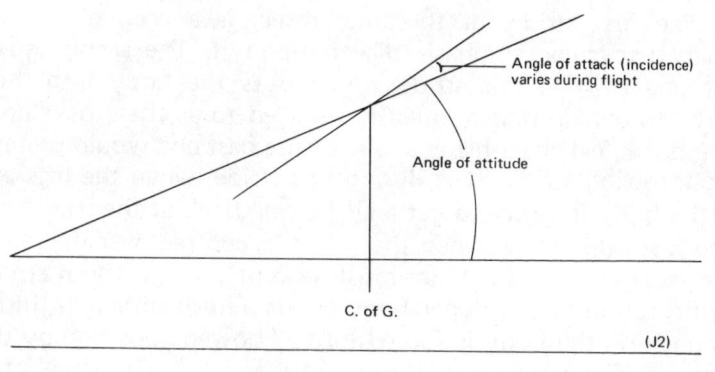

Fig. 111

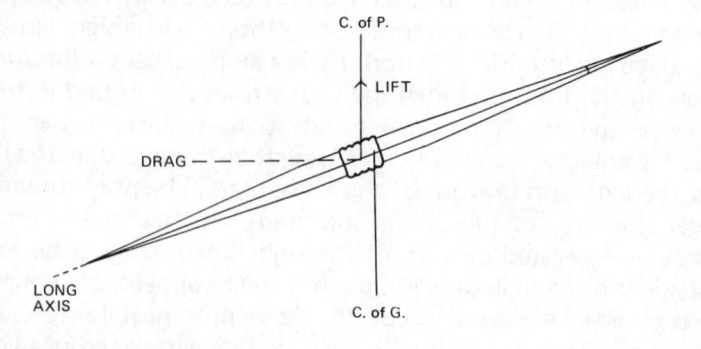

Fig. 112

all of the movements are balanced, and that the final flinging action takes place as close to the scratch line as recovery will permit. The problem facing the athlete is that during this phase, the approach speed must be kept high, but unbalancing movements have to be made with the throwing arm as it is taken to the rear. Many athletes, during the transition, use bounding-type strides, which will keep the speed fairly high and will give them more time in which to withdraw the javelin. However, the most suitable way is to synchronise the arm and leg movements so that they are complementary to each other. To achieve this the thrower must reach the withdrawal mark, at the end of the preliminary run, with the right foot. As the left foot comes forward to complete the stride, the throwing arm should be taken partially to the rear. With the right foot coming forwards to complete the next stride, the throwing arm completes the journey to the rear, thus giving the normal balanced arm action for running. Once the arm is to the rear the athlete is left with three strides before the final flinging action. These strides are essentially powerful driving ones, as the action of withdrawing the javelin has a retarding effect upon speed, and that lost during this phase must be regained. The first stride, of the final three, is a normal running stride without any particular emphasis placed upon it. The second stride is an important one as it is this stride which puts the body into the correct position for throwing. It is frequently referred to as the cross-step or cross over stride, but I feel that this is a relic of the past and would prefer to term it the pre-throwing stride. It is during this stride, when the legs are placed ahead of the body in order to get a slight lean back of the trunk, or at least on landing from this stride when the weight is centred over the rear leg. The essential aspect of it is that the hips must be kept active without any evidence of forward rotation of the upper body about a horizontal axis. Indeed soon after this position the body is forced into a "bowed" position by the action of the rear leg. The majority of throwers try to land on the heel of the right foot, with the foot pointing directly down the line of approach. Such a landing has much to commend it as it will produce a greater range of movement, and will keep the forward speed of the body fairly high. However, I no longer regard it as an essential position. I will readily accept a flat foot landing or one even on the toes, provided the foot strikes the ground in front of the body. Likewise the right foot turning out at about thirty degrees to the line of approach is equally acceptable. The essential thing is that the hip is kept active and the legs land in front of the body mass. The pre-throwing stride is often longer than any of the others, and many athletes make certain of this by a slightly exaggerated pick-up of the right knee. It must be emphasised that the stride is not a high one, although it might appear as a bound because of the extra distance covered, but the feet must pass fairly close to the ground. Viewed from the side the legs do appear to cross over. This is because the right leg must move quickly away from the left leg in order to keep the right hip active, and to produce a slight lean back. However, the

Plate 30. Ruth Fuchs (E.G.) Olympic champion 1972 demonstrates a good lean back.

right foot must not be allowed to land at right angles to the line of approach, as was favoured by the throwers of an earlier era.

Once the right foot has re-established contact with the ground, following the pre-throwing stride, the left leg must quickly move into the throwing stride so that it can serve as a brace for the right leg to drive against. Directly the body-weight has advanced in front of the right foot, the leg starts to drive the right hip to the front. The action causes the right heel to turn out and produces a marked "bow" effect in the body (see fig. 108). At this stage the arm must be prevented from striking early, and should not do so until the body has rotated so that the chest is square to the front, otherwise the flinging arm has to work against the resistance of the left shoulder. The action of the left side of the body is one forming a brace, to prevent the rotation set up in the right side, from carrying over to the left side. This does not mean to say that the left side is kept rigid. Indeed the left leg bends as it starts to take up the drive, and straightens firmly as the hip

Plate 31. Angella King (G.B.) A fine position coming up to delivery.

comes to the square on position. The rotation produced in the right side will automatically carry the throwing shoulder to the front, and will also bring with it the throwing arm. Once the chest is square to the front the only action left is that of a very fast arm. The timing, of the various parts of the movement, is very intricate, and the difference between a very long throw and a short one is often lost by this aspect of the throw being fractionally out.

When the javelin has been released, flight forces take over and these can considerably add to, or detract from, the flight range. The laws of the event stipulate that the tip of the metal head must strike the ground before any other part of the shaft. As the javelin has to be released point up, it means that rotation must take place, in the air, about the short axis of the javelin. This rule is an unfortunate one as the rotation necessary for the javelin to land correctly is not determined by the thrower but by the manufacturer.

The javelin is a good aerofoil, in that it has a streamlined shape. While the javelin is in flight it is essential that the flow of air, about the javelin, is kept in laminar layers. If the laminar flow of air breaks down then the drag forces become excessive and start to slow down the speed of flight, reducing the flight range.

Once the javelin is in flight there are two forces acting on it. They are lift and drag. Both of these forces act through the aerodynamic centre, often known as the centre of pressure (C of P) (see fig. 112). As far as the manufacturer is concerned, he regards this point as the centre of area, which is very significant in the construction of the distance rated aerodynamic javelins. The lift force is that which can aid motion while the drag force is the resistive one. The greatest lifting force is that given by the speed of release which is the one that offsets the pull of gravity. As far as the thrower is concerned it is the only significant lifting force, although theoretically it is possible for there to be one other in existence. Here I refer to the "magnus effect" related to fast rotating cylindrical bodies.

Any missile, projected for accuracy or range, must have some form of flight stabilisation. The javelin is only a good aerofoil as long as it presents the tapered point to the approaching airflow. Should it rotate in such a way, about its short axis, so as to produce a large surface to the flow of air, then it becomes a poor aerofoil. Hence any rotation about the short axis must be prevented. Unfortunately the rules of the event demand a certain amount, but the manufacturer can almost completely control this. If the javelin is forced to rotate quickly about a long axis, at right angles to the short axis, then the tendency to rotate about the short axis is considerably reduced. The thrower during the act of release imparts a spin on the javelin causing it to rotate. The thrower is seldom, if ever, conscious of this spinning action as it is determined automatically by the way the javelin is held in the hand. It is this spinning action which disturbs the air about the javelin, causing areas of differing pressures, that could produce the "magnus effect". However, it is

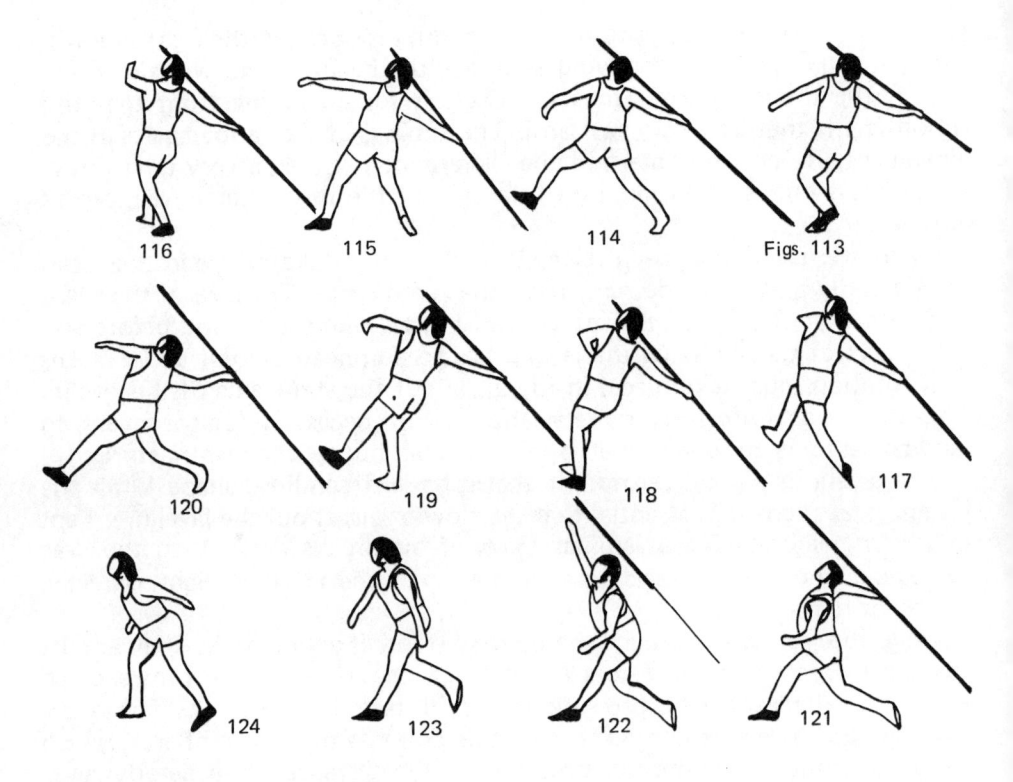

116   115   114   Figs. 113

120   119   118   117

124   123   122   121

unlikely that the thrower can spin the javelin sufficiently fast to produce such an effect.

From the above it can be realised that the way the javelin is gripped can greatly influence the stability of the flight, although the athlete can do nothing to increase the "lifting" forces. Hence, one of the prime concerns is to attempt to reduce the effect of drag. The spinning action produced at release is one such way.

The essential feature of the way the javelin is held is that it must rest along the length of the palm, with it balancing on the area of the palm nearest to the wrist. This will mean that the centre of gravity of the javelin is at about this point, and this is determined by the rules and careful manufacture. Physical effort should not be used to keep the javelin balanced, as this will certainly produce an unstable launching condition. If the javelin is permitted to rest along the complete length of the palm, this, to a large extent, will determine the grip as it will automatically place certain fingers in a position relative to the edge of the binding nearest the tail. I am personally in favour of the "V" grip, where the binding is wedged between the first and second fingers, but equally acceptable is the second finger and thumb forming the wedge behind the binding. Although a grip emphasising the position of the first finger and thumb, is probably the most natural one, it

can encourage other bad practices. With the ledge of the binding correctly wedged, the remaining fingers must overlap the javelin and keep it pressed down on the palm. Such a situation will automatically place more fingers one side of the javelin than the other, so producing greater resistance to this side on release. As the javelin leaves the hand, the little finger releases contact first, followed in succession by the remaining fingers, causing a spiralling effect that produces the spin.

Other than producing the spinning effect which retards rotation about the short axis, the second concern of the thrower, during release, is to prevent any eccentric thrust which might cause the javelin to flex or vibrate about the long axis. Vibration about this axis will disturb the laminar flow of air about the javelin, so restricting distance by increasing the drag forces. To a large extent, flexion about the long axis can be prevented by the manufacturer, but the power produced by an athlete at release can easily offset any advantage provided in manufacture. Hence the athlete must concentrate all throwing forces directly along the fundamental axis of the javelin. "Pull down the line" is a cardinal rule for the thrower.

Frequent reference has been made to the part played by the manufacturer in javelin design, and at this stage it might be worthwhile considering his role. With the added prestige given to a country, through its prowess in sport, it was only a matter of time before the technologist was forced to take an interest in this very specialised field. The first real reference one has of this effect in javelin throwing dates back to 1953 when Bud Held (U.S.A.) broke the world record for the event. To quote from a respected journal of the sport, *Track and Field News* "On August 8th 1953 Bud Held threw 260 feet to break Nikkinen's record of 258 feet 2 inches. Bud was using a 'Bud Held special' constructed from the wood of four javelins. It was a hollow affair with 27 individually fitted pieces." This was certainly the first in the range of famous "Held" javelins, which remained the favourite of the throwers from this period to about 1968 when a Swedish firm produced the Sandvick Super Elite. It would appear that the Super Elite has similar, if not identical, flight characteristics to the Held 90m. yet the Elite remains the choice of the champions. The success here could lie in the material of manufacture, the Elite being steel and the Held being alloy. Should any section of the javelin bend away from the long axis, and the impact of landing is likely to produce such an effect, then it could affect the laminar flow of air about the javelin making it less efficient. As steel is more robust than alloy it can withstand the impact of landing without distortion of shape.

The manufacture of javelins is essentially a compromise, as there are a number of factors that are not complementary to each other. The main concern of the designer is to restrict rotation about the short axis and vibration about the long axis. Unfortunately the rules governing the specifications of the implement do not give the designer the degree of

freedom he would like. This means that to a certain extent quality of design is forced by the rules of the event. However, there is a degree of latitude with the rules that allow the designer some scope for improvement.

Rotation about the short axis is determined by the relative positions of the Centre of Gravity (C. of G.) and the Centre of Pressure (C. of P.). If the C. of P. and the C. of G. were one and the same point, the javelin, if released point up, would fly through the air in the launch position and would land tail first. This, of course, would not comply with the rules. For the javelin to land point first the C. of G. must be in front of the C. of P. The further it is in front the greater is the rotation. Hence the manufacturers try to keep the moment arm, the distance between the C. of G. and C. of P., as short as possible. This lever is often termed the "pitching moment", and it is this moment arm which the manufacturers use to distance rate their javelins. For example, a javelin distance rated at 80 mtrs. is made so that it will only just rotate sufficiently, in a flight range of 80 mtrs. to land point first. A javelin of this specification would have a moment arm of about 3.5 inches.

The manufacturer takes care of the vibration about the long axis by concentrating most of the mass of the javelin about the grip. However, it is this situation that forces the javelin constructor into making a number of compromises. It is known that the stability of a javelin increases as the C. of G. moves closer to the tail. However, stability is also greater if the C. of G. is low down in the cord grip, and the position of the cord grip is partly determined by the rules governing the specifications. If the tail section is slender, the greater is the stalling effect. So the manufacturer cannot position as much of the mass about the grip as he would like to.

Thus it can be seen that world record performances are not merely influenced by the thrower alone. The technologist plays his part, although his contribution has probably reached a maximum, unless the rules concerning specifications are changed. The next decade could see this happening as the event is now becoming difficult to contain within the normal stadium. Of course the logical step would be to increase its weight but the alternatives are frightening for the throwing enthusiast. However, the problem is not one faced by the javelin throwers alone; indeed all of the long throwers are in a similar predicament that could banish the throwing events to a separate arena.

Teaching the javelin throw

The forerunner of the javelin was quite obviously the hunting spear, whose sole use was to kill. The javelin placed in careless hands is still lethal. Therefore, the strictest safety precautions must be observed when it is being thrown. It must also be remembered that the tail of the javelin is almost as dangerous as the point, and young pupils have been severely injured with this section of the javelin. However, if the safety precautions are closely followed there are not likely to be any mishaps. The rules must be:-

1. Throwing in one direction only.
2. Throwing restricted to a recognised area which is in *full view.*
3. If more than one thrower is working the order must be *All throw—all retrieve.*
4. Throwing must be carefully supervised.
5. Great care must be taken when removing the javelin from the turf after landing. The safest method is to lever the javelin to the vertical, with the point down, and at all times it should be carried in this position.

Javelin throwing is probably the most enjoyable of the throwing events for children. The essential quality is a fast arm and it is this quality which must be fostered in the early teaching situations. This aspect of the event does not have to be taught with javelins. The ideal thing is a weighted ball weighing about 800-1,000 grammes. The essential of the arm movement is the position of the elbow throughout the range of action. In the initial position the arm must be fully to the rear, the elbow joint straight. If a javelin is used it should follow the contour of the arm. In fact a safe teaching point is to aim to keep the elbow as close to the javelin as possible throughout the entire movement of this joint. By allowing an upward rotation to take place in the shoulder, the elbow can come through high and almost over the shoulder, in a fast vigorous throwing action. The elbow must come through high and close to a vertical line through the shoulder. If it is allowed to come through wide of the shoulder the movement becomes inefficient, and is also likely to produce a symptom known as "javelin elbow", which is a painful condition.

It is sound practice in education to attempt to place a newly acquired skill into a competitive situation. This will encourage the speed of the movement so essential for this event.

The next essential is to try to get the legs into a position so that they can produce the rotational effect of the right hip. A rope six feet long, with a gripping point at one end, and anchored to something about two feet above the ground at the other, is helpful in learning the way in which the hip brings the arm into the movement. However, it is a static position. With a javelin, or weighted ball, the thrower, should be encouraged to take three running strides. At the start of the run the arm should be fully behind the body. It is wise to emphasise a flat-footed run with an attempt to keep the weight over the rear leg during landing from the pre-throwing stride. Emphasis must then be placed on the driving action of the hips. It must essentially be kept simple, concentrating on only one aspect of the throw at a time.

Those who master the simple three stride movement should be encouraged to take a longer, faster run. From this point, throwing ability will be recognised, and those who have the necessary ability should be encouraged to train, and be taught a correct approach run together with the action of withdrawing the javelin.

Coaching the advanced performer

To follow the same pattern employed in the other technical events, I would like to encourage the coach to regard the event as a number of essential technical skills in which variation from these is likely to produce mediocre performances. Other aspects of technique might have a bearing on the ultimate distance achieved but are thought not to be essential aspects of the movement, and so can allow considerable scope for experimentation of individual style.

1. The right hip must be kept active

Of course this only applies to the right-handed thrower. The left-hander will place the emphasis here on the opposite hip. During the approach run the thrower will automatically keep the hips square to the front. However, during landing from the pre-throwing stride, and the reaching out effect of the left leg into the throw, the right hip will move to a position at an angle to the line of approach. The critical point is the angle to which the hip is allowed to turn, and its relative position to the rest of the body. If the hip is kept fully square to the front, and this would be very difficult to achieve, rotation could not take place about a vertical axis, only a buckling effect about a horizontal axis. If the right hip is taken fully to the side on position, so that it is parallel to the line of approach, and directly behind the left hip, it could produce rotation but it would take time and considerable power to effect. The most active position would appear to be one where the plane of the hips is at about 45° to the "square on" position. This will then permit the correct action at speed. However, it is of little value if the hip is in this position when its fast movement is hampered by the position of the trunk and legs. The essential thing is that the hips must be in advance of the shoulders. It is this which produces the bowing effect characteristic of all good throwers. The left leg must also be slightly off-set to the left of the line of approach so as to permit the speedy action.

2. The approach run must be controlled

A valuable amount of speed can be given to the javelin, during the approach run, provided it is correctly synchronised. Many novice throwers, build up too much speed in the preliminary approach run, and cannot control it, so they have to slow down in the throw itself. The approach run must be a gradual build up of speed to reach a maximum at release. In order to achieve this, the precise movements have to be practised frequently. If a little time is spent perfecting this part of the throw, so that the movements are almost self-conscious, the complete concentration can be focused on aspects of the throw which are more difficult to make reflex. The preliminary part of the run is comparatively unimportant provided it builds up gradually in speed. The important phase of the run starts when the thrower begins to withdraw the javelin, and continues right up to the point

when the javelin is released about six feet behind the line. Between the withdrawal check mark and the throw, five precise strides must be taken. If these strides vary, the rhythm of the throw is affected, so too is the position of release relative to the throwing arc. This in turn could lead to a world record throw being discounted by the thrower overstepping the scratch line. So perfect balance and control during this phase of the movement are essential (see fig. 110).

3. The arm must strike fast, but not early

Many good throwers find it difficult to distinguish between making the throwing arm act fast, and introducing it to the sequence of throwing early, and it is often this feature that prevents the good from being great. This is one of the most difficult aspects of the throw to perfect. If concentration is focused on the rapidity of the arm movement, it is uppermost in the mind of the athlete during the entire throw, so it is a fairly natural thing for this fault to creep in. It is essential that the most vigorous part of the arm movement should be left until the chest is square to the front. At this stage there should be quite a long range of action left in the lever, so that full use can be made of the fastest structure involved in the total movement.

The actual speed at which the arm strikes is probably a combination of natural ability and correct training procedures, that will help develop the strength of the muscles involved in bringing about the movement, and their correct interplay at speed. A strong arm is not necessarily a fast arm, so there is a little more to the training routine than just the development of strength.

4. The elbow must come through high and close to the vertical plane of the body

Emphasis must be placed on this for two reasons. The first is simply a safeguard against injury. It is fairly true to suggest that success in javelin throwing is partly attributed to the number of flat out training efforts the thrower can make. If these are continuously being interrupted through injury, the chances of success are essentially reduced. The second reason is to enable the very fast "whiplash" type of action to take place about the elbow joint. As this is the final lever to contribute to the movement it has to be very fast acting.

5. The javelin must be aligned correctly

Tremendous advances have been made in javelin technology, and the manufacturers have produced an almost perfect implement. The nearer one gets to perfection, the more critical certain aspects of the throw become. This is particularly true when aligning the aerodynamic javelin ready for launching. The thrower must pull directly down the line of the javelin and both the angle of release and attack should be kept fairly low. In the case of the angle of attack it should approach zero degrees and the angle of release about 35

degrees. For these to be correct the javelin must remain close to the arm once it is withdrawn. The wrist of the throwing arm must not be allowed to "cock" and permit the palm to drop below the level of the wrist. If this happens, the pull cannot be directed down the long axis, so causing it to vibrate in flight, and also giving it a steep angle of attack. Once the javelin is withdrawn, the arm must not drop below the level of the shoulder. The elevation given to the javelin is provided by the "bowing" of the back. If the arm drops below the level of the shoulder, the angle of release is affected, making it too steep.

Above all else the complete movement must be very fast. At times it should be so fast that the experienced coach even fails to see the blending of the movement. He should be left with the impression of speed, associated with the sound, made by the feet, helping to produce the final effort.

When coaching the javelin thrower the coach must make full use of the observation positions, coaching aids such as the stop watch, tape measure and motion picture machinery. Every training session is valuable so the coach must go in with a predetermined plan. The athlete must leave each coaching session elated, so the coach will have to draw on every resource possible to keep interest and motivation high. Full concentration, from both coach and athlete is essential, so distractions should be controlled and coaching points kept to a bare minimum.

Training the javelin thrower

The javelin thrower is more concerned with specific strength than almost any other athlete. If the javelin thrower were to develop the tremendous "animal" strength of the heavy thrower the chances are that both the speed and the range of movement would be sadly affected. This does not mean that the javelin thrower should neglect strength training, quite the contrary, but all strength training for the spear thrower should be directed towards the speed quality. As with all of the throwers the emphasis, placed on developing a specific quality, necessary for the event, will vary depending upon the time of the year. In the northern hemisphere the emphasis during the winter months will be directed towards the basic conditioning for the event and as the seasons change, towards the competitive one, more throwing will be included.

Development of specific strength for javelin throwing

The javelin thrower, during training, must be able to improvise in order to be able to perform strengthening type movements that will help promote the essential quality of all good throwers. The photographs on page 252 should give an idea of some of the necessary exercises. Of course it will be impossible to include all of them in each training session. However, it is recommended that about ten exercises be chosen to include in each specific strength training session, with each session being repeated two or three times

a week during the conditioning period. It must be emphasised that such exercises are supplementary to standard weight training and not in place of it. For convenience it is possible to group this section of the work under sub-headings. Throwers should select at least one from each sub-group.

(a) Throwing weighted balls. This is an identical activity to javelin throwing involving the use of weights in the shape of a ball. Each thrower should have a variety of weights ranging from 4 kilograms to 1,000 grams. The type of throwing action will be determined by the weight of the ball. With a ball weighing 4 kilograms, it will only be possible to perform the arm movement, and this at a good deal slower pace than would be possible with a javelin. Here the accent must be on strength and using the arm levers efficiently. For example, it is very difficult to throw a weight of 4 kilograms by allowing the elbow to drop low. With a weight of 1,000 grams it is possible to rehearse the complete approach run, including the final release movements. Ideally the weight should be enclosed within a plastic or rubber ball, thus permitting their use indoors. For example a 4 kilogram indoor shot is ideal for throwing against a wall, catching it, and repeating the movement in quick succession, to a total of one hundred or more repetitions, spaced throughout an evening's training session. The lighter weights can be thrown into nets without causing any damage to them.

(b) Throwing movements using medicine balls. Again these are best performed against a wall, as it will then limit the space required by a thrower in training. The best movements are those emphasising the hip and back action. In all cases the ball must be held in two hands and released from over the head. The positioning of the hands on the ball will automatically place emphasis on a certain part of the body. If the ball is picked up from the floor, and pushed to a position above the head, an excellent hip driving action can be rehearsed. (See page 252.)

(c) Throwing movements using a weight and pulley. By placing a pulley wheel, at a convenient height, on a gymnasium beam, and suspending from it a weight secured to a rope and a javelin grip, taken from a broken javelin, various aspects of the throw can be practised. It is important to make sure that the pulley wheel is higher above the ground than the complete range of the throwing action involved. Often this will mean elevating the thrower as shown in plate 37c. A pulley system should not be used for practising the arm movement but rather for strengthening the hip, back and shoulder actions.

(d) Throwing actions using friction pulleys, or a resistance applied by a partner controlling the flow of a rope over a bar. In this age of advanced technology many throwers, and gymnasia, have resistance pulleys that can graduate the flow of a rope over, or about them, by applying a controlled resistance. However, when these are not available they can be improvised, using a length of rope and a piece of apparatus like a set of gymnasium wall-bars. Here the flow of rope, over a bar, at a convenient height, is

controlled by a partner. Again complete throwing movements can be performed in this way. In fact a length of rope, about six feet long, with a ring secured at each end for the athlete to grip, is a tremendous training aid when two athletes can work together (see plates 37d/38a).

(e) Strengthening movements using elastics. Here, actions similar to those used in throwing can be performed against the resistance of elastic strands or wire springs. Alternatively the springs or elastics can be placed under stretch, and a strengthening activity can be performed by gradually controlling the tension, back to its original state, by performing the reverse movement of that required to put it under stretch. Such activities are very good for strengthening the arm and shoulder region (see plate 37b).

(f) Flexibility/strength movements using "Quoit" shaped rings made from strong plastic or metal. The discerning athlete/coach should find it easy to think of movements that can promote strength and mobility, by using the rings, in pairs, as illustrated in plate 38.

This area of specific strength is one often ignored by throwers who find greater satisfaction in handling heavy barbells. I am certain that countries, who lack the tradition of great javelin throwers, could help catch up with those more fortunate by adopting a harder and more elaborate programme for the winter conditioning. During the action of throwing the javelin, the speed of the movements involved place great strain on the body. In training the athlete must try to build up a reservoir of specific strength that will enable him to withstand even the greatest stresses likely to be experienced. Such training is more than just providing the strength for launching the javelin. It is also an insurance against injury that can considerably restrict the amount of actual throwing practice an athlete can undertake. During training an athlete will be required to make many full effort throws. Indeed, success is often determined by this very factor alone.

In addition to the specific strength exercises, listed above, the athlete will have to spend countless hours with barbells, dumb-bells and weighted discs to provide a foundation on to which specific strength can be moulded. Add to this a great variety of callisthenics, often in the hanging position, with the weight taken off the spine, and one then has a strength promoting programme that should give a booster to the "power-house".

However, it must be realised that strength alone cannot produce a javelin thrower. The javelin thrower has to be the complete athlete, as he must perform a throwing action, at the end of a fast run, in much the same way as the horizontal jumper must perform a jumping movement at the end of an approach run. To do this efficiently, the javelin thrower must be running fit, capable, if necessary, of performing as many as fifty full effort approach runs in a single session. Hence the thrower must include a certain amount of running practice, and associated activities in a training session. In fact it is often very beneficial for the javelin thrower occasionally to work-out with the horizontal jumper, doing approach work, long jumping and bounding

activities. In this field, hurdling must be considered as a very sound general conditioner, and the bounding activities described under the section for triple jumpers will certainly help to develop the explosive leg power necessary for this event.

In addition to the basic conditioning work, the javelin performer will have to spend many hours developing the technique of the event. This can only be done with a javelin, throwing it for distance. The number of throwing sessions included in a week, and the number of throws included in a session, will vary from year to year and season to season. In the formative years, before the thrower has acquired the level of strength necessary, fewer throws might be taken. A similar situation will also exist once the thrower has become really mature. During the winter conditioning period it will only be necessary to throw the javelin once or twice a week, but as the season approaches as many as four sessions a week might be felt necessary. In the winter period it might be difficult to keep the quality of throwing very high because of inadequate facilities. In this case the emphasis might be on the volume of throwing, working from a slower and shorter approach run, concentrating on specific aspects of technique. As the season approaches the emphasis will have to shift so that it is placed on speed and quality, and this in turn will restrict the number of throws possible in a session. However, at all times the athlete/coach must be conscious that it is a *speed* event and the only certain carry over from training to competition will be when the situations are almost identical. This is particularly important during the conditioning period as strength mobility and technique must progress side by side.

Chapter 16

Hammer Throwing

The hammer throw, as we know it today, is the most complex of the throwing events and probably demands more skill from the performer than any other event in the track and field programme. But the vision of a skilled athlete, gyrating with the heavy ball on the end of a length of wire, finally to hurl it almost the length of the inside perimeter of the track, is indeed one of the most captivating sights to be seen in an athletic arena. Unfortunately the event presents the administrators of the sport with tremendous problems, all of which are constantly threatening the future of the event.

The tendency in this present age is to provide multi-purpose facilities for sport. This invariably means that the central portion of our athletic stadia will also be used for a major team game when not being used for track and field athletics. The heavy head of the hammer, when dropping from the sky, buries itself deep in the ground making a large crater, and if done frequently can soon permanently damage the turf. The problem is further highlighted by the fact that the rapid development in the use of artificial turf surfaces, for major games pitches, could produce a situation, within the next twenty years, where the central areas of all of our major stadia have such a surface. This would certainly banish hammer throwing, to another area away from the main arena, something most throwers would be reluctant to accept. Enthusiasts, like myself, insist that the central area of the track must be for athletics only and a surface of hard pressed sand would be more ideal than turf. Unfortunately, the designers of recreation facilities, for the future, do not share my selfish enthusiasm.

If the damage to the turf was the only problem affecting the future of the sport, then fewer enthusiasts would express concern. However, with the greater distances being thrown the danger risk increases. With the skilled performer, hammer throwing is only dangerous to anyone standing where it is likely to land. So for world-class events it would seem logical to prevent anyone, other than the actual measuring official, to enter the central area during competition. However, bordering on most central areas are ones used for jumping, vaulting and other throwing events. Programme organisation is such that a single event could not possibly demand the sole use of the entire central area for the period of a normal competition. But future safety precautions might soon demand this and insist that the hammer

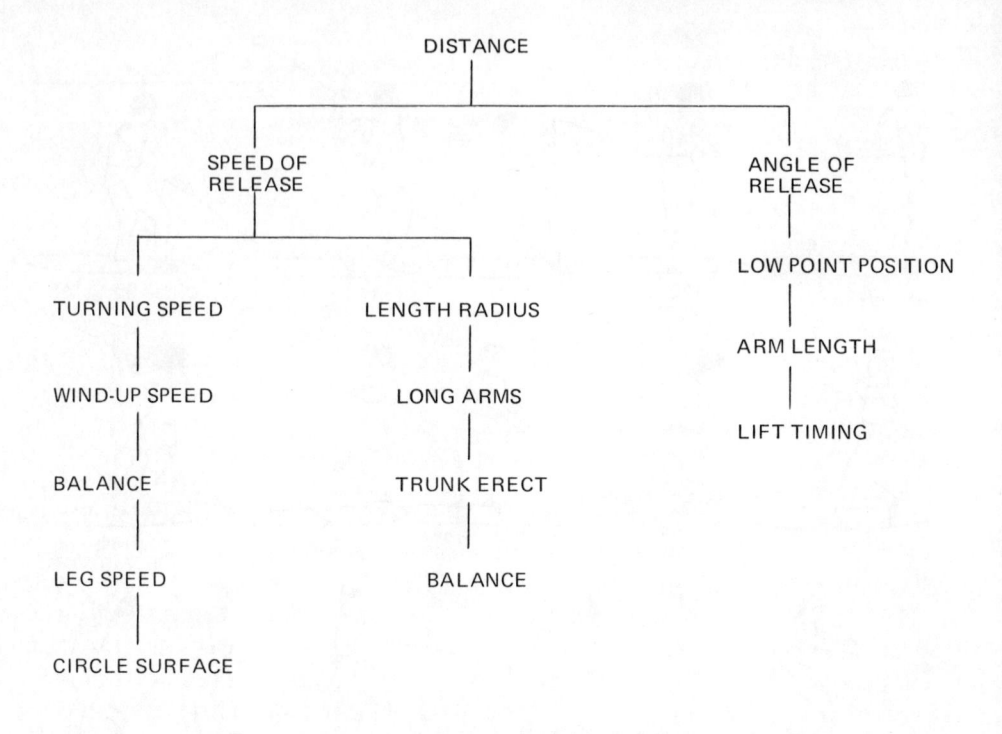

FACTORS AFFECTING RANGE OF HAMMER THROW

event be held before, or after, the normal programme of events. This of course would considerably reduce the spectator participation in the event, something cherished by all athletes.

The answer might rest in the hands of the technologist to conceive ways of restricting its flight range and its impact damage potential. Shortening the length of the wire, increasing the weight of the head, changing the material from which the head is made to a heavy yet soft substance, are all possibilities. The keen thrower does not welcome any of them but even a changed event is better than no event at all.

Compared with javelin and discus throwing, the hammer throw is a very recent addition to the sport. It would seem logical that it has developed from a rural pastime of throwing the "hammer", only in this case the hammer being of the sledge variety or that used in heavy masonry. It was certainly popular in the court of Henry VIII and there is a picture of the king, himself, making a cast. Another phase, in the history of the event, is lost in Gaelic/Celtic folk lore. Without doubt the Scots have many claims and associations with the event, particularly at their Highland Games.

Figs. 125   126   127   128   129

130   131   132   133   134

135   136   137   138   139   140

The precise competitive event, as we know it today, was developed in the United States of America where a group of men, mainly of Irish extraction, set quite incredible records. John Flanagan, a native from County Limerick, was the first man ever to throw 180 feet when in 1909 he recorded a distance of 56.19 metres (184' 4''). He was succeeded by one Matt McGrath from Tipperary, and Pat Ryan, also from County Limerick. Finally, to complete an Irish dominance that lasted from 1885 to 1949, came Pat O'Callaghan. More recent record lists have been dominated by the U.S.S.R. who seem capable of producing one world record holder after another in this event.

Basically, the rules for this event are identical to the shot event. However, it is a much longer throw, requiring rotation, and because of this the thrower throws from within a safety cage. The head of the hammer is allowed to touch the ground outside the circle, at any time during the throw, but the thrower must continue to complete the throw, otherwise it counts as a failure.

The event, as we know it today, is a multi-rotational event. In terms of very simple mechanics, two basic principles, identical to those for the shot event, apply. The distance of the throw is determined by the speed of

Plate 32a. I. Chipchase (G.B.) shows the low point.

release and the angle of projection. Provided the angle of projection is approximately forty degrees, it is not critical. Like all athletic events it is "speed" which is the controlling factor. In this case the speed of release. The speed of release will be at a maximum if the athlete turns as fast as possible, and keeps the radius as long as possible. In terms of simple body positions, the latter can be translated into meaning—keep the arms athletically straight and keep the trunk erect. These are the two factors of the body lever systems which control the radius of the hammer gyration.

The technique of hammer throwing is almost completely centred around the ability to turn fast. It demands great skill, and like *all* throwing events, *balance* is the key feature. The event, as performed by the majority of throwers, first of all involves initially accelerating the hammer, from a static position, by forcing the hammer to follow a circular path around the stationary body. This phase is known as the preliminary swings, "wind-ups" and well over half of the final speed is built up during these preliminary movements. Most athletes perform two circular movements with the hammer, before turning the whole body, and the hammer, through 360°, in

Plate 32b. I. Chipchase (G.B.) shows the high point during the single support phase.

Plate 33. I. Chipchase. (G.B.) "Up Up and away" the delivery.

what is known as the "turn". The majority of athletes perform three such turns, although some have been known to use four, each successive one faster than the previous turn, before releasing the hammer high over the left shoulder (for the normal right side orientated thrower). The number of turns performed by a thrower is partly skill dependent, but largely physique dependent. Each turn takes the thrower about twice the length of one of his feet across the circle, and the circle only measures seven feet (2.135 metres). The turning movement is made with one foot in contact with the ground all of the time; in the case of the right sided thrower the pivot foot is the left.

Basic fundamentals of hammer throwing

The throw is described for the right-handed thrower. For convenience, it is split into a number of parts, all of which blend together to form a complete fast flowing movement.

1. The hold

All good throwers wear a glove on the left hand for protection and to help consolidate the grip. The hammer should be placed between the legs so that the handle of the hammer is easy to get at. The length of the handle should be placed at right angles to the plane of the hips. The gloved left hand is inserted from the left-hand side so that the handle runs the complete width of the hand and rests on the second joint. The right hand is inserted from the right-hand side and merely folds over the left hand to close and secure its grip.

2. The stance

The thrower should take up a position with the feet, just wider than hip width apart, and back towards the direction of throw, as close to the rear of the circle as the rim will permit (see fig. 125). The hammer should either be placed in a position behind the body and slightly wide of the right foot, or rhythmically swung to this position ready to start the preliminary movements.

3. The preliminary swings

Although the hammer is held in the hands, it is wrong to think of the preliminary swings as movements involving the arms. The hammer is set in motion. from a position behind the body, with an action similar to an underarm bowling action, only considerably aided by a lateral movement of the hips. As the hammer head is thrown to a position high above the left shoulder, the arms straighten and the weight shifts wholly over the left foot. The hammer will start to drop, quite naturally, to a new low point, slightly in front of its old starting position. As it drops, the arms bend, the trunk twists slightly to permit the movement of the arms and the weight shifts back over to the right foot. The movement is repeated, only faster,

with the emphasis placed on the lateral movement from the hips. It is simple to remember: when the hammer is on the left side the hips shift to the left and vice versa when on the right side (see fig. 112). The arms play a very minor role and really serve as an extension to the hammer head. The arms must not drop over the back of the head as the hammer falls to the low point. The hands almost brush the forehead; the left elbow must be kept high to permit the hammer head to drop well back. With the hammer at the low point, usually at the end of the second preliminary swing, there follows a very critical period, of almost inactivity, known as the transition.

4. The transition

With the hammer in a position low to the thrower's right and behind the plane of the hips, the weight must start to shift across to the left foot ready for the first turn. The weight must be shifted carefully and not rushed as this will alter the natural path of the hammer head and will force the hammer to have a low position in front of the body. The arms straighten out to the low point and remain athletically straight until the hammer is released. As the weight shifts across to the left and the hammer rises towards the throwers left-hand side, the body weight pivots on the left heel. The knees must be bent and relaxed, the trunk erect. Many throwers think of pushing the knees forward. As the weight passes on to the side of the left foot the entry to the first turn is made. The turn does not start until the right foot is picked up from the ground. It is important not to rush this phase of the throw by picking the right leg up early.

5. The first turn

As the hammer sweeps high to the thrower's left, and as the weight transfers to the ball of the left foot, the right foot is picked up quickly as the turn is made on the ball of the left foot. The right foot is placed to the ground so that this foot is parallel to the left foot (see fig. 131). The right foot must not be picked up high and it must stay close to the left foot. The knees must remain flexed, and the thrower should get the sensation of turning under the hammer, with the turn completed while the hammer is at the high point. The turning force comes from the lower body, with the legs forcing the plane of the hips ahead of the hammer. During the turn the right knee is forced across the body to help speed up the turning moment. The right foot must be picked up with a straight lifting action of the right knee and most of the limb rotation necessary to perform the lifting action must come from the hip joint. The action of the right leg can be compared to a foot pumping action with the right foot remaining close to the ground. The true secret of turning with the hammer rests with the ability to keep the upper body relaxed and passive, while the turning force comes from the lower body. To keep the speed of the turn high, the right leg and hip must be pushed ahead of the hammer. The ultra fast action of the legs, pressing the

plane of the hips ahead of the plane of the shoulders, produces what is known as body torque, an important characteristic of good fast throwing.

6. Turns two and three

Each successive turn is completed in a similar manner, only faster, because the speed of the hammer head should be increasing all of the time. Because of this increased speed, the action of the right leg must be quicker to keep the hips ahead of the shoulders. However, as the hammer is exerting an increasing force on the body, the countering of this pull becomes more important as the force builds up. If this force is not countered, the thrower would be pulled up to the high point of the hammer on each turn. Such an action would lead to a loss of balance, loss of speed and a considerably decreased radius. The thrower, therefore, has to sit and hang from the hammer in order to counter this tendency to rise to the high point. The sit must be sufficient to keep the trunk erect. But while the hammer is at the high point, the weight is poised over the left leg only, hence it is the control of the left knee that is so vital. The action of the weight control over the left leg also aids the co-ordination of the right leg pick-up. The right leg must not be picked up early. The hammer should transmit the impulse to the athlete when the single contact phase should be made. The co-ordinated thrower is so balanced with the hammer that the turning movements become easy and almost reflex. There should be an easy sensation of turning with the hammer, not against it, yet always keeping ahead of it. If the movement is performed correctly, each turn should flow into the next, so that it is impossible to say where one turn finishes and the next starts. Only when the movement is stop-start-stop-start is it possible to distinguish the various phases of a throw.

At the end of the final turn the thrower must have both feet on the ground, with the hips well ahead of the hammer. Both feet must be in firm contact with the ground, before the hammer passes the horizontal position on its way to the final low point.

7. The delivery

Before the hammer reaches its final low point the back should start to arch, more as a lean back into the delivery. Both legs, which prior to this have been flexed in order to counter the pull of the hammer, lift almost vertically as the hammer is released high over the left shoulder. The thrower should experience a vertical lifting action with the hands as high as possible.

Teaching the hammer throw

This is probably one of the events which does not lend itself to class teaching, although with very careful supervision it can be done effectively. All teachers must be made aware of the potential dangers of this event and stick to a very strict code of safety precautions. If the event is being taught

in the full-class situation, the grouping of the class is of paramount importance. If the event is being taught in the small group situation, then a safety net, with just one person participating in the act of throwing at a time, is to be recommended.

For safety, and for ease of learning the skill, the event is best taught with shortened hammers. These can be constructed from a conventional hammer and handle, by joining the handle to the hammer with a short length of strong wire. Before each group is taken the short length of wire must be checked for firmness.

The first thing the novice must experience is the final delivery action. It can be done in the competitive situation. The stance is that in which a normal thrower would start, with the back towards the direction of throw. For the normal right side orientated thrower, the left hand must grasp the handle first, with the right hand over, gripping the left to secure the hold on the handle. With the knees flexed, body erect, the hammer should be swung backwards on the right side of the body, and with a type of underarm bowling action the hammer should be lifted and released high over the left shoulder. The hammer will not go very far from such a static position, but it gives the essential feeling of release and serves to illustrate the position, the body must be in before a delivery is contemplated.

From this very static position, two preliminary swings, followed by the release, can be introduced very quickly. This will give the hammer more speed, hence a greater range. Here there are a number of essential points the novice must observe. The arms bend as the hammer reaches the high point on the left-hand side, and the hands should pass close to the forehead and not be allowed to drop behind the head. The arms straighten when the hammer is low to the right side. Once the arms have straightened to the low point, on the second of the two swings, they must not bend again. The release is with high, straight, arms. The legs must be flexed to aid body balance and the trunk must be kept erect. To aid the balance of the body, and to prevent it from falling backwards, the knees should be forced forwards.

Very little time should be spent giving the novice this type of experience. The thrill of hammer throwing is got from turning at a controlled speed. Therefore, within a very short space of time a single turning movement, coupled with the release, must be introduced. As the event is essentially a competition for distance, all of the early skill training must involve the release of the hammer. The turn is best performed after two preliminary swings. As the arms straighten to the low point on the second swing a pivoting movement commences on the left heel. When the hammer goes out to the left side the right knee should be picked up quickly, forced across the body and placed down again in a similar position to that from which it started. The arms *must* remain straight throughout the turn and the release is high over the left shoulder, as in the first skill practice. The movement can be performed on grass. There must now follow a period of consolidation where

the length of the throw can be increased by lengthening the piece of wire between handle and hammer head. The single turn, with the long wire, will soon give those who have the necessary aptitude a tremendous thrill. They will be motivated to want to continue to learn more about the event. There is little point taking the novice, who does not show an aptitude for the event, beyond this stage. Whereas those who take a keen interest should be quickly taught a three turn movement. I am a firm believer in going direct from a single turn to a three turning movement and not introducing an intermediate stage of two turns.

The novice, who has got this far, will be sufficiently motivated to accept the discipline of the event. Hence the turning movements can be practised in isolation. The turning movements should again be introduced with the shortened hammer wire. The initial problem is one of orientation, getting over the "giddy" factor. In the early stages of learning, the turning movement upsets the balancing mechanisms of the body. However, after a very short space of time the body becomes accustomed to the turning movements and the "giddy" sensation disappears. To turn efficiently the weight must be centred over the left foot, the knees must be kept bent, the body must remain erect and the head kept in its natural alignment. As confidence and ability improves, the length of the wire should be increased until the turning movements can be performed with a competition-type hammer.

The safety precautions of this event cannot be over emphasised, and all movements using three turns with the conventional length hammer, must be performed from a solid base and from within a safety cage.

Coaching the advanced performer

Coaching a good performer in the hammer event probably provides the coach with more satisfaction than does coaching an athlete in any of the other athletic events. There are so many aspects of technique for the partnership to experiment with, and every session becomes one of extreme concentration. If the focus of attention of the coach strays for a fraction of a second a key feature of the throw will almost certainly be missed, since a vast number of movements are performed at such a high speed. It takes a tremendous amount of experience to coach a good hammer thrower and this experience can only be gained by working with, and observing, many throwers. It becomes a feeling where instantly a wrong pattern of movements triggers off the essential visual mechanisms of the coach. The hammer thrower in turn must rely considerably on the presence of the coach because the rotary action, performed at speed, plays havoc with one's kinesthetic awareness.

While everyone accepts that the hammer event is essentially a complex one, the simple basic essentials of "turn fast and keep the radius long" cannot be over-emphasised. Through experience I have found that the

majority of problems, with this event, stem from an unbalanced position. Hence a considerable amount of work is directed towards keeping the delicate body balance positions. Therefore, I will devote a considerable amount of this section to the emphasis of the essential positions for keeping a balanced movement.

1. *The low point of the hammer must be well back to the thrower's right.*

In this event the emphasis is always placed on the low point, probably because it is associated with something that can be seen as tangible, the ground. However, I feel that it is the position of the high point which is critical as this is the position which really has to be counterbalanced. But in correct throwing the high point will be diametrically opposite the low point, and the low point is something much easier to identify. During the turning and swinging movements, the body can only counterbalance the momentum of the hammer head in a lateral plane. If called to exert counterbalancing movements in the fore and aft plane, instability would soon result. For example, if the low point of the hammer approached a position directly between the legs, the high point would be immediately behind the head so that the instant the single foot contact phase started, the thrower would be pulled backwards across the circle. This could be countered by a forward bending movement from the body, but this would make turning impossible, by restricting the pivoting movement of the free leg about the hip joint and would considerably reduce the radius of gyration.

Hence the pull of the hammer can only be effected by a lateral counter balancing movement from the hip region.

If the hammer is dropped well back to the right, it gives the thrower more time, particularly during transition, to shift the weight across to the left as the hammer rises to its high point on this side.

2. *The weight of the body must be centred over the left foot.*

This is certainly the most obvious factor in a turning movement performed with a hammer, but nevertheless is nearly always characteristic of a good throw. In order for the body to turn through 360° in one fast movement, the right leg must be free of tension in order for it to be picked up, and later replaced, to permit the turning movement. If the weight of the body is centred over the right leg it becomes impossible to pick the leg up. If the weight is evenly distributed between the legs, the leg can be picked up but extreme muscular effort is involved, and once it has been picked up the weight will fall further to the right making subsequent lifting movements of the leg impossible. When the hammer is at the high point, it is capable of suspending a large proportion of the body weight, hence a vertical lifting action is much easier to perform when there is a force aiding this action by supporting the body weight. As the high point must be to the left, the natural counterbalance position is to the left.

3. *The hips play a most dominant role in building up the initial speed of the hammer.* It is safe to say that at least fifty per cent of the final speed of

the hammer head is developed in the preliminary swings. This is because the initial momentum of the hammer has to be overcome as the hammer is accelerated from the static position. The upper body must remain relaxed, so that the arms can remain long aided by the pull of the hammer. Hence the power for the swings must come from the lower body, and this can only be done by a lateral transference of the body weight. When the hammer is to the right the lateral transference is to the right, and vice versa. A forward-backward movement of the body will change the position of the low point, place the body in a tucked position that will make the lifting action of the free leg almost impossible, and will place the body weight centrally between the legs.

4. *The upper body must twist, in a relaxed manner, towards the right-hand side during the preliminary swings.* This is essential to enable the hammer head to be dropped fairly well back to the right. It can be further aided by keeping the left elbow high relative to the right elbow. The twist must not come from the lower body as this will change the direction of the counterbalancing movement of the hips, and will also change the low point of the hammer.

5. *During transition the weight must be shifted rhythmically across to the left foot.* A fast, forced action will create upper body tension, will almost certainly cause the body to pike and will bring the position of the low point of the hammer round to the front.

6. *The head serves as a rudder, and helps to control the balance of the throw.* The head and hips must turn together; but there must not be any attempt to lead with the head as this will create tension in the neck muscles and shoulder muscles, thus preventing the thrower from getting the true feeling of the hammer pull. The head is kept slightly higher than natural alignment and must never drop to the chest. The idea of attempting to see the hammer at the high point is a sound one.

7. *The right leg must not be picked up early.* The novice thrower often wrongly assumes that the hips can be kept ahead of the hammer by entering the first turn early. The right leg is needed to aid balance until the hammer sweeps up to the high point, and the true "lead" is got by the speed at which the hips move ahead of the hammer in the single support phase.

8. *The hammer head and pull must dictate the position of the hands.* The novice often allows a considerable vertical movement of the arms about the shoulder joint. This results from attempts to counter the hammer movements with the upper body instead of the lower body. At the low point the hammer should naturally take the hands to a position level with the right knee and at the high point they will be taken to a position approximately level with the eyes.

9. *The legs must be bent during the whole of the turning movement.* While this might be the most obvious factor in hammer throwing it cannot be overstated. Indeed, the sitting action will become slightly more pro-

nounced with each successive turn. This is because the hammer is exerting a considerable pull at the high point, during the single contact phase, hence the thrower must "hang" more from the hammer. The sitting position must be one where the head is kept up and the trunk erect. The thrower should feel the sensation of pushing the knees forward during the double-foot contact phase.

10. The right foot must move extremely quickly on the final turn. Again this is obvious because of the speed of the hammer, but it is essential if any extra speed is to be given to the hammer during delivery. The right foot must be in firm contact with the ground when the hammer is in the horizontal position (see fig. 138). If it is in this position both legs can start to lift the hammer vertically, from the low point, up to an extended delivery position.

It would be possible to list more than the ten points emphasised and enlarged in this section. The majority of the key features are interdependent and the good coach should attempt to perfect the early features of the throw. For example, a poor delivery can often be traced back to an unbalanced position in the preliminary movements. If the throwing pattern is constructed this way, there will seldom be any need for a radical change in technique.

Training for the hammer thrower

The hammer thrower really does need all of the speed, strength, mobility and skill of the "complete" athlete. His strength requirements are not as high as the shot putters. But one thing is certain there will never be a good, weak, hammer thrower. However, the hammer thrower will almost certainly need to devote more of his time to skill training and this will by necessity cause a reduction in the amount of time spent on the other facets of conditioning.

For speed, the hammer thrower should do short sprints over about 30 metres and perform any of the jumping and bounding activities described in the sections on the jumping events, and in particular in the jumps decathlon table in Appendix I.

For mobility work the thrower should work frequently with medicine balls and weights, using the momentum which can be developed in them to increase the range of movement. Activities performed in a hanging position with the body weight suspended from a beam, wall-bar or ropes and moving the lower body in a circular or lateral plane, are particularly beneficial to the hammer thrower.

Like all of the strength activities, the thrower must think of exploring two different avenues for the development of this quality. Firstly, there is the avenue for developing pure, or animal strength; this is best done by lifting heavy weights, using one of the conventional techniques, described in that section of this text. Then there is the avenue for the development of specific strength, a strength which is likely to have a carry over directly to the event.

This area is difficult for the hammer thrower to explore; however, by carefully positioning pulleys and ropes it is possible to simulate the delivery action. Turning movements with weights across the shoulders or in the hands can help with the various body positions necessary for performing the event.

Section 5

Fitness and Training

Chapter 17

Strength Training

In a book of this nature it would be very easy to devote a considerable part of it to strength training, which has played such a significant role in the development of the sport of track and field athletics. Many successes in recent years can be attributed to our better understanding of the way strength is developed.

In the sport of track and field athletics, the term "strength" is a confusing one. The shot putter has strength to hurl the heavy ball a long way; so, too, has the marathon runner who has to be on his feet for over 26 miles. The reason for the confusion is that strength is very specific; the high jumper needs a different strength from that of the long jumper. All athletes must develop the type of strength they require for their event. However, it is fairly certain that any levels of specific strength can only be moulded on to an already strong frame that has a high degree of general strength.

The analogy between the marathon runner and the shot putter suggests that the term "strength" might need to be changed and that the dictionary definition of "strength" i.e. "having powers of resistance", could give it a truer meaning. Many sources define strength training as "progressive resistance training" suggesting that the training loads should be progressively increased, and that the resistance can be provided by many different means, as detailed later.

Just as strength is difficult to define, so too it is difficult to measure or assess. For example, it is a fallacy to believe that because a person has big muscles he is automatically strong. Although there are instruments such as dynamometers which can measure strength, in certain areas, the standardisation of the equipment and testing procedures is difficult to establish.

One thing is certain, as far as strength is concerned: "Function makes an organ". If the muscles are used they will get stronger. Furthermore, strength developed before puberty is likely to be retained until age starts its decline. Strength developed artificially, after puberty, can be lost almost as quickly as it is obtained. In the area of strength, two very eminent men, from quite diverse areas of sport, have made very topical quotes:-

"No one can become strong except by the use of heavy resistance" (Percy Cerutty, Australian middle distance coach).

"The only way to gain strength of muscle is to exercise against gradually

increasing resistance" (P. Karpovitch, physiologist with a special interest in sport).

The term "resistance" frequently crops up in this section. As far as I am concerned, strength can only be developed through progressive resistance training, using the overload principle. The resistance can be in the form of weighted discs, elastics, springs, dynamometers, immovable objects, body weight or other muscle groups. There is evidence to suggest that strength can be developed by using the muscle isometrically and isotonically. Isometrically is where tension is created in the muscle, but the levers do not move significantly, and there is no visual evidence of work being performed. Isotonically is with movement, the tension developed in the muscle causing a lever to move. The latter is the most common situation in sport. However, a German research worker called Muller startled the world of sport in the 1950s when he stated that "One isometric contraction using two thirds of the fibres, once daily, was the best for an increase in strength." As many athletes had spent thousands of hours trying to develop this quality, the statement of Muller certainly came as an astounding surprise, and many tried to adopt his methods for a very short while. It soon became obvious, to those in sport, that isometric contractions might be suitable for developing strength with very weak people, but that very strong people could only become stronger through exercising the muscles isotonically.

The effect of strength training on the body is still, to a large extent, subject to unproven theories. Muscles, when exercised, certainly get bigger. This growth could be due to an increase in the diameter of each fibre. A Russian research team suggests that strength training can increase the numbers of fibres, but this is refuted by most western authorities. A most likely suggestion is that the blood supply, in the region of the muscle, is improved considerably making the capilliaries larger, activating dormant vessels, etc. Other theorists suggest that even dormant muscle fibres can be reactivated by the demands of exercise. It is theoretically possible for an efficient muscle, familiar with work, to explode more energy with a single contraction. It is also possible for the trained muscles to be able to produce greater tension per unit of "food" used in the chemical process. The theories are almost unending.

In terms of pure physiology, exercise causes a breakdown of muscle protein that can only be replenished by the complicated action of the growth hormone combining with certain essential ingredients which we take in with our food. During extreme levels of work the breakdown is excessive, and "nature" then becomes protective, building up the muscle stronger to resist further breakdowns. This is often termed the "over-compensating effect" and can also be noticed when a bone is broken, where an extra layer of bone develops about an old break.

The effects of strength training can also be psychological: for example, a egotistical feeling when the body obviously becomes bigger, and this can be further magnified if the gains in bulk are greater than one's rivals. The fact

that a heavier weight is lifted today, which could not be raised yesterday, can boost one's confidence enormously. However, the psychological effects of strength training are beyond the scope of this text.

The progressive overload principle mentioned earlier requires some definition. It expresses the idea that the muscles must be worked well beyond their normal capacity. This is done by performing the work intermittently, spacing each exercise with a period of inactive recovery. "Progressive" refers to the fact that the value of the resistance should be increased gradually as the level of strength improves with time. The stressing agent must never be so great as to involve the complete breakdown of the muscle, but the stress should be sufficient to trigger off the various adaptive mechanisms. The reader should refer to the section on middle distance running where the adaptation to stress theory is enlarged.

Frequently, throughout the text, I have referred to the terms "specific strength" and "basic or animal strength". The term "specific strength" refers to a strength specific to the athletes' chosen activity and which, of course, can be developed through performing the activity, or one very close to it, with an added resistance. The term "basic strength" refers to a general reservoir of strength which permits the body to perform increased levels of work. Basic strength is best developed by exercising the body against its own weight as in circuit training, although this is more efficient for developing local muscular endurance, and by exercising with weighted discs, known popularly as weight training. Specific strength is likely to be developed by employing the use of pulleys, elastics, springs,etc.

It is not the purpose of this chapter to delve too deeply into the numerous ideas associated with progressive resistance work. Indeed it would require a separate volume as large as this one. However, it is worthwhile to give readers some ideas to whet their appetite so that experimentation can take place and other sources of reference used.

Weight training

This activity should be used to develop basic strength. Training with weights can be dangerous, so before any training scheme is embarked upon, one should learn a good lifting technique and adopt certain safety precautions. A good lifting technique is difficult to describe in a text of this nature and it is advisable to seek the practical advice of an expert weight lifter. Basically the legs must be kept close to the bar, when lifting in the standing position, and the back must be kept straight. As far as safety is concerned, the following are cardinal points:-

1. Never attempt to lift a weight which is too heavy.
2. Make sure that the weights are secure on the bar.
3. When lifting in the supine position, or performing squats, always have a "spotter" (a person to help should one get in difficulty).

There are three main muscle groups in the body:- the arms, the trunk

and the legs. A programme designed to develop general strength should include an equal balance of each, so that harmonious growth is achieved. There are literally hundreds of different exercises with weights,and to describe them all is beyond the scope of this chapter. So the selection of exercises will be left for the reader to acquire from other sources. However, the systems, by which the various exercises are grouped together in a training schedule, are worthy of mention.

(a) Simple system. Here the performer does a number of repetitions, of an exercise, a given number of times. I favour a limit of six repetitions for track and field athletics. Once the number of repetitions has been completed, a rest period should follow before the same exercise is repeated for the same number of repetitions. After a further rest period, the exercise is performed for a third time, keeping the same number of repetitions. Ideally, the weight should be such that it is only just possible, with extreme exertion, to repeat the series of exercises three times. Once it becomes easy to repeat the series an extra weight should be added. With the first series of three exercises complete, another exercise, involving a different muscle group, should be performed in an identical manner. Ideally the athlete should select nine exercises, three for each of the main muscle regions previously mentioned.

(b) Combination system. This is almost identical to the simple system. Instead of performing one exercise and then allowing a period for recovery, two exercises are grouped together, the first being followed immediately by the second but without a recovery period. With this system one usually combines an arm and a trunk exercise together, or any two from the combination of the three main muscle groups. Once the pair of exercises has been completed three times, a rest period should follow before another pair of exercises is performed.

(c) Super-set, tri-sets, etc. Again the system is similar to the combination system but instead of selecting exercises involving different muscle groups, one group only is put under pressure for two exercises (Super-sets) or three exercises (Tri-sets) without recovery. Each exercise should be repeated six times for three successive groups before a different series of exercises takes place.

(d) Pyramid system. This is ideal for the advanced lifter. The performer starts with a weight that can be handled for six repetitions only. Once the repetitions are complete an additional weight is added and the exercise repeated five times. A further weight is added and the exercise performed for four repetitions. This is then followed, decreasing the number of repetitions until only a single lift is possible.

(e) Timed systems. I am a confirmed advocate of this system for running and horizontal jumping events. Here an exercise is performed for a period of time, rather than for a number of repetitions. For example, a 100 metres runner might perform his activity for about 11 seconds, thus giving him a

weight training time of 11 seconds without recovery. The 400 metres runner might perform his weight training exercises for a period of fifty seconds without recovery. If the exercise is performed at speed, it will produce a stressed condition identical to that which will be experienced in the event proper. Associated with this is the multi-contact system, where the number of ground contacts made by the athlete, during a race, is taken as the basis for calculating the number of repetitions performed, without recovery, during a training session. The long jumper taking seventeen strides might do seventeen fast repetitions.

(f) The Olympic lifts. These are the snatch and the clean and jerk. These should only be performed by experienced lifters, but they can add a little competition to one's weight training. It is also possible to make comparisons with other athletes as the lifts are standardised. They require skill, agility and strength which means that they are very good for the mature performer.

SPECIFIC STRENGTH

Those who do not advocate weight training as an aid to improved performance argue that weight training exercises place the athlete in unnatural positions. For example, a very popular lifting exercise is known as the bench press, where a weight is pressed vertically from the supine position. There is not an athletic event which calls for the athlete to work the muscles in this position. The carry-over of strength acquired in this way is likely to be fairly small. I only accept this theory in part, as all good throwers, at some time during their career, perform this lift. However, it is possible to choose exercises using discs, pulleys, springs, medicine balls, etc. which are likely to have a greater carry-over to the specific event for which strength is being developed.

Specific strength exercises for the sprinter/hurdler

Weight training using timed or multi-contact systems. Step-ups, dips, bent over rowing, using these systems. Harness running, hill running, elastic machine running (see plate 36b). Juggling with a medicine ball using arms, feet, knees, etc.

Specific strength training for the middle distance runner

Weight training using the combination system. Hill running, elastic machine running.

Specific strength training for the horizontal jumper.

Weight training using multi-contact system. Bounding decathlon, box work. Juggling with medicine ball.

Specific strength training for the vertical jumper

Weight training multi-contact method. Bounding activities, box work.

Juggling with a medicine ball, specific kicking activities using a medicine ball (see plates 39-40).

Specific training for the thrower

Weight training using heavy weights, with fairly frequent fast sessions and much higher repetitions. Work using pulleys, resistance pulleys, partners, elastics, medicine balls,etc. (see plates 37-38).

Strength training, like all other aspects of training, must be planned carefully to fit into the schedule designed to produce peak form to coincide with the athlete's important fixtures. This introduces the very difficult problem of phasing the weight training. Obviously there are many variables associated with the individual, such as the access to safe strength training facilities, and above all else the event for which the strength training is being done.

The jumper/sprinter, for example, might perform three strength training sessions per week during the winter months and curtail them to one during the competitive period. I believe that all athletes must keep at least one strength training session, per week, during this period. But this session must be as far removed, in time, as is possible, from the day of competition. This is because stressed muscles take several days to recover before they can produce really explosive movements again. During the winter period the jumper/sprinter should perform at least one fast strength training session, one specific strength training session and one session where the resistance is kept high and increased during the period.

However, the thrower presents an entirely different problem as he requires to keep up a very intense strength training programme the whole year round. The strength required to throw a discus, or put a shot, is not acquired overnight. It often takes many years and as such is a long term investment. Herein lies the danger. Unless the training loads are phased correctly, the thrower could reach the state where he is involved in the constant breakdown of tissue without allowing a period of recovery for repair. Therefore, the thrower must vary his training loads, exercises and approach so that the result really is a stronger athlete. Unfortunately, the thrower, for whom weight training is so important, soon begins to lift out of sheer habit in much the same way as the smoker, smokes. He tends to rely upon it and develops a "guilt complex" should it be missed; or even the intensity reduced. Such a situation is bad for the athlete. Strength training with weights must be subjected to periodic changes of loading and intensity.

It is certain that even the male human body follows a regular rhythmic cycle of function. Sport will soon find a means of detecting this rhythm, thus enabling the athlete to work hardest when the body rhythm is favourable. Without this, the athlete soon detects his own body rhythm but few, if any, apply it to their training. In future these body rhythms must be observed more carefully and the intensity of training varied accordingly.

With most athletes, I favour a four day cycle to follow, one day hard, two days fairly easy, one day very intense. Split routines, where the emphasis is placed on one area of the body one day and another area the next, might help with this phasing. Here I am referring to the very intense training programmes which, if allowed to follow from day to day, would soon produce a breakdown to the stress rather than an adaptation.

The thrower must also consider very carefully at what time during the day, relative to meals, etc. should the strength training be done, and the possible role of food supplements in this quest.

Plate 34. P. Gabbet (G.B.) Demonstrates the use of a new multi-gym weight training bay.

Plate 35a. A safe way to exercise the legs in a leg press machine.

Plate 35b. The squat with a safety rack behind.

Plate 35c. A leg extensor/flexor machine.

Plate 35d. The popular bench press with safety rack.

Plate 36a. Harness running for leg strength.

Plate 36b. Elasticated running machine made from inner-tube elastic.

Plate 37a. A javelin action with the medicine ball.

Plate 37b. A throwing action using strong elastics.

Plate 37c. A throwing action using a pulley wheel and weights.

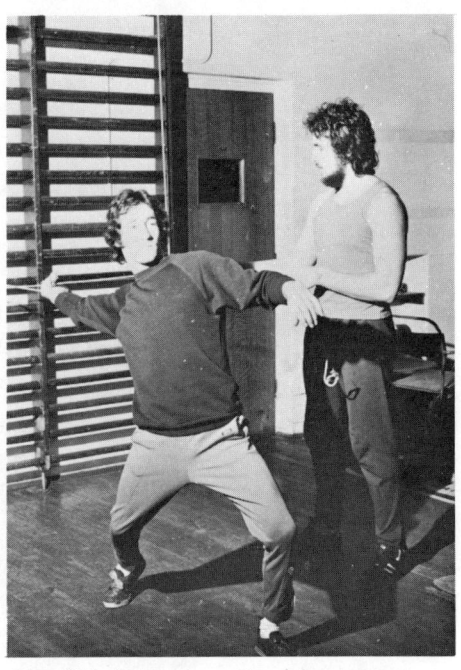

Plate 37d. A throwing action using a rope controlled by a partner.

Plate 38a. A running javelin action using a short rope with grips.

Plate 38c. A hammer action using a resistance pulley.

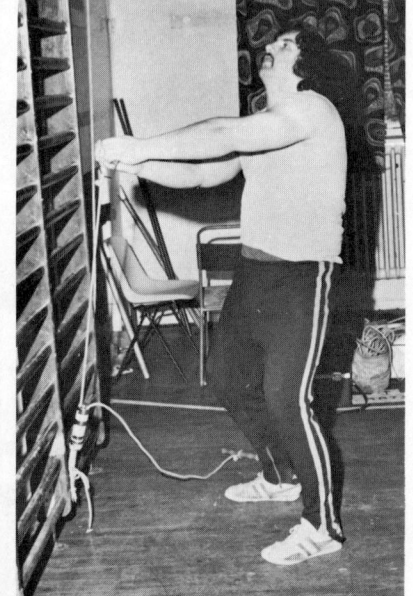

Plate 38b. A discus turning action using a rope as a form of resistance.

Plate 38d. Strength mobility using rings/rope with partner.

Plate 39a. A pole vault action using a thrown medicine ball. Here it has been kicked away by the sole of the foot.

Plate 39b. A pole vault action to kick a thrown medicine ball.

Plate 39c. Rope swing to kick a high beam.

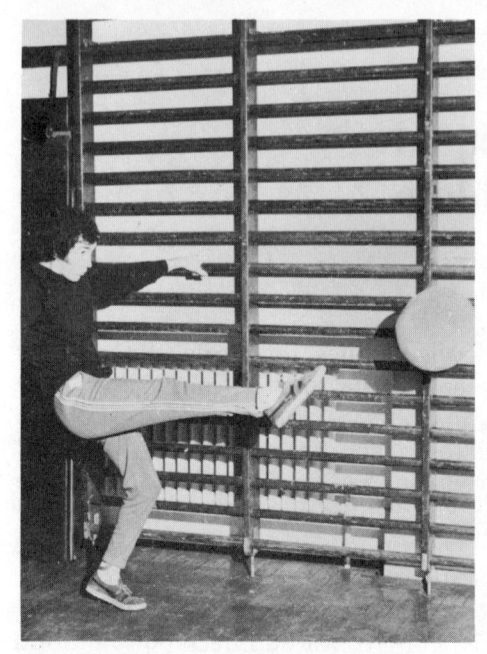

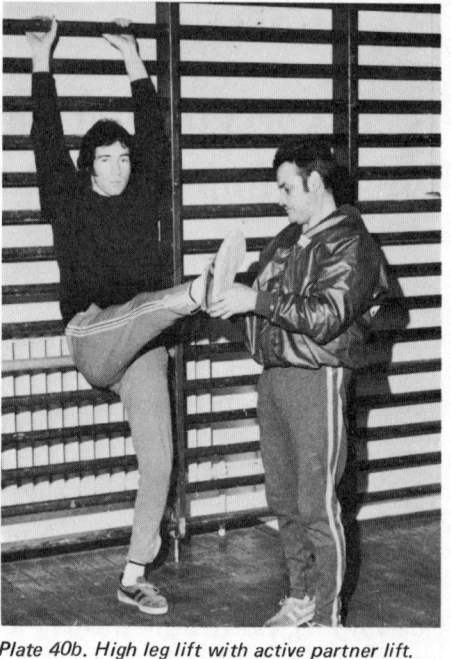

Plate 40a. Straight free leg swing to thrust a medicine ball for distance.

Plate 40b. High leg lift with active partner lift.

Plate 40c. Leg push to thrust away a thrown medicine ball for distance.

Chapter 18

Is a Normal Diet adequate for the Top-Class Athlete ?

With the present rise in performance levels, all over the world, the top-class athlete must explore every avenue open to him, or her, in order to seek improvement. I believe that success in sport is directly proportional to the amount of quality work one is able to do, and this is obviously restricted by the amount of time one has available for training. Some fortunate athletes can train three, or more times a day, others have to settle for just a single session after a hard day's work. The truth is that world standards are almost forcing an era of the full-time athlete due to the intensity of work necessary for Olympic success. Most athletes, in recent years, have considerably increased their training loads and are fast approaching saturation point in this area; some have sought the expert advice of coaches in exploring the realm of improved performance and training techniques; others have sought the use of ergogenic aids, both legal and illegal. However, very few have carefully examined the most basic requirement of all—*food.*

At a recent international symposium on nutrition I posed the question "Is a normal diet adequate for a top-class sportsman?" Coming from a very rural area, with an abundant supply of fresh foods, I have always been conscious of the present-day neglect we show for our diet. The various processes of freezing, canning, processing and cooking destroy a considerable amount of the natural value in the foods which we eat. Even the "so-called fresh" ones have spent some time in storage before they come to the shops. This situation made me study the topic of nutrition and seek the advice of experts. The world of nutrition is full of contradictions and it is almost impossible to find a satisfactory answer to our problems. However, a number of European countries, which enjoy tremendous success in sport, have examined the matter very carefully and their papers offer us excellent guidelines. In this country our dieticians and doctors are satisfied by the idea that the "normal diet is adequate for the average person". Around the two words "average" and "normal" must lie the reason for confusion and misunderstanding.

According to the 1971 census the U.K. had a population of 55,347,000. In 1972 it sent a team of 157 men and women, representing the cream of amateur sport, to the Olympic Games in Munich. In terms of total population this represents a figure of .00028%, which illustrates that the top-class

sportsman is unique and cannot be brushed aside as an "average person".

The energy requirements of an average person are about 2,750 calories per day and most texts list the active person as one who requires 3,600 calories per day (this is probably based on the research work carried out on Canadian lumber jacks or on British miners). I have calculated myself, and this is supported by work done in Finland, that the top-class athlete requires something in excess of 6,000 calories per day and our throwers, who have been known to lift as much as 70 tons of weights in a single training session, certainly exceed this level. So it can be seen that the statistics used by our dieticians can be most inaccurate when applied to people who train three or even four times a day, as is often the case with those of world-class.

As far as the supply of energy is concerned, the foods which we eat can be divided into three categories: protein, carbohydrates and lipids (Fats). The subject of vitamins and minerals will be discussed later. It is fairly simple for any dietician to assess the approximate daily requirements of each. But it will be very approximate and the diet of the top-class sportsman cannot afford to be approximate. The skilled movements of the sportsman are very precise and many training routines are geared to split-second accuracy, so it would seem illogical to consider his nutritional requirements in any other terms. The sportsman is involved in attempting to limit the number of things that can be left to chance. This includes diet, since the energy requirements for very active people can be calculated with some degree of accuracy. This is certainly done in several Eastern European countries, and the following table, which might help to calculate the requirements, emerged from one of them.

Energy output per K gm body weight per hour

Activity	Calories
Sleeping	.93
Standing	1.5
Dressing/undressing	1.69
Running 400 metres/minute	85.0
Javelin throwing	11.0

This lists just a few of the activities an athlete could be involved in every day. If all of the activities are timed, with a stop watch, and carefully logged, in much the same way as a training diary would be kept, a more accurate assessment of the nutritional needs can be calculated.

The table on page 258 gives a breakdown of the calorie "C" requirements, into the various food components, per K gm body-weight, for some aspects of the sport.

Most readers will know that energy is derived from the sun through the food we eat. The act of exercise involves the expenditure of energy derived from the combustion of certain chemical matters, which are part

	Protein	Lipids (Fats)	Carbohydrates	"C"
Jumping	2.4	1.6	9.6	65
Throwing	2.7	2.0	10.0	72
Sprinting	2.4	1.8	10.0	70
Middle distance running	2.5	2.3	13.0	85.0

of the body, and the loss arising from this conversion of energy must be replaced. The energy equivalent of our food can be calculated through a scientific process, and is measured in kilocalories or large "C" as it is more frequently termed. The energy equivalent derived from our food must balance that expended during work. If the body consumes more food than is converted to energy, then the digestive system is overloaded and the excess is converted to fatty tissue and deposited about the body. If the food intake does not match up to the energy expenditure, then exhaustion will set in once any reserves have been used up. In simple terms, this will mean that those involved in high levels of work must eat more of everything in order to remain healthy and active.

In the final calculation it must be remembered that each gram of protein or carbohydrates yields 4.1 calories and each gram of fat 9.3 calories.

The subject of protein is frequently raised in the sporting press and at sporting functions, and I hope by now the pre-match steak fallacy has been fully understood. The main constituent of any living organism is *protein* and our body requires a constant supply of it. Of the three categories already mentioned, it is the only one that can supply nitrogen. The body can manufacture fats from carbohydrates and carbohydrates from proteins, but protein itself can only be obtained from essential amino acids. Of the twenty-plus amino acids known, only about eight are essential to the body. Food containing substances from which these eight can be derived is of greater value to the body.

Exercise causes a breakdown of muscle protein, which is restored under the complicated action of the growth hormone, coupled with certain chemicals derived from our food. So it would appear that any controlled stimulation of growth hormone activity would be helpful in building stronger and more efficient muscle tissue. Working with a group of medical students/athletes we tried protein extracts to stimulate such activity, but it only caused minor alimentary discomforts. However, an article by Scilla Miller, in *Athletics Coach* entitled "Flower Power Pills" prompted the use of pollen in a similar experiment. Pollitabs were administered to only four good class athletes who could be seen regularly for measurements. The body fat folds were measured by using a caliper reading in millimetres. The following formula was used and the results were processed by computer:

Caliper readings . . . mild bicep, mild tricep, scapula and iliac crest.

x = Log 10 sum of caliper readings

y = 1.1610 − 0.0632 x ± 0.0069 = body density

% = body fat = (4.95/y − 4.5) 100

RESULTS.

	Athlete A Mean fat	wt.	Athlete B Mean fat	wt.	Athlete C Mean fat	wt.	Athlete D Mean fat	wt.
Start	8.430	10st. 9	5.526	10st. 12	7.902	12st. 0	17.362	16st. 8
Jan.	8.22	10st. 9	5.040	10st. 12	6.278	12st. 0	17.246	16st. 8
Feb.	7.10	10st. 8	5.040	10st. 12	5.021	11st. 13	17.293	16st. 7
Mar.	7.15	10st. 8	4.441	10st. 12	4.138	11st. 13	15.183	16st. 6
April	7.30	10st. 8	4.468	10st. 12	4.662	11st. 13	14.72	15st. 10

Pollitabs were given only during the months of January and March. The experiment was not a piece of nutritional research but was intended to help validate my own empirical ideas. As far as research is concerned it has many weaknesses, i.e. small sample, no control group, period of testing, etc.

Three of the athletes found that during the period when taking pollitabs the work load could be increased, but that the increased load could not be sustained when not taking the extract. It would be easy to dismiss the findings as a "placebo effect" but I would rather support the view that a substance like pollitabs can improve athletic performance by helping athletes to recover from very high levels of work. However, I am certain that it could merit further study under research conditions.

The recommendations of the 1936 League of Nations Committee are that the body requires 1 gram of protein for each kilogram of body weight, and 4 grams/kilogram for a child. The problem, as I see it, is where, in this spectrum, does the very active athlete fit,' who is constantly requiring to rebuild broken down muscle tissue. Is 1 gram/kilogram sufficient? I am not qualified to say but the Russian work suggests an intake of between 2.5 and 3 grams/ kilogram, with an increase above this level for those continually involved in sustained endurance events like distance running, cycling, swimming, etc. Contradictory evidence comes from Astrand (Sweden) who found that there was not a significant rise in nitrogen output after activity, and this is supported by Szanto (England) who suggests that "The athletes' extra intake of protein is probably due to psychological factors rather than sound physiological factors". In the face of such conflicting evidence it leaves the athlete/coach with little choice except play safe and try to take extra protein in the form of supplements as no harm can be done anyway.

While on the subject of proteins, it might be worthwhile considering the time of training, relative to food intake, especially for those involved in strength promoting exercise. It is generally accepted that there is peak amino acid activity about two hours after ingestion and that this activity subsides considerably after this time lapse. It would seem logical to the layman that the stimulus for promoting strength, i.e. weight training, etc. should coincide with this peak availability of raw materials. Most sportsmen, because of their work, are forced to do their strength training well removed from their last meal, hence the stimulus and the availability of raw materials do not coincide. In this area I have found the pollen extract valuable as it does not involve the time consuming factor of eating. I think that in this country we should spend some time examining the time of a meal, and its content, relative to the time of training so that the stimulus for an improved response coincides with the availability of raw materials.

The lipids (fats) are an area of nutrition which is very quickly glossed over by most dieticians and one gets the impression that they should be avoided, particularly those of animal extraction. However, there is evidence to suggest that vegetable oils have a very relevant place in the diet of sportsmen. The Russian Institute suggests a ratio of 1:1:4 for proteins, fats and carbohydrates but that sportsmen should take more carbohydrate and less fat due to the oxygen consumption involved in the exchanges.

However, there are two areas under this category which might be of interest to sportsmen. The first is a phospholipid known as lecithin. Studies conducted in the U.S.S.R. proved that 1 milligram/200 grams body weight of lecithin increased cortical excitability and improved motor response. An unpublished thesis from U.S.A. suggested that lecithin improved the forearm reaction time of tennis players considerably. Lecithin could loosely be described as the insulator around nerve fibres. Such a finding is also significant for our skilled field events.

The second area is that of steroids and one must accept the fact that anabolic steroids (testosterone) tend to increase protein retention and are extremely effective for building up the body. However, there is an official ban on them in amateur sport, but it has been suggested that they have been used in professional sport as well as in the amateur versions. However, coaches must be made aware of the dangers of playing with the hormone balance of the body. The recent T.V. series, introduced by an ex-Olympic gold medallist, must have horrified most people (the incidence of vaginal cancer in the offspring of women subjected to a certain contraceptive steroid). However, this takes us into the realms of pharmacology and not nutrition.

The carbohydrate group forms nature's richest source of energy and since it includes all sugars and starches it is unlikely that any diet will be lacking in this group. However, there could be a danger in including a greater proportion of the carbohydrate requirements as simple sugars. Sugars appear

to be an irritant of both the nervous system and certain endocrine organs. It is therefore suggested that the starches should form at least 60% of the carbohydrate requirement. However, under certain circumstances larger amounts may be taken, particularly before prolonged endurance events where the blood sugar level is likely to fall very low. In this case the quickly assimilated sugars, such as fructose and glucose (grape sugar), should be used. Honey is an excellent source of easily assimilated sugar but it should form part of the remaining 40%.

A very rich carbohydrate diet can be used to improve performances immediately prior to sustained endurance events. Astrand found that if the muscles were exhausted, improved performances resulted by depleting the glycogen reserve, followed by an almost exclusively fat/protein diet for three days and then by four days of a rich carbohydrate diet. This has been successfully applied by several British athletes.

The most controversial topic of all is that of vitamins. Again the material evidence in this field is very conflicting. Also at times an athlete must make a compromise since certain aspects of vitamin therapy are not compatible. For example, Vitamin B1 (Thiamine) is essential for the final metabolism of carbohydrates, but an excess of it might restrict maximum oxygen uptake. However, research in the U.S.A. and Russia found that the addition of Vitamin B1 and Vitamin C (Ascorbic Acid) to the athlete's diet is conducive to better athletic results, through more effective training.

For athletes training by contemporary methods the need for vitamins is great. It is suggested that vitamin requirement is very closely associated with energy expenditure as can be seen in the table below.

1. For sprints, throws, gymnastics

Period	A1	B1	B2	Ncn.	C.	E.
Active rest	2.0	2.5	2.0	20	75	3
Principle training	3.0	5.0	2.5	20	150	3
Competition	2.0	10.0	5.0	25.0	250	3

All milligrams
Ncn = Niacin

2. For endurance sports

Period	A1	B1	B2	Ncn.	C.	E.
Active rest	2.0	3.0	2.0	20	100	3
Principle training	3.0	10.0	5.0	25	250	6
Competition	2.0	15.0	5.0	25	300	6

The use of vitamins presents various problems. For instance, Vitamins A and C are subject to seasonal changes. What might be suitable for Australia and New Zealand would not be so for Finland. Also, storage and cooking destroy some of the natural vitamins. Many of them are interdependent and a deficiency of one does not permit the correct action of another.

They are not stimulants but must be obtained from natural sources, and cannot be produced within the body.

Vitamins form two natural groups: Water Soluble, including Vitamins B and C, and fat soluble Vitamins A, D, E, K. It is possible than an excess of the fat soluble vitamins could prove toxic, but this is most unlikely with top-class sportsmen whose demands for vitamins are considerably increased. In particular, it has been found that Vitamin A therapy improves the performance of table tennis and tennis players who play in artificial light. This is due to an association the vitamin has with optic purple.

The whole subject of vitamins is so vast that I could not do justice to it in a short space of time at the end of a lengthy chapter. However, I am certain that athletes requiring extra vitamins should obtain them from natural sources. I am a firm believer in Wheat Germ Oil and Brewers Yeast and would include them in all diets for top-class sportsmen.

Furthermore there are the minerals such as calcium, which is essential for the assimilation of protein; iron, together with Vitamin C and B12, for the production of red blood cells, and the efficient transportation of oxygen; and, of course, liquid intake to balance that lost during high activity. The problem is what to leave out, not what to put in.

As mentioned at the beginning of this chapter, very few have carefully examined the subject of food. One thing is certain. Increased training loads require increased food intake and this will remain a problem for the sports dietician and the athlete to sort out. It is not just the total energy requirement that is significant. It is the way in which the various foods are combined to provide the most efficient sources of raw material. With increased training loads, more time has to be spent training. In consequence, there is less time available for eating, especially if it is food which requires timely digestion before a training routine can follow it. I am fairly certain that the athlete will have to resort to quickly and easily digested food supplements.

My aim in this chapter is solely to encourage coaches, athletes and officials to look carefully at the topic of food and consider "Is a normal diet adequate for a top-class athlete?". In particular, if the athlete/nutritionist/physiologist examines the issue, the sport will certainly be a healthier one.

Appendix 1 The Jumping Decathlon Table

Points	1 Stand Long Jump	2 Stand Triple Jump	3 2 Hops Step & Jump	4 2 Hops 2 Steps & Jump	5 2 Hops 2 Steps 2 Jumps	6 Spring Jumps	7 Stand 4 Hops & Jump	8 Run 4 Hops & Jump	9 25 yards Hop Dom Leg	10 5 Strides Long Jump
100	12' 3"	34' 6"	42' 8"	51' 0"	62' 10"	56' 0"	58' 0"	78' 0"	2.5	23' 11"
99	—	34' 3"	42' 4"	50' 9"	62' 4"	55' 6"	57' 6"	77' 6"	—	—
98	12' 0"	34' 0"	42' 0"	50' 6"	61' 10"	55' 0"	57' 0"	77' 0"	2.6	—
97	—	33' 9"	41' 8"	50' 3"	61' 4"	54' 6"	56' 6"	76' 6"	—	23' 10"
96	11' 9"	33' 6"	41' 4"	49' 6"	60' 10"	54' 0"	56' 0"	76' 0"	2.7	—
95	—	33' 3"	41' 0"	49' 3"	60' 4"	53' 6"	55' 8"	75' 6"	—	—
94	11' 6"	33' 0"	40' 8"	49' 0"	59' 10"	53' 0"	55' 4"	75' 0"	2.8	23' 9"
93	—	32' 9"	40' 4"	48' 10"	59' 4"	52' 8"	55' 0"	74' 6"	—	—
92	11' 3"	32' 6"	40' 0"	48' 6"	58' 10"	52' 4"	54' 6"	74' 0"	2.9	—
91	—	32' 3"	39' 8"	48' 2"	58' 4"	52' 0"	54' 0"	73' 4"	—	23' 8"
90	11' 0"	32' 0"	39' 4"	47' 10"	57' 10"	51' 8"	53' 8"	72' 2"	3.0	—
89	—	31' 9"	39' 0"	47' 6"	57' 4"	51' 4"	53' 4"	71' 6"	3.1	23' 7"
88	10' 9"	31' 6"	38' 8"	47' 2"	56' 10"	51' 0"	53' 0"	71' 0"	—	—
87	—	31' 3"	38' 4"	46' 10"	56' 4"	50' 6"	52' 6"	70' 6"	3.2	23' 6"
86	10' 6"	31' 0"	38' 0"	46' 6"	55' 10"	50' 0"	52' 0"	70' 0"	—	—
85	—	30' 9"	37' 8"	46' 2"	55' 4"	49' 8"	51' 8"	69' 6"	—	23' 5"
84	10' 3"	30' 6"	37' 4"	45' 10"	54' 10"	49' 4"	51' 4"	69' 0"	3.3	—
83	—	30' 3"	37' 0"	45' 6"	54' 4"	49' 0"	51' 0"	68' 3"	3.4	—
82	10' 0"	30' 0"	36' 8"	45' 2"	53' 10"	48' 8"	50' 8"	67' 9"	3.5	23' 4"
81	—	29' 9"	36' 4"	44' 10"	53' 4"	48' 4"	50' 4"	67' 0"	3.6	—
80	9' 9"	29' 6"	36' 0"	44' 6"	52' 10"	48' 0"	50' 0"	66' 6"	3.7	23' 3"
79	—	29' 3"	35' 8"	44' 2"	52' 4"	47' 8"	49' 6"	66' 0"	3.8	—
78	9' 6"	29' 0"	35' 4"	43' 10"	51' 10"	47' 4"	49' 0"	65' 6"	3.9	—
77	—	28' 9"	35' 0"	43' 2"	51' 4"	47' 0"	48' 8"	65' 0"	4.0	23' 2"

	1 Stand Long Jump	2 Stand Triple Jump	3 2 Hops Step & Jump	4 2 Hops 2 Steps & Jump	5 2 Hops 2 Steps 2 Jumps	6 5 Spring Jumps	7 Stand 4 Hops & Jump	8 Run 4 Hops & Jump	9 25 yards Hop Dom Leg	10 5 Strides Long Jump
76	9' 3"	28' 6"	34' 8"	42' 10"	51' 6"	46' 2"	48' 4"	64' 3"	4.1	23' 1"
75	—	28' 3"	34' 4"	42' 6"	51' 0"	45' 10"	48' 0"	63' 9"	4.2	23' 0"
74	9' 0"	28' 0"	34' 0"	42' 4"	50' 6"	45' 6"	47' 6"	63' 0"	4.3	22' 10"
73	8' 10"	27' 9"	33' 8"	41' 10"	50' 0"	45' 0"	47' 0"	62' 6"	4.4	22' 8"
72	8' 9"	27' 6"	33' 4"	41' 6"	49' 8"	44' 8"	46' 8"	62' 0"	4.5	22' 6"
71	8' 8"	27' 3"	33' 0"	41' 0"	49' 4"	44' 4"	46' 4"	61' 6"	4.6	22' 4"
70	8' 7"	27' 0"	32' 8"	40' 9"	48' 10"	43' 10"	46' 0"	61' 0"	4.7	22' 2"
69	8' 6"	26' 9"	32' 4"	40' 4"	48' 4"	43' 6"	45' 6"	60' 6"	4.8	22' 0"
68	8' 5"	26' 6"	32' 0"	40' 0"	48' 0"	43' 0"	45' 0"	60' 0"	4.9	21' 9"
67	8' 4"	26' 3"	31' 8"	39' 8"	47' 6"	42' 8"	44' 8"	59' 6"	5.0	21' 6"
66	8' 3"	26' 0"	31' 4"	39' 4"	47' 0"	42' 4"	44' 4"	59' 0"	5.1	21' 3"
65	8' 2"	25' 9"	31' 0"	39' 0"	46' 8"	42' 0"	44' 0"	58' 3"	5.2	21' 0"
64	8' 1"	25' 6"	30' 8"	38' 8"	46' 2"	41' 8"	43' 8"	57' 9"	5.3	20' 9"
63	8' 0"	25' 3"	30' 4"	38' 4"	45' 10"	41' 4"	43' 4"	57' 0"	5.4	20' 6"
62	7' 11"	25' 0"	30' 0"	38' 0"	45' 4"	41' 0"	43' 0"	56' 6"	5.5	20' 3"
61	7' 10"	24' 9"	29' 8"	37' 8"	45' 0"	40' 6"	42' 6"	56' 0"	5.6	20' 0"
60	7' 9"	24' 6"	29' 4"	37' 4"	44' 6"	40' 0"	42' 0"	55' 6"	5.7	19' 9"
59	7' 8"	24' 3"	29' 0"	37' 0"	44' 0"	39' 6"	41' 6"	55' 0"	5.8	19' 6"
58	7' 7"	24' 0"	28' 8"	36' 8"	43' 6"	39' 0"	41' 0"	54' 3"	5.9	19' 3"
57	7' 6"	23' 9"	28' 4"	36' 4"	43' 0"	38' 8"	40' 8"	53' 9"	6.0	19' 0"
56	7' 5"	23' 6"	28' 0"	36' 0"	42' 6"	38' 4"	40' 4"	53' 0"	6.1	18' 9"
55	7' 4"	23' 3"	27' 9"	35' 8"	42' 0"	38' 0"	40' 0"	52' 6"	6.2	18' 6"
54	7' 3"	23' 0"	27' 6"	35' 4"	41' 6"	37' 8"	39' 8"	52' 0"	6.3	18' 3"
53	7' 2"	22' 9"	27' 3"	35' 0"	41' 0"	37' 4"	39' 4"	51' 6"	6.4	18' 0"
52	7' 1"	22' 6"	27' 0"	34' 8"	40' 6"	37' 0"	38' 0"	51' 0"	6.5	17' 9"
51	7' 0"	22' 3"	26' 9"	34' 4"	40' 0"	36' 8"	37' 6"	50' 6	6.6	17' 6"

50	17' 3"	6.7	50' 0"	37' 0"	36' 4"	39' 6"	34' 0"	26' 6"	22' 0"	6' 11"
49	17' 0"	6.8	49' 6"	36' 8"	36' 0"	39' 0"	33' 8"	26' 3"	21' 9"	6' 10"
48	16' 10"	–	49' 0"	36' 4"	35' 8"	38' 6"	33' 4"	26' 0"	21' 6"	6' 9"
47	16' 8"	6.9	48' 6"	36' 0"	35' 4"	38' 0"	33' 0"	25' 9"	21' 3"	6' 8"
46	16' 6"	–	48' 0"	35' 6"	35' 0"	37' 6"	32' 8"	25' 6"	21' 0"	6' 7"
45	16' 4"	7.0	47' 6"	35' 0"	34' 8"	37' 0"	32' 4"	25' 3"	20' 9"	6' 6"
44	16' 2"	–	47' 0"	34' 6"	34' 4"	36' 8"	32' 0"	25' 0"	20' 6"	6' 5"
43	16' 0"	7.1	46' 6"	34' 0"	34' 0"	36' 4"	31' 8"	24' 9"	20' 3"	6' 4"
42	15' 10"	–	46' 0"	33' 6"	33' 8"	36' 0"	31' 4"	24' 6"	20' 0"	6' 3"
41	15' 8"	7.2	45' 6"	33' 0"	33' 4"	35' 8"	31' 0"	24' 3"	19' 9"	6' 2"
40	15' 6"	–	45' 0"	32' 6"	33' 0"	35' 4"	30' 8"	24' 0"	19' 6"	6' 1"
39	15' 4"	7.3	44' 6"	32' 0"	32' 8"	35' 0"	30' 4"	23' 9"	19' 3"	6' 0"
38	15' 2"	–	44' 0"	31' 6"	32' 4"	34' 8"	30' 0"	23' 6"	19' 0"	5' 11"
37	15' 0"	7.4	43' 6"	31' 0"	32' 0"	34' 4"	29' 8"	23' 3"	18' 9"	5' 10"
36	14' 10"	–	43' 0"	30' 8"	31' 8"	34' 0"	29' 4"	23' 0"	18' 6"	5' 9"
35	14' 8"	7.5	42' 6"	30' 4"	31' 4"	33' 8"	29' 0"	22' 9"	18' 3"	5' 8"
34	14' 6"	–	42' 0"	30' 0"	31' 0"	33' 4"	28' 8"	22' 6"	18' 0"	5' 7"
33	14' 4"	7.6	41' 6"	29' 8"	30' 8"	33' 0"	28' 4"	22' 3"	17' 9"	5' 6"
32	14' 2"	–	41' 0"	29' 4"	30' 4"	32' 8"	28' 0"	22' 0"	17' 6"	5' 5"
31	14' 0"	7.7	40' 6"	29' 0"	30' 0"	32' 4"	27' 8"	21' 9"	17' 3"	5' 4"
30	13' 10"	–	40' 0"	28' 8"	29' 8"	32' 0"	27' 4"	21' 6"	17' 0"	5' 3"
29	13' 8"	7.8	39' 6"	28' 4"	29' 4"	31' 8"	27' 0"	21' 3"	16' 9"	5' 2"
28	13' 6"	–	39' 0"	28' 0"	29' 0"	31' 4"	26' 8"	21' 0"	16' 6"	5' 1"
27	13' 4"	7.9	38' 6"	27' 8"	28' 8"	31' 0"	26' 4"	20' 9"	16' 3"	5' 0"
26	13' 2"	–	38' 0"	27' 4"	28' 4"	30' 8"	26' 0"	20' 6"	16' 0"	4' 11"
25	13' 0"	8.0	37' 6"	27' 0"	28' 0"	30' 4"	25' 8"	20' 3"	15' 9"	4' 10"
24	12' 10"	–	37' 0"	26' 8"	27' 8"	30' 0"	25' 4"	20' 0"	15' 6"	4' 9"
23	12' 8"	–	36' 6"	26' 0"	27' 4"	29' 8"	25' 0"	19' 8"	15' 3"	4' 8"
22	12' 6"	8.1	36' 0"	26' 0"	27' 0"	29' 4"	24' 8"	19' 4"	15' 0"	4' 7"
21	12' 4"	–	35' 6"	25' 8"	26' 8"	29' 0"	24' 4"	19' 0"	14' 9"	4' 6"

	1 Stand Long Jump	2 Stand Triple Jump	3 2 Hops Step & Jump	4 2 Hops & 2 Steps & Jump	5 2 Hops 2 Steps 2 Jumps	6 2 Hops 5 Spring Jumps	7 Stand 4 Hops & Jump	8 Run 4 Hops & Jump	9 25 yards Hop Dom Leg	10 5 Strides Long Jump
20	4' 5"	14' 6"	18' 8"	24' 0"	28' 8"	26' 4"	25' 4"	35' 0"	–	12' 2"
19	4' 3"	14' 0"	18' 4"	23' 8"	28' 4"	26' 0"	25' 0"	34' 6"	8.2	12' 0"
18	4' 2"	13' 9"	18' 0"	23' 4"	28' 0"	25' 8"	24' 8"	34' 0"	–	11' 10"
17	4' 1"	13' 6"	17' 8"	23' 0"	27' 8"	25' 4"	24' 4"	33' 6"	–	11' 8"
16	4' 0"	13' 3"	17' 4"	22' 8"	27' 4"	25' 0"	24' 0"	33' 0"	8.3	11' 6"
15	3' 11"	13' 0"	17' 0"	22' 4"	27' 0"	24' 8"	23' 8"	32' 6"	–	11' 4"
14	3' 10"	12' 9"	16' 8"	22' 0"	26' 8"	24' 4"	23' 4"	32' 0"	–	11' 2"
13	3' 9"	12' 6"	16' 4"	21' 8"	26' 4"	24' 0"	23' 0"	31' 6"	8.4	11' 0"
12	3' 8"	12' 3"	16' 0"	21' 4"	26' 0"	23' 8"	22' 8"	31' 0"	–	10' 8"
11	3' 7"	12' 0"	15' 8"	21' 0"	25' 8"	23' 4"	22' 4"	30' 6"	–	10' 4"
10	3' 6"	11' 9"	15' 4"	20' 8"	25' 4"	23' 0"	22' 0"	30' 0"	8.5	10' 0"
9	3' 5"	11' 6"	15' 0"	20' 4"	25' 0"	22' 8"	21' 8"	29' 6"	–	9' 8"
8	3' 4"	11' 3"	14' 8"	20' 0"	24' 8"	22' 4"	21' 4"	29' 0"	–	9' 4"
7	3' 3"	11' 0"	14' 4"	19' 8"	24' 4"	22' 0"	21' 0"	28' 6"	8.6	9' 0"
6	3' 2"	10' 9"	14' 0"	19' 4"	24' 0"	21' 8"	20' 8"	28' 0"	–	8' 8"
5	3' 1"	10' 6"	13' 8"	19' 0"	23' 8"	21' 4"	20' 4"	27' 6"	–	8' 4"
4	3' 0"	10' 3"	13' 4"	18' 8"	23' 4"	21' 0"	20' 0"	27' 0"	8.7	8' 0"
3	2' 11"	10' 0"	13' 0"	18' 4"	23' 0"	20' 8"	19' 8"	26' 6"	–	7' 8"
2	2' 10"	9' 9"	12' 8"	18' 0"	22' 8"	20' 4"	19' 4"	26' 0"	–	7' 4"
1	2' 0"	9' 6"	12' 4"	17' 8"	22' 0"	20' 0"	19' 0"	25' 6"	8.8	7' 0"

Events 1-5 should be performed with the starting foot flat on the ground.

Event 6. This is five bounding movements with both legs together and without stopping during the five movements.

Event 9. Is a hopping race using the dominant leg.